THE BEDFORD SERIES IN HISTORY AND CULTURE

The Salem Witch Hunt

A Brief History with Documents

Related Titles in
THE BEDFORD SERIES IN HISTORY AND CULTURE
Advisory Editors: Lynn Hunt, *University of California, Los Angeles*
David W. Blight, *Yale University*
Bonnie G. Smith, *Rutgers University*
Natalie Zemon Davis, *Princeton University*
Ernest R. May, *Harvard University*

THE BEDFORD SERIES IN HISTORY AND CULTURE

The Salem Witch Hunt
A Brief History with Documents

Richard Godbeer
University of Miami

BEDFORD / ST. MARTIN'S   Boston ◆ New York

For Bedford/St. Martin's

Publisher for History: Mary V. Dougherty
Director of Development for History: Jane Knetzger
Executive Editor: William J. Lombardo
Senior Editor: Heidi L. Hood
Developmental Editor: Debra Michals
Editorial Assistant: Jennifer Jovin
Production Supervisor: Samuel Jones
Executive Marketing Manager: Jenna Bookin Barry
Project Management: Books By Design, Inc.
Index: Books By Design, Inc.
Text Design: Claire Seng-Niemoeller
Cover Design: Andrea M. Corbin and Marine Miller
Cover Art: An Execution of Witches in England (engraving) by English School
    (seventeenth century), Private Collection/The Stapleton Collection/The Bridgeman
    Art Library
Composition: Achorn International
Printing and Binding: Haddon Craftsmen, Inc., an RR Donnelley & Sons Company

President: Joan E. Feinberg
Editorial Director: Denise B. Wydra
Editor in Chief: Karen S. Henry
Director of Marketing: Karen R. Soeltz
Director of Production: Susan W. Brown
Associate Director, Editorial Production: Elise S. Kaiser
Manager, Publishing Services: Andrea Cava

Library of Congress Control Number: 2010933562

Manufactured in the United States of America.

5   4   3   2   1   0
f   e   d   c   b   a

For information, write: Bedford/St. Martin's, 75 Arlington Street, Boston, MA 02116
(617-399-4000)

ISBN-13: 978-0-312-48455-2

Acknowledgments

Distributed outside North America by PALGRAVE MACMILLAN.

Foreword

The Bedford Series in History and Culture is designed so that readers can study the past as historians do.

The historian's first task is finding the evidence. Documents, letters, memoirs, interviews, pictures, movies, novels, or poems can provide facts and clues. Then the historian questions and compares the sources. There is more to do than in a courtroom, for hearsay evidence is welcome, and the historian is usually looking for answers beyond act and motive. Different views of an event may be as important as a single verdict. How a story is told may yield as much information as what it says.

Along the way the historian seeks help from other historians and perhaps from specialists in other disciplines. Finally, it is time to write, to decide on an interpretation and how to arrange the evidence for readers.

Each book in this series contains an important historical document or group of documents, each document a witness from the past and open to interpretation in different ways. The documents are combined with some element of historical narrative—an introduction or a biographical essay, for example—that provides students with an analysis of the primary source material and important background information about the world in which it was produced.

Each book in the series focuses on a specific topic within a specific historical period. Each provides a basis for lively thought and discussion about several aspects of the topic and the historian's role. Each is short enough (and inexpensive enough) to be a reasonable one-week assignment in a college course. Whether as classroom or personal reading, each book in the series provides firsthand experience of the challenge—and fun—of discovering, recreating, and interpreting the past.

Lynn Hunt
David W. Blight
Bonnie G. Smith
Natalie Zemon Davis
Ernest R. May

for my students

Preface

The Salem witch hunt of 1692 ranks among the more infamous events of American history. Indeed, it may be one of the few incidents from colonial history that students have heard of and think they know something about. It has inspired an enormous and varied literature, ranging from novelistic treatments and Arthur Miller's acclaimed play *The Crucible* to an ever-growing body of scholarship in which historians seek to explain the occurrence of the witch hunt. Given the enduring popular fascination with this subject, it is not surprising that the scholarship on Salem has reached a much broader audience than academic books on most other topics. Some of these books are regularly assigned in undergraduate courses. Yet instructors who want to use primary documents to bring the witch hunt to life for students have had few options. There are two scholarly editions of the surviving court records from 1692, but until now there has been no volume of documents on the Salem panic presented within an explanatory framework designed to help undergraduates understand the documents and appreciate their significance. This volume fills that gap.

The witch hunt of 1692 is a gripping and fascinating story in its own right. That Salem has proven to be so compelling to readers over the centuries is hardly surprising, given the sheer scale and intensity of the hysteria that spread throughout eastern Massachusetts that year, the mounting fears of a demonic conspiracy to undermine New England, and a colorful cast of characters, including the group of apparently terrified girls who wielded, through their accusations, the power of life and death over their neighbors. Yet as this book immerses students in that story, it also situates the 1692 witch hunt within a broad historical context. It introduces students to the supernatural world that colonists inhabited. It examines the influence of Puritanism on their worldview, the social structure of early New England, the workings of the legal system, and the transatlantic context in which colonists operated. It addresses the colonists' increasingly fraught relations with local Indian nations and the broad changes taking place in the region toward the end of the seventeenth century. This volume is designed not only to teach students about the Salem witch hunt but also to place it within the larger context of New England's colonial experience. As such, it will prove an effective teaching tool for survey courses as well as more specialized courses on colonial America, religious history, legal history, and witchcraft.

The introductory essay in Part One encourages students to think about the crisis from a range of perspectives: religious, cultural, gendered, psychological, social, economic, political, and legal. It discusses the supernatural beliefs that influenced those involved in the panic. It introduces students to the history of witch trials in New England and across the Atlantic in England and Europe, discussing the challenges involved in prosecuting an invisible crime. It examines the kinds of tensions among neighbors that produced witch accusations and the characteristics that made some people—particularly some women—more vulnerable to accusation than others. And it describes the specific crises in the region during the years prior to 1692 that help us understand the timing of the panic.

Part Two is divided into five groups of documents, each with its own brief introduction that helps students understand and contextualize that specific set of documents. The first introduces students to supernatural beliefs in early New England and the mounting sense of crisis in the region during the years leading up to 1692. The second group includes two contemporary accounts of the initial accusations, as well as the crucial response of the local minister, Samuel Parris, to what was happening. The third and longest group contains legal documents from six sample cases that were chosen to highlight particular themes and issues that played a significant role in the crisis. These vivid selections from the court records enable students to consider why particular women and men were accused and the kinds of evidence with which the court had to work. The fourth group details growing opposition to the trials. The fifth contains anguished attempts by those involved in the witch hunt to come to terms with what they had done. To help students as they read, gloss notes throughout the documents explain the meaning of words no longer in common usage.

The documents are followed by a chronology of events, a list of questions for consideration, a selected bibliography, and an index. Taken together, this collection enables students to immerse themselves in the events of 1692 and to develop explanatory frameworks for the witch hunt that are sensitive to the colonists' own beliefs, assumptions, and fears. It treats the witch hunt not as a peculiar aberration that burst out of nowhere but as a product of seventeenth-century attitudes and problems. The ultimate goal of this book is to introduce students to a colonial world in which the natural and supernatural were tightly interwoven.

ACKNOWLEDGMENTS

It is now a quarter century since I first started as a doctoral student to explore witchcraft in seventeenth-century New England. One of my professors at the time warned me, with a rueful smile, that once you begin writing about witchcraft, there is no escape. He was right. Since then I have produced books and articles on other topics in colonial and revolutionary history, but again and again I find myself returning to witchcraft. Over the decades, I have accumulated many intellectual debts that would take a long time to itemize in full. Many of these are acknowledged in my previous books and essays, but I would like to mention three individuals who played a central role in making this subject such a rich part of my intellectual life. John Demos was my first adviser at Brandeis University; it was his provocative scholarship that drew me into early American history. John's ability to tease out individual stories and their larger significance has remained an important inspiration ever since. Benson Saler introduced me to anthropological scholarship on witchcraft and broadened my perspective in ways for which I am deeply thankful. I hope that Benson realizes what a profound influence he had on my work. Soon after John Demos left for Yale, Christine Heyrman arrived at Brandeis and became my dissertation adviser. This turned out to be an amazing stroke of luck: Christine's combination of uncompromising rigor and unerring support has been, as the Puritans would say, a remarkable providence. Sustained as I was by the unfailing kindness and wisdom of these three mentors, my life as a young scholar was never a solitary endeavor.

Many years later, I continue to accumulate debts. Virginia DeJohn Anderson, University of Colorado, Boulder; Wendy Lucas Castro, University of Central Arkansas; Erika Gasser, California State University, Sacramento; Richard Johnson, University of Washington; Daniel Mandell, Truman State University; Elizabeth Reis, University of Oregon; Daniel Blake Smith, University of Kentucky; and James H. Williams, Middle Tennessee State University, provided invaluable comments on a draft of this book. The final version owes much to their insights and suggestions. I am grateful to the Boston Public Library, the Colonial Society of Massachusetts, the Connecticut Historical Society, the Danvers

Archival Center, the Massachusetts Historical Society, the Massachusetts Archives at Columbia Point, the Massachusetts Supreme Judicial Court Archives, the New York Public Library, and the Peabody Essex Museum for permission to include in this volume documents from their collections. My undergraduate research assistant, Christian Cameron, provided important help at an early stage of the project as he entered the documents into computer files. At Bedford/St. Martin's, Mary Dougherty has been a sage and supportive presence throughout this project's gestation. Debra Michals, my project development editor, has been consistently thoughtful, constructive, and sensitive to the challenges of making this topic accessible to students. Debra's acuity, good cheer, and wit make her a delight to work with. Jennifer Jovin has been gracious and efficient in shepherding the project through turnover to production.

But my principal debt is to my students. I have been teaching courses on witchcraft for over twenty years as well as discussing the subject more briefly in survey courses. How I teach this rich but challenging material has changed significantly over the years as I experiment with ways of making a world that produced witch accusations comprehensible to modern students. Most teachers come to realize that they learn as much from their students as their students learn from them, and I am no exception. I hope that I never stop appreciating their enthusiasm and insights, which go a long way toward explaining my sustained interest in this topic. It is to my students—past, present, and future—that I dedicate this volume.

Richard Godbeer

A Note about the Documents

The documents that survive from the Salem witch hunt are rich and varied. They include published accounts by observers, sermons in which ministers commented on the crisis, letters and journal entries in which contemporaries responded more privately to what was happening, and of course the official trial records. Most of these sources reflect the views of literate and educated men from the upper ranks of New England society. Yet the legal records also include hundreds of depositions from less privileged townsfolk and villagers who came forward to testify, whether against or in support of the accused. Many of those who did so could not write for themselves, but court officials recorded their oral testimony for future reference—and for posterity. Those transcriptions enable us to move beyond a reliance on theological treatises, sermons, legal manuals, and court judgments (important though these are), giving us access to the beliefs, experiences, and fears of ordinary people who played a central role in what happened that year.

When preparing documentary collections for use in undergraduate courses, historians have to decide whether it is more important to provide a literal transcription, even if that is sometimes at the expense of intelligibility, or whether some degree of adaptation is worthwhile as a helping hand to students unversed in the vagaries of premodern spelling and grammar. In preparing this volume, my priority has been to make the documents accessible and comprehensible. Some of the documents included in this volume were published in the seventeenth or early eighteenth century, in a few cases while the witch hunt was still going on; others were not originally intended for publication but were later transcribed and published. Even those documents that were produced for a public audience and made their way immediately into print require some adaptation. Early American printers often capitalized the first letters of words in ways that can seem to us and often were quite arbitrary. I have eliminated those capital letters in accordance with modern practice; I have also modernized spellings, filled out occasional contractions, and eliminated unnecessary commas.

Documents that were not originally meant for publication and that survive as handwritten manuscripts tend to be much more erratic in their spelling, grammar, and use of capitalization. This is particularly true of legal documents from the trials, many of which were written in haste and under considerable stress. The spelling, punctuation, and syntax used by those who recorded the claims, counterclaims, and decisions of those involved in the witch hunt are often breathtaking in their lapses and idiosyncrasies. Misspellings, contractions, and sentences that run on for many lines with little or no punctuation can make these documents seem at times quite incomprehensible. For these handwritten documents I have corrected misspellings, inserted the missing letters in contractions, and provided some minimal punctuation to guide the reader. I have also provided clarification in square brackets when it may not be immediately clear which person is indicated by a pronoun such as *he* or *she*. The result looks quite different from a literal transcript of the original document. (Instructors or students who wish to compare the versions included in this book with the original, unmodified documents can consult the recent scholarly edition of the court records edited by Bernard Rosenthal. See the Selected Bibliography.) These editorial interventions may disturb some purists, but it has been my experience that students find unmediated versions of these documents utterly perplexing. The corrections and clarifications that I have inserted will hopefully ensure that students and general readers stick with the documents and become gripped by the amazing story that they have to tell us.

Contents

The Salem Witch Hunt

A Brief History with Documents

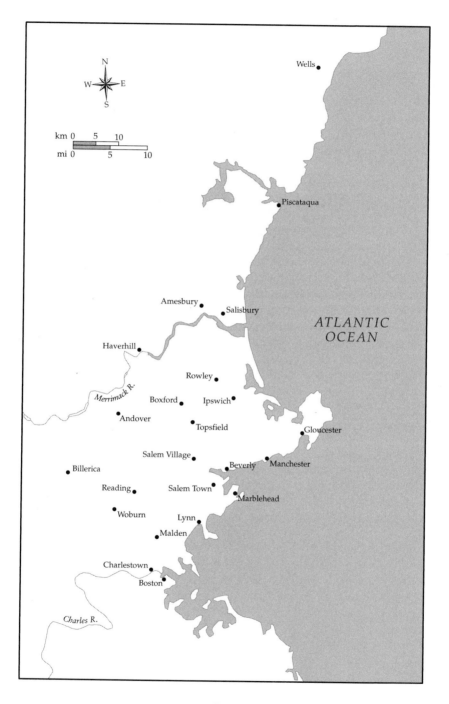

PART ONE

Introduction:
Explaining the Salem
Witch Hunt

In 1692, a witch panic swept through Essex County in Massachusetts. The panic began in Salem Village, a tiny farming community some fifteen miles north of Boston, but during that year over 150 women and men from roughly two dozen different towns and villages were formally charged with the crime of witchcraft (Map 1). Many other individuals were named informally. The tally of formal indictments might have continued to increase had the trials not been suspended that October amidst bitter controversy over the evidence used to convict accused witches. By the time the court halted its proceedings, nineteen people had been hanged; several others had died in prison awaiting trial; and one man who refused to plead "innocent" or "guilty" had been killed by the weight of stones that officials piled on his chest in a failed attempt to extract a plea from him. The Salem witch hunt convulsed an entire region of New England. It destroyed lives, devastated families, and left neighborhoods scarred by shared tragedy, resentment, and recrimination. More than three centuries later, the witch hunt of 1692 continues

Map 1. *Massachusetts in the Year of the Witch Hunt (opposite)*
The towns shown are those in which accused individuals resided in 1692.

to fascinate and horrify. It is perhaps not surprising that this lurid story has become one of the most notorious events in early American history. Indeed, it figures as one of the very few events from the colonial period that most modern Americans have heard of.

The panic began in January 1692, when several girls and young women in Salem Village began to have strange fits. The violence of these fits and the anguish of the afflicted girls horrified their families and neighbors. As the fits spread from household to household, local residents became increasingly worried. Not surprisingly, the parents, guardians, masters, and mistresses of those who had been struck down were especially eager to determine what or who was causing the afflictions and how to stop them. Two of the afflicted girls lived in the household of the village minister, thirty-nine-year-old Samuel Parris. Nine-year-old Elizabeth Parris was his daughter; eleven-year-old Abigail Williams was his niece. The minister's initial response was to seek the advice of William Griggs, the local physician. Parris was quite willing to consider the possibility that his daughter and niece were suffering from a physical ailment; he did not simply assume that the afflictions were supernatural. But Griggs concluded that medical treatment would not help the situation. In his view, the girls were "under an evil hand." Parris consulted with neighboring ministers, and they agreed with Griggs. The ministers advised Parris "to be much in prayer for the discovery of what was yet secret" and to "wait upon the Providence of God" (Document 10).

Parris and his family accordingly prayed for deliverance. But other villagers were reluctant to "sit still and wait," as the ministers had counseled. They wanted to find out who was afflicting the girls and to punish those responsible. Mary Sibley, the aunt of Mary Walcott, another of the afflicted girls, decided to take matters into her own hands. She had the minister's Indian slaves, Tituba and John, bake a cake made of meal mixed with Mary Walcott's urine, which they then fed to a dog. This was a traditional English technique for identifying witches: if all went well, the person responsible for Mary Walcott's affliction would now be exposed. Tituba, whom Parris had purchased while living in Barbados, had a reputation for occult skill and later admitted that "her mistress in her own country . . . had taught her some means to be used for the discovery of a witch." When Parris found out about the urine-cake, he was horrified and condemned the practice as "going to the Devil for help against the Devil" (Documents 10, 11, and 13).

But Parris himself now changed his strategy. Perhaps under pressure from worried and frightened neighbors, he encouraged the girls to name their tormentors. At the end of February, the girls accused three women of bewitching them, one of whom was Tituba, and local magistrates issued warrants for their arrest. This was not the first time in New England's history that officials had had to deal with accusations of witchcraft against several suspects at once, but over the next few weeks, accusations proliferated on a scale that was unprecedented. Not only did the girls from Salem Village identify a growing number of women and men who were allegedly tormenting them, but people in neighboring towns and villages came forward with accusations of their own. Before long, the entire county was in the grip of a major witch panic.

The explosion of witch accusations could not have come at a worse time since in early 1692 Massachusetts had no legally established government. In 1684 the government in London had withdrawn the charter that for over sixty years had enabled colonists in Massachusetts to arrange their own affairs with little interference from London. The much more authoritarian structure that replaced it two years later proved extremely unpopular. James II, the king who had imposed that new system of governance, was deposed in 1688, and colonists responded by carrying out a bloodless coup against his representatives in New England. Once a new monarch was installed in London, colonists dispatched agents to lobby for a government more to their liking. In early 1692, the colonists were waiting for a new governor to arrive from England. Until he arrived, no trials could take place. Meanwhile, the accusations continued to proliferate.

When Sir William Phips arrived in Boston on May 14 as the newly appointed governor of Massachusetts, he discovered that over four dozen people had been arrested on charges of witchcraft and that the number of accused witches was growing daily. A governor could at his discretion create special courts of Oyer and Terminer (meaning "to hear and determine") to address extraordinary situations such as a rapid accumulation of cases that might overwhelm the regular court system. These special courts followed the same evidentiary guidelines and procedures as regular courts, including trial by jury. Phips decided that this would be the most effective way to handle the mounting crisis. The governor moved swiftly, appointing six members of his council to sit as magistrates, with his deputy governor, William Stoughton, serving as chief justice of the court. None of these men were professional lawyers. But Stoughton had been trained for the ministry at Harvard College and so did have a thorough grounding in theology, which would presumably prove helpful in dealing with supernatural crimes.

The special court started its work two weeks later on June 2, meeting in Salem Town. The court turned out to be swift and ruthless in dispatching witch suspects. At its opening session, it convicted the first suspect to stand trial, Bridget Bishop, and sentenced her to death. Bishop was hanged outside Salem Town on June 10 (Documents 42–51). At its second sitting, which started on June 28 and lasted for five days, the court tried and convicted five women; they were hanged on July 19. Six more individuals appeared before the court during its third session, which convened on August 2 and lasted four days. All six were sentenced to death. One of these, Elizabeth Proctor, was granted a reprieve because she was pregnant, but the other five went to their deaths on August 19. The court's fourth session began on September 6 and ended on September 17, with a two-day break on September 11 and 12. During those two sets of five days, the court convicted another fifteen accused witches. One of these escaped from prison, and six were granted a reprieve because they had confessed and agreed to assist the court by identifying other witches. The remaining eight were hanged on September 22. So far, the conviction rate had been 100 percent.

But by this point the trials were mired in controversy. The court's proceedings had been dogged by criticism from the first day that it met. One of the judges, Nathaniel Saltonstall, had resigned in protest following the condemnation of Bridget Bishop. In mid-June the governor's council had asked a group of ministers to advise them on how best to proceed, presumably because officials were already on the defensive. The ministers' response raised serious concerns about the evidence being used to justify conviction, especially information that came from apparitions, referred to by contemporaries as "specters" (Document 81). The afflicted girls claimed that specters in the shape of particular individuals appeared to them and tried to recruit them as witches through combinations of temptation and torment. The accusers and their supporters insisted that the women and men so represented must have given their permission for devils to appear in their likeness and must be witches in league with Satan. The court evidently took the same view. Though the magistrates claimed that they were not convicting solely on the basis of spectral testimony, it was clear to observers that the chilling scenes in which afflicted girls claimed to be attacked by the specters of accused witches had a profound impact on the court. Though a few local ministers defended the proceedings, many of their colleagues became increasingly vocal in their criticism of the court during the summer. By early fall a growing chorus of concerned residents was voicing opposition to the trials. The court's trump card against these critics was that over fifty of the accused had confessed to their crimes, but a growing number of these confessors now recanted, claiming that they had incriminated themselves and other suspects under pressure from officials and in the hope that their lives would be spared for cooperating with the court (Documents 77–80).

At this point, Governor Phips decided that the fiasco had to end. In early October he informed the government in London that he had prohibited further arrests for witchcraft, excepting cases that were "unavoidable" (Document 85). On October 26, the Massachusetts assembly asked local ministers to meet in a formal convocation that would then advise how to deal with those of the accused still awaiting trial. On October 29, Phips dissolved the Court of Oyer and Terminer, referring all remaining cases to the regular court system, which had been reorganized in accordance with the new charter. In early 1693 the Supreme Court of Judicature convened to consider the cases of those fifty-two individuals who had survived the rigors of confinement (several had died in prison). The court acquitted forty-nine, but convicted three and immediately issued a warrant for their execution. The governor intervened again and reprieved all three before they could be taken away to be hanged. There now began a lengthy and painful period of reckoning as those involved in the witch panic had to come to terms with their roles in what had happened, especially the deaths of two dozen people (Documents 86–95).[1]

PUTTING SALEM INTO A LARGER CONTEXT

The beliefs and fears that made the witch hunt of 1692 possible did not appear out of nowhere in the early months of 1692. Over sixty trials for witchcraft had taken place in New England prior to those at Salem. And the Salem panic was not the only witch crisis to afflict the region that year. In Stamford, Connecticut, a servant girl who began to have fits that same spring accused several women, two of whom were tried and narrowly escaped with their lives.[2] Fear of witches was embedded within the culture that English migrants brought with them when they crossed the Atlantic to settle in North America. The Salem trials took place at the tail end of a European witch hunt that spanned three centuries (from roughly 1450 to 1750). Prosecutions varied in number and ferocity from place to place and from decade to decade, but over this period many thousands of accused women and men were convicted and executed.[3]

England's history of witch-hunting was relatively mild compared to that of some European countries. It had only one major witch panic (in 1647), though hundreds of English women and men were tried as witches during the second half of the sixteenth century and the first half of the seventeenth century. Across the Atlantic, accusations of witchcraft occurred throughout the British colonies. But there were far fewer prosecutions in the middle and southern colonies than in New England. There was one execution in Maryland and five in Bermuda. Even excluding the Salem trials, New England courts convicted sixteen women and men on charges of witchcraft during the second half of the seventeenth century (at least fourteen were hanged).[4] The disproportionate number of cases in New England was due to the powerful influence of religious culture in that region. As we will see, Puritan beliefs encouraged a preoccupation with evil forces that seemed to endanger individual souls and New England as a whole. The Devil's agents posed a constant threat, whether in the form of Indians threatening to invade English settlements or neighbors who used witchcraft to harm their enemies while masquerading as godly members of the community (Document 12).

What happened at Salem was, then, an exceptional manifestation of beliefs and fears that were commonplace in this period. Placing Salem within that broader context of witch beliefs and witch-hunting has become a major priority for recent historians. Scholars have paid close attention to contemporary witch beliefs that were shaped as much by traditional folk culture as by Puritan theology. They have also examined the social tensions and conflicts that often lay behind accusations of witchcraft, asking why those accusations tended to emerge from particular kinds of interaction and why some New Englanders were much more vulnerable than others to accusations of witchcraft. Of those accused as witches in seventeenth-century New England, almost four of every five were women. The documents surviving from witch trials have much to tell us about gender relations in early New England.

Yet even as scholars insist, quite rightly, that witch fears and accusations were a persistent feature of New England life, they also recognize that the panic of 1692 was very different from other trials for witchcraft in seventeenth-century New England—both in the scale of the witch hunt and in the intensity of the fears that gripped local residents that year. Early scholars of the witch hunt tended to focus on the issue of blame: some defended those involved as well-meaning but misguided; others condemned them as superstitious zealots or accused them of taking part in a murderous conspiracy.[5] Recent scholars have been more inclined to seek explanations for why a witch panic of this magnitude erupted at this particular time and in this specific locale. Some of these explanations have proved more convincing than others. For example, a graduate student in biology at the University of California, Santa Barbara, proposed in 1976 that the fits suffered by Salem Villagers were symptoms of a disease, convulsive ergotism, which came from eating contaminated grain. Scholars have scrutinized this argument and exposed its fundamental flaws, yet it has proved resilient outside academic circles.[6] More compelling explanations make the most sense when considered in combination. In seeking to understand any historical event or process, a multicausal approach is generally more helpful than a monocausal one.

The remainder of this introductory essay provides a brief overview of recent scholarship on witch beliefs and trials in seventeenth-century New England, paying particular attention to the Salem panic and its causes. It approaches the subject from a range of interwoven perspectives: religious, cultural, political, social, economic, gendered, and legal. The intention is to suggest some of the ways in which recent studies can help us make sense of the documents that follow in Part Two.[7] This introduction also provides background information about the legal system in colonial New England, the procedures that officials involved in the trials were supposed to follow, and the guidelines available to them as they embarked upon the challenging task of trying individuals in a court of law for what were, after all, invisible crimes.

PURITANISM AND THE SUPERNATURAL WORLD

To understand what happened in 1692, we must be willing to take seriously the ways in which English colonists in general and Puritans in particular viewed the world around them, including the interplay of natural and supernatural phenomena. It is all too easy to dismiss early American witch beliefs and accusations as the result of "superstition" or "ignorance." Many of the assumptions made by those involved in seventeenth-century witch trials may strike modern readers as bizarre, perhaps even laughable, yet those assumptions seemed neither peculiar nor unreasonable to accusers or to the officials who took their allegations seriously. At least some of those involved were remarkably intelligent and highly educated. Explaining illness or misfortune in terms of witchcraft would have made good sense to early New Englanders, given the ways in which they viewed and experienced the world around them. We do not need to agree with their perspective or condone their actions, but we do need to take them seriously if we are to understand why they thought and acted as they did.

In common with most Europeans and also the Indians who inhabited North America, New England settlers believed that the world was an enchanted place, filled with supernatural forces that could influence events and bring about changes in the natural world. Colonists believed that the supernatural realm could intrude upon their lives at any time. People living in this era did not believe in accidents or coincidence; they were always looking for the cause and meaning of events. Puritans in particular believed that each and every occurrence in this world, however seemingly trivial, was willed by God, without whom (as one minister put it) "not a sparrow falls unto the ground" (Document 3). Any extraordinary event that seemed to interrupt the natural order—comets and eclipses, dramatic fires and epidemics, deformed births and inexplicable crop failures, dreams and visions—carried supernatural significance (Documents 1 and 2).[8]

According to the worldview embraced by most New Englanders, God was constantly at work in their day-to-day lives, testing and tempting, rewarding and punishing, as each individual deserved. Puritans believed that no man or woman could ever deserve salvation: everyone inherited from Adam and Eve, the disobedient parents of all humankind, a basic moral deficiency that made it impossible for them to succeed in obeying God's laws. But God was willing to forgive those who tried earnestly to live virtuous lives, even though they could never entirely succeed. God had predestined certain men and women to be saved, not because they were virtuous but because they were sincerely striving to become virtuous in a constant battle against sinful thoughts and temptations. No one could know for certain whether they belonged to that select group until the Day of Judgment, but Puritans constantly searched within themselves for signs that they might be truly faithful. They also kept a close watch for any indication that God approved or, more likely, disapproved of their efforts. Ministers argued that any misfortune or mysterious illness carried a divine message: usually God was prompting sinners to self-examination, repentance for sinful thoughts or actions, and a renewed commitment to obey God's commandments (Documents 40 and 88). On some occasions God inflicted the warning himself; on others he allowed the Devil to act on his behalf, perhaps through a human witch. In either case, ministers insisted that the appropriate response was to repent and reform (Documents 3 and 4).

Yet devout New Englanders looked outward as well as inward for the source of their afflictions. When Samuel Parris became convinced that witchcraft was causing the fits that tormented his daughter and niece, he concluded that God must be punishing him and his family for their sins. At first he led his household in focusing on a course of prayerful self-examination and repentance. But eventually Parris struck outward at the more immediate cause of his problems, pressuring the afflicted girls to name their human tormentors so that those responsible could be brought to justice. There was nothing unorthodox about such a strategy, given that the Bible declared unequivocally, "Thou shalt not suffer a witch to live" (Exodus 22.18, King James Version). Scripture taught that witches were real and that they should be hunted down for punishment.

But self-examination and legal prosecution were not the only options available to colonists. They could also turn to traditional folk remedies that promised to identify and punish those who used witchcraft against them. On both sides of the Atlantic, there survived and flourished alongside Christianity deeply rooted folk beliefs that governed the use of magic. Folk magic was based on the assumption that men and women could wield supernatural power for their own benefit. Many settlers believed that through the use of simple techniques passed down from one generation to the next over hundreds of years, they could harness occult forces to achieve greater knowledge and control over their lives. They could, for example, predict the future by suspending an egg white in a glass to make a primitive crystal ball (Document 10). They could inflict harm on an enemy by stabbing a doll (sometimes called a "poppet") representing that person (Documents 44, 47, and 50). They could heal their physical ailments by combining herbal remedies with charms or spells. And they could defend themselves against occult attack through countermagic. Countermagic involved inflicting damage on a bewitched object or on something associated with an afflicted person, perhaps burning the ear of an afflicted sow or the hair of a bewitched child; this would undo the bewitchment and identify the witch, either by drawing her to the scene or by burning her (itself a gratifying form of retribution). This is what Mary Sibley had in mind when she asked Tituba to bake a urine-cake in hope of identifying whoever had bewitched her niece (Documents 10, 11, and 13).[9]

Most of these divining, healing, and defensive techniques were quite straightforward, and so it was not unusual for colonists to experiment on their own. But New Englanders also turned to magical experts in times of need. These experts—often called "cunning folk"—performed an important social service as they told fortunes, claimed to heal the sick, and offered protection against witchcraft. But contemporaries believed that cunning folk could also use their skills to harm or destroy those who crossed them. The belief that magic could be used for both good and

evil purposes placed cunning folk in an ambiguous and potentially perilous position. Anyone known for their occult skill had reason to worry if
they argued with a neighbor who then suffered a mysterious illness or
mishap. Neighbors might conclude that skills previously used for their
benefit were now being turned against them. Dorcas Hoar of Beverly
claimed to be able to tell fortunes and was known for the accuracy of her
predictions; she was accused of witchcraft in 1692 (Documents 57–59),
as was Tituba (Documents 28–32).

The basic assumption underlying folk magic—that those in need
could harness occult powers for their own ends—contrasted sharply
with the teachings of Puritan theology, which placed supernatural power
firmly in God's hands and insisted that those in adversity could hope to
end their affliction only by reaffirming their deference to God's authority. Clergymen were horrified by the popularity of magical techniques,
especially among supposedly devout settlers. They insisted that human
beings could not wield supernatural power and that scripture gave no
sanction for such experiments. The Puritan clergy did not doubt that
magic worked, but according to them it did so because the Devil intervened to assist whoever used magical techniques. Individuals might
think that they were successfully harnessing occult powers, but in fact
the Devil was doing it for them and so luring them into his service (Document 13).[10]

Yet in general, colonists who turned to magic do not seem to have
given much thought to where such powers came from. Ministers were
trained in theology and were deeply concerned with issues of causation.
Some of their congregants shared that concern, but others cared more
about results. Tradition taught that certain occult techniques were effective, so why not put them to the test? Colonists often combined religious
and magical strategies in a composite worldview that made little logical
sense but that worked for them. Some settlers may not have understood
why magic was objectionable from a theological perspective; others may
have understood quite well their ministers' objections but quietly ig-
nored official warnings or set aside their own misgivings—for the
simple reason that magic seemed to work. It also met needs for knowledge and control that Puritan theology reserved only for God. Some
colonists encouraged neighbors who were apparently bewitched to use
countermagic; others rejected such measures and condemned those
who advocated using them. These disagreements could become bitter
and fraught. After all, lives and souls were at stake (Documents 4 and 5).
Yet when colonists turned to magic, they were not necessarily rejecting
religious faith. More likely they were turning to whatever supernatural

resource seemed helpful at a given moment. Mary Sibley was a church member and presumably prayed to God for her niece's deliverance from affliction as well as asking Tituba to bake a urine-cake. She may well have felt that the child needed all the help she could get.

Neither magical belief nor the use of magical techniques was gender-specific. Both men and women functioned as cunning folk. The power wielded by these experts was potentially dangerous whether in the hands of a male or a female. Yet cunning women were much more likely than cunning men to be accused of witchcraft. For a female to wield mysterious and potentially lethal gifts contradicted the widespread assumption that power should rest in male hands, so magical skill was especially threatening if possessed by a woman. The disproportionate prosecution of female cunning folk testified to the colonists' fear of female power and a general conviction that witchcraft was for the most part a female offense.

DANGEROUS WOMEN

Witch accusations in Europe, England, and New England targeted far more women than men. Seventy-eight percent of all accused witches in New England were women. In this regard the Salem witch hunt was typical of prosecutions during the seventeenth century as a whole: 76 percent of those accused during the Salem panic were female. Roughly half of the men charged with this crime in New England were either married to or otherwise closely associated with accused women. They were, as historian John Demos puts it, suspect "by association" with female witches.[11] Puritan ministers did not teach that women were by nature more evil than men. But as historian Elizabeth Reis has pointed out, "colonists shared with their English brethren the belief that women's bodies were physically weaker than men's" and that therefore "the Devil could more frequently and successfully gain access to and possess women's souls."[12] Ministers reminded their congregations that it was Eve who first gave way to Satan and then seduced Adam, when instead she should have continued to serve his moral welfare in obedience to God. All women, pastors warned, had inherited from their first mother that dangerous blend of vulnerability and power. It was not only the male population that subscribed to this argument: both men and women internalized the claim that women were more vulnerable to the Devil's influence. As women accused other women, they participated in negative assumptions about their own sex.[13]

Yet most women in seventeenth-century New England were not accused of witchcraft. They became vulnerable to such allegations only if they seemed to be challenging their place in a gendered hierarchy that Puritans held to be ordained by God. New England colonists inhabited a hierarchical world in which people were expected to obey and respect those in authority over them. Like the majority of people during this period, they believed that the most fundamental of hierarchical relationships was that of man over woman: the authority of a patriarch within the family household over his wife, children, and servants was a model for all other hierarchical relations. Although the basic assumption underlying patriarchal order was that authority should rest with men, women had nonetheless a range of active and valued roles to play within New England society. Puritans argued that everyone, however humble or subordinate, deserved respect if they carried out faithfully their responsibilities within the hierarchy of God's creation. Women who accepted and fulfilled their allotted roles as wives, mothers, household mistresses, and church members were praised by relatives and neighbors as Handmaidens of the Lord. Puritan ministers taught that women were not "a necessary evil," as Catholic theologians had often claimed, but instead "a necessary good," provided by God as a "sweet and intimate companion" for men.[14] Puritan thinkers needed to believe this because wives and mothers played such an indispensable role in the raising of self-disciplined and godly children. "There was no place in this vision," historian Carol Karlsen writes, "for the belief that women were *incapable* of fulfilling such a role. Nor was there a place in the ideal Puritan society for women who refused to fill it."[15]

That cautionary note served as a none-too-subtle threat. Women whose circumstances or behavior seemed to disrupt social norms and hierarchies could easily lose their status as Handmaidens of the Lord and become branded as Servants of Satan. Especially vulnerable were women who had passed menopause and thus no longer served the purpose of procreation, women who were widowed and so neither fulfilled the role of wife nor had a husband to control them or protect them from malicious accusations, and women who had inherited or stood to inherit property, violating expectations that wealth would remain under male ownership as it passed from one generation to the next. Women who seemed unduly aggressive and contentious or who failed to show deference toward men in positions of authority and seemed not to accept their place in the social hierarchy were also more likely to be accused (Document 15). Such conduct would have struck contemporaries as problematic if exhibited by a man, but it was utterly unacceptable in a woman.[16]

Even as New England Puritans stressed the important roles played by wives and mothers within the family household, lingering fears complicated and compromised their celebration of women as "a necessary good." Behavior or circumstances that seemed disorderly could easily become identified as diabolical and associated with witchcraft: Satan had, after all, led a rebellion against God's rule in heaven. Colonists associated subversive women with witchcraft because they seemed to reenact the behavior of Eve and of the Devil, both of whom were real historical figures in the minds of New Englanders. Eve's legacy as a female prototype was double-edged: on the one hand, she had served as a successful helpmeet in the Garden of Eden; on the other, she was Satan's first human ally. Eve was worthy of honor as Adam's companion prior to their fall from grace, but her disobedience to God at the Devil's bidding made her the first witch.

MALEVOLENT NEIGHBORS

When seventeenth-century New Englanders suspected that they were bewitched, whether by a woman or a man, the person they blamed was usually a close neighbor with whom they had a history of personal tension or conflict. In most cases the antagonism developed according to one of three scenarios. In the first of these, neighbor A requested a favor such as temporary shelter or the loan of a household implement from neighbor B, who refused and then felt guilty for having done so. Neighbor A was disappointed and resentful, perhaps cursing neighbor B and vowing to get even. Neighbor B now displaced his own sense of guilt onto neighbor A, blaming neighbor A's vengeful anger for subsequent misfortunes, such as the unexplained death of livestock or a mysterious illness within neighbor B's family. According to neighbor B, witchcraft was at work and neighbor A was responsible (Documents 22, 24, and 25). In the second scenario, an exchange of goods between neighbor A and neighbor B went awry; neighbor A felt aggrieved and became angry. In the weeks, months, or even years that followed, neighbor B's family suffered a series of misfortunes and became convinced that neighbor A was taking revenge by using occult forces against them (Documents 46 and 50). In the third scenario, neighbor A and neighbor B quarreled because neighbor A had allegedly damaged property belonging to neighbor B. Neighbor A was enraged by the allegation. Members of neighbor B's family were subsequently troubled by mysterious misfortunes and accused neighbor A of bewitching them (Documents 49 and 60). The assumption underlying accusations of witchcraft in each scenario was that an individual who felt mistreated (neighbor A) had turned to witchcraft as a form of revenge, becoming the ultimate nightmare neighbor. Indeed, neighborliness (or lack thereof) was the fundamental issue for all those involved.[17]

If we are to understand why these kinds of arguments between neighbors escalated as frequently as they did into accusations of witchcraft, we need to appreciate the ways in which patterns of social interaction in New England settlements intersected neatly with belief in witchcraft. Most New Englanders lived in tiny communities where everyday life was intensely personal. Each resident not only knew everyone else in the town but also interacted with neighbors in many different roles and contexts. Most of us live in large towns or cities with populations in the tens of thousands and upward. Many of us have not even met all the neighbors on our street or in our apartment complex, let alone those who live in other parts of the town or city. Different people fulfill distinct and isolated functions in our lives. When we go to the bank, a government office, or a shopping mall, the chances are that the teller, official, or salesperson with whom we deal will be a stranger. Even if we have dealt with the person before, it is unlikely that we know him or her in any other capacity. The experience of a New England settler could not have been more different. Because personal interactions and influence were central to the experience of early New Englanders, it made good sense to account for misfortune or suffering in personal terms. A particular neighbor had quarreled with you and was now taking revenge for a perceived injury by bewitching you.

New Englanders were well aware that they depended on each other for their survival. Townsfolk and villagers helped each other put up new buildings or harvest crops; they exchanged food and simple products such as candles or soap in a local barter economy; and they gave each other emotional support as they navigated life's challenges and tragedies. The Puritan faith in which most of the colonists believed (albeit to varying degrees) taught that being a good neighbor had its spiritual as well as practical dimensions. Settlers must keep watch over one another, warn each other when they seemed to be in danger of giving way to sinful urges, and trust that others would keep an equally close eye on them. This emphasis on a spirit of community and mutual support meant that arguments between neighbors became not only irritating but also a betrayal of larger values on which their spiritual and practical welfare depended. It is, then, hardly surprising that such disputes gave rise to festering resentments.

In many instances there was no institutional outlet for the tensions and hostilities that resulted. If someone trespassed upon a neighbor's property or assaulted another town resident, a law had been broken and the malefactor would be dealt with accordingly. But refusing to lend a neighbor food or a tool was not a crime, and so the resulting animosity could not be expressed or mediated directly through civil or criminal proceedings. Witchcraft allegations provided an outlet for feelings of guilt or hostility rooted in confrontations between neighbors over issues of mutual support and responsibility. Yet we should be wary of concluding that New Englanders used such allegations merely as a cynical ploy to get rid of their enemies. Settlers saw the natural and supernatural worlds as tightly interwoven. Issues of mutual support and neighborliness were tied to spiritual endeavors, and anything that seemed to threaten spiritual integrity could be traced to the Devil and his minions. Most of those who accused their neighbors of bewitching them believed quite sincerely that they were guilty as charged. The histories of tension and conflict between neighbors that witnesses recounted for court officials reveal a web of resentment and fear that cast long, sometimes deadly, shadows over these seventeenth-century communities. Allegations of witchcraft brought together three important components of premodern culture: the inability to explain or control illness and other forms of misfortune, a deeply embedded belief in supernatural forces that could be used to inflict harm, and the densely personal nature of human interactions. The mysterious and the supernatural converged with what historian John Demos refers to as "things most tangible and personal." Along "the seam of their convergence" emerged accusations of witchcraft.[18]

THE WITCH PANIC OF 1692

But how helpful are these various interpretive approaches as we try to make sense of the Salem witch hunt? Several of those who stood trial in 1692 were cunning folk. These women and men had allegedly used their occult skills not only to divine the future and heal the sick but also to afflict and destroy, as in the case of Dorcas Hoar (Documents 57–59). Yet fear of magical cunning cannot explain all of the accusations or the scale of what happened that year. The Salem witch hunt continued a general tendency to associate witchcraft primarily with women. Many of the accusations in 1692 substantiate the argument that witch-hunting functioned as a way to rid the community of women who were perceived as disorderly and thus dangerous. Yet visions of gendered evil were by no means always consistent. After all, the witches at Salem had a male leader, George Burroughs (Documents 62–75). Those who accused Burroughs of being the "chief" witch reaffirmed patriarchal norms by claiming that even disorderly women would ultimately defer to men. Once the accusations spread beyond Salem Village, many people came forward to describe quarrels with their neighbors that had festered over the years and had given rise to suspicions of witchcraft; these histories of personal antagonism often conform to the patterns that emerge from earlier accusations (Documents 22, 24, 25, 46, 49, 50, and 60). Yet why these townsfolk and villagers chose to come forward with these stories and allegations in such large numbers at that particular point in time requires additional explanation. Furthermore, many of the accusations brought by the afflicted girls in Salem implicated women and men whom they had never even met, suggesting that the tensions and fears at work in 1692 transcended personal conflicts between neighbors.

The witch hunt of 1692 was extraordinary in its scale and in the intensity of the fears that it expressed. The witch panic makes most sense if we step back from events in Salem itself and place them in a broader context of military, political, and religious crisis. A succession of attacks directed against the settlements of New England during the two decades prior to 1692 had created intense anxiety among those who lived in the region. Perhaps the most terrifying of these were Indian raids that came in two waves, the first in 1675–1676 and the second beginning in 1689. Relations with local Indian nations had become increasingly tense as the colonists expanded further inland and became increasingly imperious in their treatment of the Indians. In 1675, a court in Plymouth executed three Wampanoags for having murdered an Indian convert to Christianity, instead of handing them over for punishment by their own people. Indians throughout the region were outraged and joined together to launch a major attack on English settlements, led by the chief of the Wampanoags, Metacomet (sometimes referred to by colonists and historians as King Philip). The warfare that ensued brought New England to the brink of destruction. Although the English colonists did eventually repel the Indians, they sustained devastating losses. The physical, economic, and psychological impact shook New England to its foundations.

A second wave of Indian attacks began just over a decade later. When James II, a close ally of the Catholic French, was removed from the

English throne and replaced with his daughter Mary and her Protestant husband, the French king Louis XIV declared war on England and its colonies. The French in Canada now encouraged Indian forces to launch a series of raids on the northeastern frontier of New England. This offensive resurrected memories of Metacomet's War and created widespread anxiety as people wondered where the "hell-hounds" would next strike (Document 6). In the summer of 1691, Indians attacked communities in western Massachusetts, and the panic intensified.

Puritans believed that New England and its native inhabitants had belonged to the Devil until the Protestant English arrived and secured the region for God. Many colonists were convinced that Indians worshipped the Devil and practiced witchcraft. Given that association and the recent shift of Indian raids in a southward direction, it is hardly surprising that anxiety about the Indian threat surfaced repeatedly in the trial depositions at Salem. Accusers and confessors described the Devil as appearing to them in the shape of an Indian man.[19] Some of the accusers were orphaned refugees from Maine, and several men who did not fit the usual witch stereotype became suspect because they were linked in various ways to Native Americans and the frontier. John Proctor, for example, had been fined for selling alcohol to Indians.[20] One of the confessing witches told the court that she had been "troubled with fear about the Indians and used often to dream of fighting with them." The Devil, she said, had promised that "if she would serve him she should be safe" because "he was able to deliver her from the Indians." Another claimed that French Canadians and Indian chiefs had attended witch meetings "to concert the methods of ruining New England." The prospect of Catholics, Indians, and witches joining forces to invade God's stronghold in the New World would have horrified godly colonists, and yet it would also have seemed to them a natural alliance.[21]

Indians were by no means the only enemies to have launched assaults on New England during the years preceding 1692.[22] Political reforms imposed by the government in London had also threatened to undermine the colonists' way of life. In 1684 the crown revoked the charter that had granted Massachusetts something akin to self-government. Two years later, the northern colonies were incorporated into a single entity, to be known as the Dominion of New England. There would henceforth be no representative assemblies, and all power would be vested in the governor and his councilors. The man appointed to rule as governor, Sir Edmund Andros, was a career soldier with an autocratic temperament. He was also an Anglican, much to the outrage of Puritans, who saw their new governor's religion as one short step away from

Roman Catholicism, which they in turn associated with the Antichrist. Andros attempted unsuccessfully to negotiate a peace with the Indians and then led an equally unsuccessful military expedition against them in Maine. Some suspected that the governor had traveled northward not to attack Indians but to make a secret pact with them and also with French Catholics in Canada, plotting the destruction of Puritan New England. Opponents of the Andros regime characterized dominion officials as "tools of the Adversary" (a term used to describe Satan), and one of the governor's friends was even denounced as a "Devil."[23]

Anglicanism was not the only heresy intruding on New England. In the summer of 1688, a Quaker preacher named George Keith arrived in New England and launched an evangelical campaign. Quakers rejected many of the beliefs that other Protestants held dear. Their egalitarian ideals—refusing to bow, kneel, or remove their hats out of respect for a person of higher rank—challenged basic assumptions about hierarchy and horrified even those who did not care much about their religious views. Quakers claimed to receive revelation from God, but Puritans declared that these so-called revelations were really diabolical. The Quakers were so called because they sometimes shook when receiving revelation; the similarities between these convulsions and demonic possession did not go unnoticed by their enemies. And just as women who challenged social norms could end up being associated with Satan and his rebellion against rightful authority, so Quakers who refused to show respect for social hierarchy were seen as aligning themselves with the prince of disorder and sin.

Though Quakers remained a tiny minority, the vehemence of anti-Quaker tracts that appeared in the early 1690s testifies to the danger that some Puritans believed Quakers posed. What made matters worse was that the new charter of 1691 gave freedom of worship to *all* Protestants. Until 1684 only the male members of Puritan churches had been allowed to vote in political elections, but now the right to vote would be based instead on landownership (as in England and the other North American colonies), thus including property-owning dissenters such as Anglicans and Quakers in the political process. These changes struck a direct blow to Puritan dominance in New England.

Puritans had felt for some time that their godly society was under threat. Most of the colonists who settled in New England during the first few decades of settlement were committed Puritans, but during the second half of the seventeenth century the population became more diverse in its values and priorities. Some of those who migrated in these later decades were drawn more by economic opportunity than by religious ideals; and as the original settlers produced children, not all of these native-born New Englanders grew up to share their parents' values. Those who identified closely with the religious goals of the early settlers feared that they were losing control of the region's culture and that New England was in a state of moral decline. A more diverse population and a more worldly way of life struck them as the Devil's work.

That sense of decline and the siege mentality that it created among devout settlers provided an important context for the ways in which colonists responded to crises that struck New England during the years prior to the Salem panic. Indian raids, the Dominion, Quaker evangelism, and the dramatic implications of the new charter left many colonists feeling imperiled — "like a company of sheep torn by wolves" (Document 6). From a modern perspective, these events seem unconnected to witchcraft, but not so in the minds of seventeenth-century New Englanders. The colonists described these various threats in much the same language used to characterize witches: as alien, invasive, and malevolent. To be ruled by Andros and his cronies, to be attacked by Indians, or to be evangelized by Quakers was equivalent to being assaulted by Satan. From this perspective, the witch crisis of 1692 was not an isolated event, but rather the climax of a devilish assault upon the region (Documents 6–9).

The pattern of witch accusations that year suggests an intense preoccupation with invasion. Those who could be linked in some way to recent experiences of physical and spiritual assault proved most vulnerable to accusations of witchcraft. Fear of Indians resonated through the testimony given at the trials. And a significant number of the accused had close Quaker associations.[24] Many of the accused were clearly perceived as outsiders, either literally or figuratively. Eight of the Andover suspects were marginalized by ethnic affiliation. (Martha Carrier, for example, was Scottish and had married a Welshman.)

Meanwhile, deepening fears and tensions in the tiny community of Salem Village paralleled the anxieties gripping New England as a whole.[25] Salem Village developed as an outgrowth of Salem Town, one of the region's largest seaports. It was situated within the territorial bounds of Salem Town and had no civil government of its own; it was legally joined with and subordinate to the nearby seaport. Salem Town needed the food that Salem Villagers produced and benefited from the taxes that they paid. But some villagers wanted independence from the town, in part because the latter had proved remarkably insensitive to their concerns. The church in Salem Town, for example, refused to let the villagers form a congregation of their own, despite the inconvenience of having to travel so far to the town meetinghouse. At least part of this reluctance was financial since ecclesiastical independence would result in villagers paying taxes to support their own church instead of the congregation in Salem Town. Farmers who were committed to time-honored values of stability and moral community also wanted to separate themselves from the social mobility and self-interested individualism that increasingly characterized the nearby seaport. These villagers tended to perceive neighbors who lived nearer to the town or associated with its commercial interests as morally suspect and untrustworthy. Two competing visions of New England's future turned a conflict over practical issues into a culture war.

Salem Village became increasingly conflict-ridden as those who associated with the town aligned against those who were eager to separate and form an autonomous community. Proponents of separation from the town eventually secured the establishment of an independent church in 1689 and the ordination of Samuel Parris as their pastor. Parris proved to be an unfortunate choice: a failed and bitter merchant who resented those who succeeded in the world of commerce, he fueled local hostilities. Parris gave a series of inflammatory sermons that translated factional division into a cosmic struggle between the forces of good and evil. In the minds of his supporters, Salem Town became the symbol of an alien, corrupt, and even diabolical world that threatened the welfare of Salem Village (Document 12).

Because supporters of Samuel Parris perceived their enemies as nothing less than evil, it was but a short step for them to become convinced that those aligned with the town and its interests were servants of Satan. Historians Paul Boyer and Stephen Nissenbaum have argued that divisions within the village were reproduced in the pattern of accusations in 1692, so that a disproportionate number of accused witches and their defenders lived on the side of the village nearest to Salem Town, while most of the accusers lived on the western side.[26] Many of the accused had personal histories or interests that either associated them with Salem Town or otherwise marked them as threatening outsiders. But this was not just a cynical bid to dispose of enemies by labeling them as witches. Villagers pointed the finger of accusation at particular individuals because they truly believed them to be morally deficient and thus likely members of a diabolical conspiracy. Those people who had become identified with forces of change, which their enemies construed as disorder and immorality, were now accused of having allied with radical evil, namely, the Devil.

Boyer and Nissenbaum's perspective on the witch panic has been influential but also controversial. Perhaps the most serious problem with their argument is its focus on Salem Village, given that the witch hunt of 1692 was, after all, a regional phenomenon involving two dozen towns and villages. Salem did not even produce the most accusations; that dubious distinction fell to Andover.[27] Yet the tense situation within Salem Village itself paralleled crises in the region at large as those villagers who feared and resented Salem Town came to see all those associated with it as the agents of a corrupt and evil world that threatened to destroy their way of life. The afflictions in Salem Village unleashed fears of alien, invasive, and diabolical forces that had accumulated throughout the region during the last two decades. "The usual walls of defense about mankind," declared a minister in Boston, "have such a gap made in them that the very devils are broke in upon us" (Document 9).

THE AFFLICTED GIRLS

And what of the afflicted girls and young women who claimed that witches wanted them to join a satanic conspiracy and tortured them when they refused? It was their fits that began the witch hunt, and they remained the focus of attention throughout the trials.[28] Whenever an accused witch came before the magistrates, the girls were also brought in so that officials could observe whether they would be struck down by the defendant (they almost always were). Observers at the time and commentators ever since have struggled to understand the behavior and motives of these girls and young women. Yet we know very little about the circumstances under which the fits began. (What little we do know is contained in the accounts by John Hale and Deodat Lawson; see Documents 10 and 11.) The attitudes of contemporary observers toward the girls and their accusations tended to be colored by each observer's overall position on the crisis. And the one surviving statement from an afflicted girl in the aftermath of the panic (Document 91) followed a general tendency to explain what had happened in terms of delusion by the Devil; it tells us next to nothing of her individual motives or feelings during the panic. The information at our disposal is, then, woefully incomplete. Equally frustrating is that the questions we might like to ask are not necessarily those asked by those involved in the panic.[29]

It is possible that the torments were faked. Given that so many of the people whom the afflicted girls accused were also disliked or feared by their parents, masters, and mistresses, it is tempting to see the girls as embroiled in a cynical and deadly conspiracy, whether as the puppets of murderous adults or as active and willing participants in their own right. Yet we should think carefully before leaping to this conclusion. The afflicted girls were almost certainly influenced by the attitudes and fears of the adults with whom they lived, but that does not necessarily mean that those adults actually told them what to say and whom to accuse. The girls may simply have named people whom they had heard their parents or masters and mistresses condemn as evil and malign. It seems quite likely that there was an element of performance in their fits, and they may well have relished the power that they exercised during the court's proceedings, a power that children and young women would not otherwise have attained in seventeenth-century New England. But that does not necessarily mean that they were lying when they told officials that they believed their fits to be caused by witchcraft. This was, let us not forget, a culture in which most people believed that supernatural forces could and did impinge on the natural world; the colonists assumed witchcraft to be a real threat. And even if the girls' fits were partly or wholly feigned, the responses of those around them could very easily have ended up scaring them into believing that they really were afflicted. The line between counterfeit and sincerity can sometimes be very hazy.

It does seem clear that the afflicted girls were angry as well as afraid and that their anger was not directed solely against those whom they accused of witchcraft. They rarely missed an opportunity to shock and insult those in authority over them. When the Reverend Deodat Lawson gave a guest sermon in Salem Village on March 20, two of the afflicted disrupted the service with impertinent remarks that under normal circumstances would have been unthinkable in a Puritan meetinghouse. Lawson later wrote:

> After psalm was sung, Abigail Williams said to me, "Now stand up, and name your text!" And after it was read, she said, "It is a long text." In the beginning of sermon, Mrs. Pope, a woman afflicted, said to me, "Now there is enough of that." And in the afternoon, Abigail Williams, upon my referring to my doctrine, said to me, "I know no doctrine you had. If you did name one, I have forgot it." (Document 11)

During the weeks and months that followed, the afflicted girls and women accused respectable members of the Puritan community such as Rebecca Nurse of bewitching them (Document 11) and alleged that an ordained minister was leading the witch conspiracy. According to them, at least some of those who posed as the servants and handmaidens of God were really the Devil's disciples.

To understand why the afflicted girls and young women behaved in this way, we need to consider their recent histories and the ways in which their upbringing would have shaped their responses to the circumstances in which they now found themselves. A significant number of these accusers had been orphaned in the recent Indian attacks and had come south to live with relatives or family friends, some of them as servants. The farms on which their families had depended for their livelihood had been either badly damaged or completely destroyed. As a result, they had little or no dowry to offer, and so their marital prospects were dismal. In a society that valued women largely in terms of their husbands' social and economic standing, they must have known that they were almost certainly doomed to obscurity.[30] No wonder, then, that at least one of them had apparently experimented with divination during the winter of 1691–1692 in an attempt to find out who her future husband would be (Document 10). And no wonder, too, that they used their temporary power and prestige during the witch crisis to attack, none too subtly, the Puritan establishment that taught members of its flock to accept unquestioningly the fate handed down to each of them by God.

Having grown up in devout households and communities, these young women doubtless understood that their anger and resentment made them potential recruits for the Devil's cause. As good Christians, they would have feared rebellious emotions that they equated with disorder and evil, personified in the Devil and his first recruit, Eve. But by claiming and perhaps convincing themselves that they were bewitched, they could express anger and discontent without having to acknowledge full responsibility for such feelings. After all, the Devil and his followers were speaking through them. And by accusing others of being witches, they shifted attention away from their own moral failings to those of the women and men whom they now accused of allegiance to Satan. This is not to suggest that they were using their fits simply to express opinions that they would not otherwise have dared to articulate and to deflect criticism away from themselves. They may have feared quite sincerely that the Devil and his disciples were after them; their faith taught them that the resentment they felt made them likely recruits. They may have feared above all else the thoughts and feelings that lurked within themselves. Ultimately, the afflicted girls were fighting a war against their own inner demons.[31]

TRYING A WITCH

When people became convinced, for whatever reason, that a neighbor had used witchcraft against them, they could respond in a number of ways. They could focus on their own spiritual failings as the ultimate reason for God's having unleashed the Devil and his minions. They could seek revenge through the use of countermagic. Or they could lodge a formal complaint and so initiate a criminal prosecution. The first response treated the situation as a spiritual challenge and placed at least some blame for what was happening on the victims themselves. The second responded to supernatural affliction by blaming someone else and seeking retribution through occult means. The legal response offered victims the possibility of official and public retribution, but it also required that accusers come forward with hard evidence of the suspect's guilt. And there lay the rub: subjecting a supernatural crime to judicial scrutiny was no small challenge.

To convict someone on charges of witchcraft, the accusers had to produce clear evidence of guilt that corresponded with the law's definition of witchcraft. In New England, that definition focused on the witch's identity as a heretic. Theologians on both sides of the Atlantic depicted witches as servants of the Devil who had forsaken Christianity and sworn allegiance to Satan. In return for committing to serve him, each witch was assigned a familiar spirit, or demon, that would do the witch's bidding; this included inflicting harm on the witch's enemies and their property. In England and its New England colonies, allegations of witchcraft were handled by secular courts, not ecclesiastical courts of inquisition like those that conducted witch trials in Spain, Italy, and other Catholic countries. But the legal code in Massachusetts was, nonetheless, framed in theological terms. It defined a witch as "any man or woman . . . [who] hath or consulteth with a familiar spirit."[32] To convict a witch in a Massachusetts court, there had to be proof that the accused had sworn allegiance to the Devil or had inflicted occult harm through a familiar spirit (in which case the court could assume that a covenant had been signed).

Yet ordinary men and women were much more inclined to think about witchcraft as a practical problem; they were interested less in causation than in results. They wanted to know who the witch was, and they wanted her punished. Depositions in most witch cases reflected that practical preoccupation and rarely made any mention of the Devil. The evidence that witnesses produced against witch suspects in New England prosecutions generally fell into one of four categories. Most frequently, accusers described quarrels with the defendant, followed by mysterious illnesses or misfortunes that were presumably brought on by vengeful witchcraft (Documents 22, 24, 25, 46, 49, 50, and 60). Sometimes witnesses related in their depositions that the accused had a reputation for magical cunning, perhaps because they told fortunes or used spells to heal the sick; this suggested that the accused had occult powers that may have been deployed for malicious as well as benign purposes (Documents 57–59). Witnesses also described having turned to countermagic in the hope of identifying and perhaps injuring whoever had bewitched them; they reported the results of such experiments to the court as incriminating testimony. Finally, neighbors of the accused would describe generally suspicious behavior, such as extraordinary and perhaps superhuman strength (Documents 62, 68, and 74).

Neither legal nor theological experts were impressed by these kinds of evidence. They dismissed descriptions of mysterious illness or misfortune following an argument with the accused as insufficient grounds for conviction. They also warned that Satan was a malicious liar. When people turned to countermagic, for example, he might exploit their credulity and produce misleading effects that incriminated the innocent. Judges were occasionally willing to conclude that divination or other magical practices proved collusion between the accused witch and the Devil (theologians did, after all, argue that magic was not condoned by God and so must rely on a diabolical agency); but for the most part New England courts were loathe to convict unless the evidence presented against the defendant made explicit mention of the Devil.

The fact that witnesses did not adapt their testimony to fit legal requirements, peppering their depositions with helpful references to the Devil, suggests that ordinary colonists focused quite doggedly on practical issues when thinking about witchcraft and that they were less thoroughly schooled in official ideology than our stereotypes of early New Englanders would lead us to expect. Other than letters or word of mouth, there was no way of transmitting information about these cases (not even newspapers, let alone radio, television, or the Internet). Townsfolk preparing to give testimony against a neighbor suspected of witchcraft might be aware that a recent prosecution in another county or colony had failed to secure a conviction, but they did not necessarily know exactly why.

In Europe, England, and New England alike, there was a significant gulf between the ways in which theologians thought about witchcraft and the practical preoccupations of most ordinary folk. That discrepancy mattered most when people turned to the legal system for protection against suspected witches, since courts had to mediate between these two perspectives as they assessed the evidence before them. The witchcraft laws in European countries generally defined witchcraft as a diabolical heresy, potentially a serious problem for those applying the laws in judicial proceedings, but in many jurisdictions the courts could use torture to extract the kinds of evidence that would justify conviction.[33] In England, by contrast, the courts of common law that presided over witchcraft cases were prohibited from using torture during the questioning of suspects. But the English statutes enacted against witchcraft in 1542 and 1563 defined the crime as a hostile act rather than as heresy, so that the preoccupation of most accusers with practical harm was less problematic.[34]

The New England authorities operated under English jurisdiction and so had no legal recourse to torture when questioning defendants in witchcraft cases. But unlike their English counterparts, New England courts had to operate according to a biblically inspired definition of witchcraft that demanded proof of the Devil's involvement. As a result, they were uniquely ill-equipped to secure convictions, which was very bad news for those who believed in the guilt of the accused. The only occasion on which New England courts presiding over witch trials gathered extensive evidence of diabolical allegiance was the Salem witch hunt, which was also the one occasion on which the authorities used extreme psychological pressure and physical torture, illegally, to extract a large number of confessions (Documents 37, 77–80, and 84). In other seventeenth-century New England cases, the discrepancy between legal requirements and popular testimony more often than not resulted in acquittal. Of those sixty-one known prosecutions, sixteen at most resulted in conviction and execution, a rate of just over 26 percent.[35]

New England courts were willing to convict accused witches, but only if the evidence satisfied strict standards of proof. In a capital case, this meant a voluntary confession or at least two independent witnesses to an incident demonstrating the individual's guilt. Most magistrates had no legal training; they sat on the bench as a part-time public service, not as a full-time professional career. But at least some of these magistrates worked hard to prepare for witchcraft cases by reading legal manuals and theological works on the subject. During the previous two centuries, English writers had produced a vast body of scholarship examining witchcraft from theological, legal, and medical perspectives. The two most influential studies of witchcraft as a legal problem were *A Discourse on the Damned Art of Witchcraft* by William Perkins (1608) and *A Guide to Grand-Jury Men* by Richard Bernard (1627). Both authors wanted to establish a straightforward and reliable procedure for trying witches. Perkins and Bernard rejected time-honored practices such as "ducking," which involved throwing suspects into a pond or river. (If they floated, the water had rejected their bodies as unholy and so they must be guilty as charged; if they sank, they must be innocent.) The two authors argued that there was neither biblical nor scientific justification for such procedures.[36] According to Perkins and Bernard, unless an accused witch confessed, courts could justify conviction only if two or more trustworthy witnesses had seen the accused witch either invoke the Devil or perform deeds that could only have been achieved through the assistance of a demon. In addition to consulting books such as those by Perkins and Bernard, magistrates also turned to ministers for advice during witch trials. After all, clergymen were learned men of God with a detailed knowledge of the supernatural world who could help to make sense of the often perplexing evidence on which such cases depended.[37]

The combined impact of legal guides and ad hoc consultation was generally heartening for defendants, but less so for those who wanted them convicted. Hard evidence of any kind was difficult to secure in cases that centered on invisible crimes. Yet one type of evidence that could potentially overcome this difficulty was the witch's teat. Contemporaries believed that when a witch signed a covenant with the Devil, she or he was assigned a demon, usually in the form of an animal, which would become her or his familiar and carry out malevolent deeds on her or his behalf. The witch fed the familiar by allowing it to suck blood from a third nipple, otherwise known as the witch's teat. This was an aspect of witch lore that ministers, legal experts, and laypeople agreed on. The laws passed against witchcraft in New England focused specifically on a witch's relationship with her familiar spirit, presumably because this offered the possibility of physical evidence. Many witnesses giving testimony at witch trials claimed that they had seen familiars feeding from accused witches (Documents 11, 18, 28, and 52). Court officials responded to such claims by having suspects examined (preferably by male doctors or women experienced in midwifery, but sometimes by locals with no medical experience whatsoever) to see if they did indeed have a third nipple (Documents 35, 45, and 72). However, there was a problem: many people have marks or lumps on their bodies, and the examiners were more often than not uncertain as to whether the marks that they found on accused witches were natural or witch's teats. As a result, courts were rarely in a position to conclude definitely that the defendant had a third nipple.

The neighbors and enemies of accused witches had given what they considered to be damning testimony and were often infuriated by the reluctance of the court to treat their depositions as legally compelling. Magistrates feared that if they approved the conviction of a witch suspect on the basis of dubious evidence, they might very well be executing an innocent person. But accusers felt that they had risked their lives in speaking out against a witch who lived in their midst; if she was freed back into their community, the irate and vengeful creature might give them good reason to regret ever having come forward to testify. In the minds of men and women who did not doubt witchcraft's malevolent power, this pattern of acquittal was a gross miscarriage of justice. Neighbors sometimes refused to accept the verdict, conferred with each other, gathered new evidence against the suspect, and then renewed legal charges.[38]

Yet as the difficulty of securing a legal conviction for witchcraft became increasingly apparent, New Englanders became less inclined to initiate legal prosecutions against suspected witches. Nor were officials eager to take on such cases. There were nineteen witch trials in New England during the 1660s, but only six during the 1670s and eight during the 1680s. The dramatic fall in the number of prosecutions for witchcraft during the 1670s and 1680s was not due to any decline in fear of witches. That became only too clear in 1692 when official encouragement of witch accusations in and around Salem Village resulted in over 150 formal charges, some of which doubtless represented a backlog of festering suspicions from the past decade or so.

THE COLLAPSE OF THE TRIALS

The magistrates charged with handling the panic of 1692 proved much more willing to convict than had those who presided over previous witch trials. During the summer and early fall of that year, the special court tried twenty-seven individuals and found all of them guilty as charged. The magistrates must have been heartened by a fundamental difference between the trials over which they were presiding and earlier cases: the testimony accumulating at Salem contained plentiful evidence of the Devil's involvement in the alleged bewitchments and so seemed much more likely to satisfy legal requirements. Over fifty of those indicted in 1692 confessed that they were indeed witches who had covenanted with Satan. These women and men described, often in graphic detail, their initiation into the Devil's service and also named others who had allegedly joined the satanic conspiracy (Documents 28, 29, 61, and 76). Legal experts such as Perkins and Bernard argued that confession was by far the most satisfactory basis for conviction in a witchcraft case. Yet by the end of the summer many of these confessing witches had recanted, claiming that their admissions of guilt had been forced from them through the use of psychological pressure and physical torture. Some of those recanting revealed that they had given false confessions because officials promised to spare their lives on condition that they admit their guilt, renounce their allegiance to Satan, and cooperate with the authorities in naming other witches. It is not clear whether court officials intended these reprieves of execution to be temporary or permanent, but in a ghastly irony, only those who refused to perjure themselves went to their deaths (Documents 37, 77–80, and 84).

Apart from confessions, almost all of the testimony that made reference to the Devil came from the afflicted girls and young women. Most of their information came, they claimed, from the specters of witches that appeared to them, as in the cases of Sarah Good (Documents 16, 17, 19, and 21), Tituba (Documents 30 and 31), John Proctor (Documents 33, 34, and 36), Bridget Bishop (Documents 44 and 51), Dorcas Hoar (Documents 53–56), and George Burroughs (Documents 65, 67, and 71). Theologians taught that human beings could not themselves turn into or produce specters; instead, devils assumed their form and acted on their behalf. The magistrates took the position that devils could appear in the image of a particular individual only with that person's permission, so that the appearance of a specter could be treated as proof that the individual represented was, in fact, a witch. Officials also noted when a movement by the accused in court produced a corresponding torment in the afflicted girls (Documents 11, 42, and 52). The court placed considerable emphasis on the touch test, whereby witch suspects were required to place their hands on the afflicted girls. If the girls recovered from their fits, which they usually did, the accused witch must be guilty. The magistrates were apparently convinced that unless courts treated touch test results as incriminating evidence, "it would scarce be possible ever to convict a witch."[39]

Yet critics of the court argued that neither spectral evidence nor the touch test was reliable as a basis for conviction. Documents 81 to 84 lay out those arguments in detail. But it is worth noting here that none of those attacking the court questioned the reality of witchcraft. What they did doubt was the possibility of proving who exactly was responsible for witchcraft, unless the witch freely confessed. If no confession was forthcoming, they insisted, evidence must be based, as in any criminal prosecution, on "that which one man can know concerning another by his senses, and that according to the true nature and use of them."[40] How that kind of evidence could be secured when dealing with supernatural acts was open to question. Equally troublesome was that the Devil was a notorious liar, so that any information subject to his influence might well be misleading and part of a scheme to incriminate the innocent.

Once spectral testimony and the touch test came under attack and once confessors began to recant, the court found itself in an extremely awkward position. An impressive number of townsfolk and villagers from communities across Essex County had come forward to testify against witch suspects; their depositions testified eloquently to a widespread and profound fear of witchcraft. But unlike the confessors and afflicted girls, these other witnesses rarely mentioned the Devil's involvement as the law demanded. The evidence that they provided in their depositions bore a close resemblance to the testimony presented at earlier trials (such as descriptions of quarrels with the accused followed by mysterious illnesses or misfortunes) that had usually failed to convince magistrates and had resulted in acquittal. As the eagerness of the court to convict collided with a growing chorus of outrage and condemnation, the governor felt that he had no choice but to suspend the proceedings and reassess the situation.[41]

Neither critics of the court nor posterity would look kindly on the proceedings of 1692 and the deaths that resulted, but from the perspective of people who wanted the courts to take decisive action against witches in their midst, the acquittal and release of so many suspects in the weeks and months following the suspension of the trials must have been both galling and frightening. That witch trials disappeared from the history of New England shortly thereafter owed as much to popular disillusionment with the legal process as to any reluctance on the part of officials to accommodate witch accusations.[42] Belief in witchcraft and fear of witches would persist throughout the eighteenth century, despite growing doubts about the reality of supernatural phenomena within educated circles. Countermagic remained a popular defense against occult attack, and sometimes people used more direct means to punish those whom they believed to be witches. In the summer of 1787, Philadelphians lynched a woman suspected of witchcraft in a street near the building where the Constitutional Convention was taking place. In the minds of many people, witchcraft was still a very real threat.[43]

NOTES

[1] For more detailed narratives of the witch hunt, see Chadwick Hansen, *Witchcraft at Salem* (New York: George Braziller, 1969); and Mary Beth Norton, *In the Devil's Snare: The Salem Witchcraft Crisis of 1692* (New York: Knopf, 2002).

[2] For more on the Stamford witch hunt, see Richard Godbeer, *Escaping Salem: The Other Witch Hunt of 1692* (New York: Oxford University Press, 2005).

[3] For a balanced synthesis of the massive scholarship on this subject, see Brian P. Levack, *The Witch-Hunt in Early Modern Europe*, 3rd ed. (New York: Pearson, 2006).

[4] For witchcraft cases elsewhere in the British colonies on the mainland of North America, see John Demos, *The Enemy Within: 2,000 Years of Witch-Hunting in the Western World* (New York: Viking, 2008), 87–92. For witch trials in Bermuda, see Michael Jarvis, "Bermuda," in *Encyclopedia of Witchcraft: The Western Tradition*, ed. Richard M. Golden (Santa Barbara: ABC-Clio, 2006), 111–12.

[5] For examples of works more sympathetic to those involved, see George L. Kittredge, "Notes on Witchcraft," *Proceedings of the American Antiquarian Society* 18 (1907):

148–212; and Samuel Eliot Morison, *The Puritan Pronaos: Studies in the Intellectual Life of New England in the Seventeenth Century* (New York: New York University Press, 1936). For more condemnatory works, see Charles W. Upham, *Salem Witchcraft*, 2 vols. (Boston: Wiggin and Lunt, 1867); and James Truslow Adams, *The Founding of New England* (Boston: Little, Brown, 1921). Two recent books that do not flinch from placing blame for what happened at Salem are Enders A. Robinson, *The Devil Discovered: Salem Witchcraft 1692* (New York: Hippocrene Books, 1991), which sees the witch hunt as driven by conspiracy; and Bernard Rosenthal, *Salem Story: Reading the Witch Trials of 1692* (New York: Cambridge University Press, 1993), which places much emphasis on the role played by "simple fraud" in the trials (185).

[6]Linnda R. Caporael, "Ergotism: The Satan Loosed in Salem?" *Science*, Apr. 2, 1976, 21–26. For a critique of Caporael's thesis, see Nicholas P. Spanos and Jack Gottlieb, "Ergotism and the Salem Village Witch Trials," *Science*, Dec. 24, 1976, 1390–94.

[7]For a more detailed account of how historians, scientists, and playwrights have sought to explain the witch hunt over the past three hundred years, see Demos, *The Enemy Within*, 189–212.

[8]David D. Hall, *Worlds of Wonder, Days of Judgment: Popular Religious Belief in Early New England* (New York: Knopf, 1989), chap. 2.

[9]For a detailed discussion of magical beliefs and practice, see Richard Godbeer, *The Devil's Dominion: Magic and Religion in Early New England* (New York: Cambridge University Press, 1992), esp. chap. 1.

[10]For discussion of clerical opposition to magic, see ibid., chap. 2.

[11]John Demos, *Entertaining Satan: Witchcraft and the Culture of Early New England* (New York: Oxford University Press, 1982), 60. See also Carol F. Karlsen, *The Devil in the Shape of a Woman: Witchcraft in Colonial New England* (New York: Norton, 1987), 47–48.

[12]Elizabeth Reis, *Damned Women: Sinners and Witches in Puritan New England* (Ithaca, N.Y.: Cornell University Press, 1997), 108, 110.

[13]Reis argues that women were more inclined than men to see themselves as wholly "unfit and unworthy." Whereas men differentiated between their sinful deeds and their inner selves, women conflated the two. See Reis, *Damned Women*, chap. 1 (quotation on 38).

[14]John Cotton, *A Meet Help* (Boston, 1699), 14, 21. Laurel Thatcher Ulrich discusses the positive and active roles envisaged for and performed by women in New England communities, many of which drew inspiration from biblical models, in *Good Wives: Image and Reality in the Lives of Women in Northern New England, 1650–1750* (New York: Knopf, 1982).

[15]Karlsen, *The Devil in the Shape of a Woman*, 165.

[16]Karlsen discusses the demographic, economic, and temperamental characteristics of accused witches in ibid., chaps. 2–4.

[17]See Demos, *Entertaining Satan*, chap. 9.

[18]Ibid., 312. For the links between social tension and witch accusations in early modern England, see Alan Macfarlane, *Witchcraft in Tudor and Stuart England: A Regional and Comparative Study* (London: Routledge and Kegan Paul, 1970); Keith Thomas, "Anthropology and the Study of English Witchcraft," in *Witchcraft Confessions and Accusations*, ed. Mary Douglas (London: Tavistock, 1970); and Max Marwick, "Witchcraft as a Social Stress Gauge," in *Witchcraft and Sorcery: Selected Readings*, ed. Max Marwick (Harmondsworth, U.K.: Penguin, 1970).

[19]See, for examples, Bernard Rosenthal et al., eds., *Records of the Salem Witch-Hunt* (New York: Cambridge University Press, 2009), 491; and Cotton Mather, "A Brand Pluck't Out of the Burning," in *Narratives of the Witchcraft Cases, 1648–1706*, ed. George Lincoln Burr (New York: Charles Scribner's Sons, 1914), 261.

[20]*Records and Files of the Quarterly Courts of Essex County, Massachusetts*, 9 vols. (Salem, Mass., 1911–1975), 7:135.

[21]Mather, "A Brand Pluck't Out of the Burning," 281–82; and Rosenthal et al., eds., *Records of the Salem Witch-Hunt*, 491. Many historical studies have examined the links

between Indian attacks and the witch hunt. These include Richard Slotkin, *Regeneration through Violence: The Mythology of the American Frontier, 1600–1860* (Middletown, Conn.: Wesleyan University Press, 1973); David Konig, *Law and Society in Puritan Massachusetts: Essex County, 1629–1692* (Chapel Hill: University of North Carolina Press, 1979); James E. Kences, "Some Unexplored Relationships of Essex County Witchcraft to the Indian Wars of 1675 and 1689," *Essex Institute Historical Collections* 120 (1984): 179–212; Karlsen, *The Devil in the Shape of a Woman*, 226–30; Godbeer, *The Devil's Dominion*, chap. 6; John McWilliams, "Indian John and the Northern Tawnies," *New England Quarterly* 69 (1996): 580–604; Elaine G. Breslaw, *Tituba, Reluctant Witch of Salem: Devilish Indians and Puritan Fantasies* (New York: New York University Press, 1996); and most recently Norton, *In the Devil's Snare*.

[22] For a more detailed version of the argument put forward in the following paragraphs, see Godbeer, *The Devil's Dominion*, 182–203.

[23] "Declaration of the Gentlemen, Merchants, and Inhabitants of Boston," in *The Andros Tracts*, ed. William Whitmore, 3 vols. (Boston, 1868–1874), 1:13; and M. Halsey Thomas, ed., *The Diary of Samuel Sewall*, 2 vols. (New York: Farrar, Straus and Giroux, 1973), 1:108.

[24] Attacking Quakers themselves as witches was not feasible now that the charter of 1691 had made their beliefs, at least officially, acceptable; but accusing their friends and relatives provided an alternative way of expressing anxieties about their invasion of New England. See Christine Leigh Heyrman, "Specters of Subversion, Societies of Friends: Dissent and the Devil in Provincial Essex County, Massachusetts," in *Saints and Revolutionaries: Essays on Early American History*, ed. David D. Hall, John M. Murrin, and Thad. W. Tate (New York: Norton, 1984), 60.

[25] The following three paragraphs summarize the argument made by Paul Boyer and Stephen Nissenbaum in *Salem Possessed: The Social Origins of Witchcraft* (Cambridge, Mass.: Harvard University Press, 1974).

[26] Ibid., 34.

[27] Elinor Abbot provides a thought-provoking analysis of divisions within seventeenth-century Andover in *Our Company Increases Apace: History, Language, and Social Identity in Early Colonial Andover, Massachusetts* (Dallas, Tex.: SIL, 2007), though she declines to suggest specific connections between those divisions and the accusations of 1692. See also Chadwick Hansen, "Andover Witchcraft and the Causes of the Salem Witchcraft Trials," in *The Occult in America: New Historical Perspectives*, ed. Howard Kerr and Charles Crow (Urbana: University of Illinois Press, 1983); and Godbeer, *The Devil's Dominion*, 197. Critics of *Salem Possessed* have chipped away at various components of its argument; see the forum entitled "Salem Repossessed" in *William and Mary Quarterly* 65 (2008): 391–534.

[28] There were more mature women among the afflicted, including Sarah Bibber (born c. 1656), Bathshua Pope (born 1652), and Ann Putnam Sr. (born 1661). But attention focused on the children and young women.

[29] We should also bear in mind that there is no modern consensus on how to interpret physical and emotional symptoms such as those exhibited by the afflicted girls. Even if we could send a team of physicians, psychiatrists, social workers, paranormal experts, and pastors back in time to examine the afflicted girls and young women, they would almost certainly not agree as to what was causing the fits.

[30] See Karlsen, *The Devil in the Shape of a Woman*, 226–30; and Norton, *In the Devil's Snare*.

[31] This paragraph is much indebted to Karlsen, *The Devil in the Shape of a Woman*, chap. 7. See also Godbeer, *The Devil's Dominion*, chap. 3; and Godbeer, "Chaste and Unchaste Covenants: Witchcraft and Sex in Early Modern Culture," in *Wonders of the Invisible World, 1600–1900*, ed. Peter Benes (Boston: Boston University Press, 1995), 53–72. For a very different perspective on the afflicted girls, see Peter Charles Hoffer, *The Devil's Disciples: Makers of the Salem Witchcraft Trials* (Baltimore: Johns Hopkins University Press, 1996). According to Hoffer, some of the afflicted showed symptoms

of child abuse. The psychological impact of that abuse would, he argues, help to explain at least some of their behavior. John Demos suggests that adolescent girls may have accused older women who symbolized their mothers, against whom they could not openly rebel (and some of whom were no longer present); see Demos, *Entertaining Satan*, 157–65.

[32] *The Book of the General Laws and Liberties Concerning the Inhabitants of the Massachusetts* (1648; San Marino, Calif.: Huntington Library, 1975), 5.

[33] See Levack, *The Witch-Hunt in Early Modern Europe*, esp. 80–88.

[34] The only known occasion on which English officials subjected witch suspects to torture was during the witch hunt of 1647, led by Matthew Hopkins, the so-called Witch-Finder General. (This was the only major witch panic to occur in early modern England.) See Macfarlane, *Witchcraft in Tudor and Stuart England*, chap. 9; Richard Deacon, *Matthew Hopkins: Witch Finder General* (London: Frederick Muller, 1976); Malcolm Gaskill, ed., *English Witchcraft, 1560–1736*, vol. 3, *The Matthew Hopkins Trials* (London: Pickering and Chatto, 2003); and Malcolm Gaskill, *Witchfinders: A Seventeenth-Century English Tragedy* (London: John Murray, 2005). See also Matthew Hopkins, *The Discovery of Witches* (London, 1647).

[35] In two of the sixteen cases resulting in conviction it is not clear whether the individual was in fact executed. Four of those convicted had confessed, which made the court's job much easier. If those cases are omitted, the conviction rate falls to just under one-fifth (19.7 percent).

[36] The only occasion on which ducking is known to have been used during a New England witch prosecution was during the Connecticut witch hunt of 1692, when Mercy Disborough and Elizabeth Clawson both underwent this test; see Godbeer, *Escaping Salem*, 97–100.

[37] Increase Mather, a respected clergyman in Boston, discussed a range of supernatural phenomena, including witchcraft, and the opinions of learned authors on issues such as ducking in his *Essay for the Recording of Illustrious Providences*, published locally in 1684. Mather's book would have been a valuable resource for magistrates who did not have access to imported volumes such as those by Perkins and Bernard.

[38] See Godbeer, *The Devil's Dominion*, 172–73.

[39] Cotton Mather, *Magnalia Christi Americana*, ed. Kenneth B. Murdock (Cambridge, Mass.: Harvard University Press, 1977), 331.

[40] Samuel Willard, *Some Miscellany Observations on Our Present Debates Respecting Witchcrafts* (Philadelphia, 1692), 7.

[41] That the accusers were now naming individuals from prominent families, including the governor's own wife, doubtless also figured in the decision to halt the trials. But that decision seems to have been driven primarily by controversy surrounding the magistrates' assessment of the evidence before them.

[42] For witch trials in New England after 1692, see Godbeer, *The Devil's Dominion*, 225.

[43] *Independent Journal* (New York), July 18, 1787; and *Massachusetts Centinel*, Aug. 1, 1787. For further discussion of witch beliefs in the eighteenth century, see Herbert Leventhal, *In the Shadow of the Enlightenment: Occultism and Renaissance Science in Eighteenth-Century America* (New York: New York University Press, 1976), chap. 3; Demos, *Entertaining Satan*, 387–400; Alan Taylor, "The Early Republic's Supernatural Economy: Treasure Seeking in the American North-East, 1780–1830," *American Quarterly* 38 (1986): 6–34; Jon Butler, *Awash in a Sea of Faith: Christianizing the American People* (Cambridge, Mass.: Harvard University Press, 1990), 228–36; and Godbeer, *The Devil's Dominion*, 226–30.

PART TWO

The Documents

1

Signs and Assaults from the Supernatural World

When people in and around Salem Village decided in 1692 that they were the victims of witchcraft, they made several important assumptions about the reality of the supernatural and its role in cause and effect. Most people on both sides of the Atlantic—Europeans, Indians, and Africans—believed that the natural and supernatural worlds were equally real and closely intertwined. Puritans were convinced that every incident in this world, however seemingly trivial, came about through God's will and contained a heaven-sent message that God communicated to humankind via the physical world. For Puritans, there was no such thing as a random occurrence or coincidence. For example, when Boston minister John Cotton died in 1652, grief-stricken members of his congregation saw the arrival of a comet that same month as a commentary on Cotton's life (Document 1). Thinking along the same lines, Samuel Sewall, a Boston merchant and magistrate who served as a judge in the Salem witch trials, pondered in one of his diary entries the meaning of a brilliant rainbow that appeared over Boston (Document 2).

When Puritans faced illness or misfortune, they assumed that their suffering had a supernatural cause and meaning: God sent these "afflictions" to test, warn, and punish them. Sometimes God acted indirectly by unleashing the Devil, who was always eager to torment and tempt men and women in hope of recruiting them to his cause. The Devil's disciples would then inflict harm on other human beings through acts of witchcraft. But the ultimate cause of all such devilish assaults was God's anger in response to human sin; any affliction should prompt self-examination, repentance, and reformation. Some people responded to misfortune primarily in terms of the judgments and warnings that they represented, praying for God's forgiveness and guidance; others focused on more immediate and subordinate agents—human witches—against whom they could take action, either legally or via extralegal means such as countermagic. Minister Cotton Mather resisted the temptation to blame his son's death on a local woman suspected of witchcraft, deferring instead to God's will (Document 3). Yet when the children of a stoneworker named John Goodwin fell victim to strange fits in 1688 (Document 4), a woman with whom the Goodwin family had quarreled was arrested and condemned to death on charges of witchcraft. Early on in the crisis, some of Goodwin's neighbors urged him to use countermagic against the suspected witch, but he preferred to rely on prayer.

Goodwin was by no means alone in condemning countermagic, and the use of such techniques could create considerable tension between neighbors, as in the case of Goodwife Chandler and her protective horseshoe (Document 5). The saga of the horseshoe might strike some modern readers as farcical, but for Goodwife Chandler this was a matter of life and death; yet some neighbors believed that her actions invited the Devil into their midst, endangering her immortal soul and the entire community. These diverse responses had two common characteristics: they assumed, first, that the cause of the illness was not random but a deliberate act of will; and second, that supernatural forces were at work.

The Salem witch hunt was preceded by a succession of regional crises that shook New England to its foundations and that contemporaries understood in supernatural terms. From a modern point of view, these military, political, and religious afflictions (described in the introduction to this volume) might seem unconnected to witchcraft, but seventeenth-century New Englanders understood them as a series of concerted attacks by the Devil and his minions. The remaining documents in this section enable us to appreciate the cumulative impact of these crises, as they heightened the sensitivity of colonists to the influence of supernatural forces in their lives.

Document 6, an extract from Mary Rowlandson's famous account of her capture by Indians during their raid on Lancaster, Massachusetts, in early 1675, describes that experience not just as a physical ordeal but also as a religious lesson, teaching her much about God's relationship with her and with New England. The language used by colonists to describe missionary efforts by non-Puritans (Document 7) and equally unwelcome initiatives by imperial officials (Document 8) deserves close attention. Like the Indians, these enemies were seen as predatory, invasive, and demonic. In Document 9, Cotton Mather captured effectively the ways in which these various attacks on New England made sense to him and other colonists as components of "the same history," a history of divine anger and demonic assault.

1

The Arrival of a Comet and the Death of a Star Preacher

There was a star appeared on the 9th [day] of the 10th month 1652, dark and yet great for compass,[1] with [a] long blaze dim also to the east, and [it] was quick in the motion, and every night it was less and less until the 22nd of the same month, and then it did no more appear, it being the night before our reverend teacher Mr. John Cotton died, the greatest star in the churches of Christ that we could hear of in the Christian world for opening and unfolding the counsels of Christ to the churches, and all the Christian world did receive light by his ministry.

[1] Circumference.

"Records of the First Church in Boston," *Publications of the Colonial Society of Massachusetts* 39 (1961): 9–10.

2

Samuel Sewall Finds Reassurance in a Rainbow

At Boston upon the Lord's Day, August 11, 1728, about 6 p.m. a noble rainbow was seen in the cloud, after great thundering and darkness and rain: one foot thereof stood upon Dorchester neck,[2] the eastern end of it; and the other foot stood upon the town. It was very bright, and the reflection of it caused another faint rainbow to the westward of it. For the entire completeness of it, throughout the whole arch, and for its duration, the like has been rarely seen. It lasted about a quarter of an hour. The middle parts were discontinued for awhile; but the former integrity and splendor were quickly recovered. I hope this is a sure token that

[2] A narrow promontory, or peak of high land jutting out into a body of water.

"Letter Book of Samuel Sewall," 2 vols., *Massachusetts Historical Society Collections*, 6th ser., vols. 1–2 (Boston, 1886–1888), 2:248.

Christ remembers his covenant for his beloved Jews under their captivity and dispersion, and that he will make haste to prepare for them a city that has foundations, whose builder and maker is God.[3]

[3] Puritan New Englanders believed that God had inspired them to establish a New Israel in North America; like the Israelites of the Old Testament, the colonists now had to prove themselves worthy of God's favor.

3

The Death of Cotton Mather's Infant Son

On March 28, [1693,] Tuesday, between 4 and 5 a.m., God gave to my wife a safe deliverance of a son. It was a child of a most comely and hearty[4] look, and all my friends entertained his birth with very singular expressions of satisfaction. But the child was attended with a very strange disaster; for it had such an obstruction in the bowels as utterly hindered the passage of its ordure[5] from it. We used all the methods that could be devised for its ease; but nothing we did could save the child from death. It languished in its agonies till Saturday, April 1, about 10 p.m., and so died, unbaptized. There was a conjunction of many and heavy trials in this dispensation of God; but God enabled me to bear them all with an unexpected measure of resignation unto his Holy Will. . . . When the body of the child was opened, we found that the lower end of the *rectum intestinum*, instead of being musculous, as it should have been, was membranous,[6] and altogether closed up. I had great reason to suspect a witchcraft in this preternatural accident; because my wife, a few weeks before her deliverance, was affrighted with a horrible specter[7] in our porch, which fright caused her bowels to turn within her; and the specters which both before and after tormented a young woman in our neighborhood bragged of their giving my wife that fright in hopes, they said, of doing mischief unto her infant at least, if not unto the mother. And besides all this, the child was no sooner born, but a sus-

[4] Attractive and healthy.
[5] Excrement.
[6] In other words, it consisted of membrane instead of muscle.
[7] Apparition.

pected woman sent unto my father a letter full of railing against myself, wherein she told him, "He little knew what might quickly befall some of his posterity." However, I made little use of, and laid little stress on, this conjecture, desiring to submit unto the will of my heavenly father, without which not a sparrow falls unto the ground.

4

Strange Afflictions in the Goodwin Household

Joshua Moody's Account

We have a very strange thing among us which we know not what to make of except it be witchcraft, as we think it must needs be. Three or four children of one [John] Goodwin, a mason,[8] that have been for some weeks grievously tormented, crying out of head, eyes, tongue, teeth breaking their neck, back, thighs, knees, legs, feet, toes, etc., and then they roar out, "Oh my head, oh my neck," and from one part to another the pain runs almost as fast as I write it. The pain is (doubtless) very exquisite,[9] and the cries most dolorous[10] and affecting, and this is notable, that two or more of them cry out of the same pain in the same part at the same time, and as the pain shifts to another place in one, so in the other, and thus it holds them for an hour together and more; and when the pain is over, they eat, drink, walk, play, laugh, as at other times; they are generally well at night. A great many good Christians spent a day of prayer there, Mr. Morton[11] came over, and we each spent an hour in prayer, since which the parents suspecting an old woman and her daughter living hard by,[12] complaint was made to the justices, and compassion had so far that the women were committed to prison, and are there now. . . . We cannot but think the Devil has a hand in it by some

---

[8] An artisan who works in stone.
[9] Intense.
[10] Sorrowful.
[11] Charles Morton, the minister in Charlestown, Massachusetts. The Goodwin family lived in Boston but belonged to the Charlestown church.
[12] Nearby.

Joshua Moody to Increase Mather, Oct. 4, 1688, *Massachusetts Historical Society Collections*, 4th ser., vol. 8 (1868), 367–70; and Cotton Mather, *Memorable Providences* (Boston, 1689), 49–53.

instrument. It is an example in all the parts of it not to be paralleled. You may enquire further of Mr. Oakes, whose uncle administered physic[13] to them at first, and he may probably inform you more fully. There are also sundry in the country that remain distracted since the measles last spring. Some have lately made away with themselves, one redcoat[14] and another man. . . . They are solemn warnings and presages.

John Goodwin's Account

It was a thing not a little comfortable to us, to see that the people of God was so much concerned about our lamentable condition, remembering us at all times in their prayers, which I did look at as a token for good; but you must think it was a time of sore temptation with us, for many did say (yea, and some good people too), were it their case, that they would try some tricks,[15] that should give ease to their children. But I thought [that] for us to forsake the counsel of good old men and to take the counsel of the young ones might ensnare our souls, though for the present it might offer some relief to our bodies, which was a thing I greatly feared. . . . If God be pleased to make the fruit of this affliction to be to take away our sin, and cleanse us from iniquity, and to put us on with greater diligence to make our calling and election[16] sure, then, happy affliction! The lord said that I had need of this to awake me. I have found a prosperous condition a dangerous condition. I have taken notice and considered more of God's goodness in these few weeks of affliction than in many years of prosperity. I may speak it with shame, so wicked and deceitful and ungrateful is my heart, that the more God hath been doing for me, the less I have been doing for him. . . . Now I earnestly desire the prayer of all good people that the Lord would be pleased to perfect that work he hath begun, and make it to appear that prayer is stronger than witchcraft.

[13] Medicine.
[14] An English soldier.
[15] Countermagic.
[16] Puritans referred to those whom God had chosen to be saved as the elect.

5

The Horseshoe Controversy in Newberry, Massachusetts

May 17, 1680

The testimony of Esther Wilson, aged about 28:

That she living with her mother, Goodwife[17] Chandler, when she was ill, she would often cry out and complain that Goodwife [Elizabeth] Morse was a witch and had bewitched her, and every time she came to see her she was the worse for her. . . . One coming to the house asked why we did not nail a horseshoe on the threshold (for that was an experiment to try witches). My mother, the next morning, with her staff made a shift[18] to get to the door and nailed on a horseshoe as well as she could. Goodwife Morse, while the horseshoe was on, would never be persuaded to come into the house, and though she were persuaded[19] by the deponent and Daniel Rolfe to go in, she would not, and being demanded the reason, she would not tell me now, and said it was not her mind to come in, but she would kneel down by the door and talk and discourse, but not go in, though she would come often times in a day, yet that was her practice. William Moody, coming to the house and understanding that there was a horseshoe nailed on to the door, said it was a piece of witchery and knocked it off and laid it by; very shortly after, [on] the same day, Goodwife Morse came in and thrust into the parlor where my mother lay before she was up; and my mother complained of her, and I earnestly desired her that she would be gone, and I could very hardly with my importunity[20] entreat her to do it. The horseshoe was off about a week and she would very often come in that time. About a week

---

[17] Women of elite status were addressed as Mistress (Mrs.); other women were referred to as Goodwife or Goody. The male equivalents were Mister (Mr.) and Goodman.

[18] A great effort.

[19] Urged. The word *persuade* could mean (a) trying to convince someone to do or think something or (b) succeeding in that effort. It was used in both senses within this one sentence.

[20] Persistent urging.

Samuel G. Drake, *Annals of Witchcraft in New England* (Boston: W. Elliot Woodward, 1869), 275–76.

after, my mother, to keep her out of the house, got Daniel Rolfe to nail on the shoe again, which continued for about seven or eight days, and at that time she would not come over the threshold to come in, though often importuned to do it. Then William Moody, coming again, took off the horseshoe and put it in his pocket and carried it away; then the said Goodwife Morse came as before and would go in as before.

6

Mary Rowlandson's Account of the Indian Attack on Lancaster

Now is the dreadful hour come that I have often heard of (in time of war, as was the case with others) but now mine eyes see it. Some in our house were fighting for their lives, others wallowing in their blood, the house on fire over our heads, and the bloody heathen ready to knock us on the head if we stirred out. Now might we hear mothers and children crying out for themselves and one another, "Lord, what shall we do?" Then I took my children (and one of my sister's) to go forth and leave the house: but as soon as we came to the door and appeared, the Indians shot so thick that the bullets rattled against the house as if one had taken a handful of stones and threw them, so that we were fain to give back.[21] We had six stout dogs belonging to our garrison, but none of them would stir, though another time, if an Indian had come to the door, they were ready to fly upon him and tear him down. The Lord hereby would make us the more to acknowledge his hand, and to see that our help is always in him. But out we must go, the fire increasing and coming along behind us roaring, and the Indians gaping before us with their guns, spears, and hatchets to devour us. No sooner were we out of the house but my brother-in-law (being before wounded in defending the house, in or near the throat) fell down dead, whereat the Indians scornfully shouted, and hallooed, and were presently upon him, stripping off his clothes. The bullets flying thick, one went through my side, and the same (as would seem) through the bowels and hand of my dear child

[21] Obliged to retreat.

Mary Rowlandson, *The Sovereignty and Goodness of God* (Cambridge, 1682), 2–5, 62–63.

in my arms. One of my elder sister's children, named William, had then his leg broken, which the Indians perceiving, they knocked him on the head. Thus were we butchered by those merciless heathens, standing amazed, with the blood running down to our heels. My elder sister being yet in the house, and seeing those woeful sights, the infidels hauling mothers one way and children another, and some wallowing in their blood, and her eldest son telling her that her son William was dead, and myself was wounded, she said, "Lord, let me die with them," which was no sooner said, but she was struck with a bullet and fell down dead over the threshold. I hope she is reaping the fruit of her good labors, being faithful to the service of God in her place. In her younger years she lay under much trouble upon spiritual accounts, till it pleased God to make that precious scripture take hold of her heart, [from] 2 Corinthians 12.9, "And he said unto me, my grace is sufficient for thee." More than twenty years after, I have heard her tell how sweet and comfortable that place [22] was to her. But to return: the Indians laid hold of us, pulling me one way and the children another, and said, "Come, go with us." I told them they would kill me. They answered [that] if I were willing to go along with them, they would not hurt me.

Oh the doleful sight that now was to behold at this house! "Come behold the works of the Lord, what desolations he has made in the earth." Of thirty-seven persons who were in this one house, none escaped either present death or a bitter captivity save only one, who might say as he, "And I only am escaped alone to tell the news" (Job 1.15). There were twelve killed: some shot, some stabbed with their spears, some knocked down with their hatchets. When we are in prosperity, oh the little that we think of such dreadful sights, and to see our dear friends and relations lie bleeding out their heart-blood upon the ground. There was one who was chopped into the head with a hatchet, and stripped naked, and yet was crawling up and down. It is a solemn sight to see so many Christians lying in their blood, some here, and some there, like a company of sheep torn by wolves, all of them stripped naked by a company of hellhounds, roaring, singing, ranting, and insulting, as if they would have torn our very hearts out. Yet the Lord by his almighty power preserved a number of us from death, for there were twenty-four of us taken alive and carried captive. . . .

It is said, "Oh that my people had hearkened to me, and Israel had walked in my ways, I should soon have subdued their enemies, and turned my hand against their adversaries" (Psalm 81.13–14). But now

---

[22] Biblical passage.

our perverse and evil carriages in the sight of the Lord have so offended him that, instead of turning his hand against them, the Lord feeds and nourishes them up to be a scourge[23] to the whole land.

Another thing that I would observe is the strange Providence of God, in turning things about when the Indians [were] at the highest and the English at the lowest. I was with the enemy eleven weeks and five days, and not one week passed without the fury of the enemy, and some desolation by fire and sword upon one place or other. They mourned (with their black faces) for their own losses, yet triumphed and rejoiced in their inhumane, and many times devilish, cruelty to the English.... Now the heathen begins to think all is their own, and the poor Christians' hopes to fail (as to man) and now their eyes are more to God, and their hearts sigh heavenward; and to say in good earnest, "Help Lord, or we perish." When the Lord had brought his people to this, that they saw no help in anything but himself, then he takes the quarrel into his own hand, and though they [the Indians] had made a pit (in their own imaginations) as deep as hell for the Christians that summer, yet the Lord hurled themselves into it. And the Lord had not so many ways before to preserve them but now he hath as many to destroy them.

[23] A lash, figuratively an instrument of divine anger.

7

Cotton Mather on the Quaker Threat

But while the Indians have been thus molesting us, we have suffered molestations of another sort, from another sort of enemies which may with very good reason be cast into the same history with them. If the Indians have chosen to prey upon the frontiers and outskirts of the province, the Quakers have chosen the very same frontiers and outskirts for their more spiritual assaults; and finding little success elsewhere, they have been laboring incessantly and sometimes not unsuccessfully to enchant and poison the souls of poor people in the very places where the bodies and estates of the people have presently after been devoured by the savages.

Cotton Mather, *Decennium Luctuosum [A Sorrowful Decade]* (Boston, 1699), 162.

8

The Dominion of New England

Thus did Sir Edmund Andros[24] and his creatures, who were deeply concerned in the illegal actions of the late unhappy reigns, contrary to the laws of God and men, commit a rape on a whole colony; for which violence it is hoped they may account and make reparation (if possible) to those many whose properties as well as liberties have been invaded by them.

Captain Palmer,[25] in the close of his partial[26] account of New England, entertains his readers with an harangue[27] about the sin of rebellion and misapplies several scriptures that so he might make the world believe that the people of New England have been guilty of wicked rebellion by their casting off the arbitrary power of those ill men who invaded liberty and property to such an intolerable degree, as hath been proved against them. But does he in sober sadness think that if, when wolves are got among sheep in a wilderness, the shepherds and principal men there shall keep them from ravening,[28] that this is the sin of rebellion condemned in the scripture?

[24] Sir Edmund Andros, a professional soldier, was appointed by James II as governor of the Dominion of New England, a new administrative structure imposed in 1686 which did away with all representative institutions. See the introduction for a more detailed description of the dominion and its alienation of New England colonists.

[25] Captain Palmer was a defender of the dominion.

[26] Partisan.

[27] A lengthy and scolding speech or tirade.

[28] Plundering or devouring.

The Revolution in New England Justified (Boston, 1691), 66–67.

9

Cotton Mather on the Recent History of New England

I believe there never was a poor plantation more pursued by the wrath of the Devil than our poor New England; and that which makes our condition very much the more deplorable is that the wrath of the great God himself at the same time also presses hard upon us. It was a rousing alarm to the Devil when a great company of English Protestants and Puritans came to erect evangelical churches in a corner of the world where he had reigned without any control for many ages; and it is a vexing eye-sore to the Devil that our Lord Christ should be known and owned and preached in this howling wilderness. Wherefore he has left no stone unturned, that so he might undermine this plantation and force us out of our country.

First, the Indian Powwows[29] used all their sorceries to molest the first planters here; but God said unto them, "Touch them not!" Then, seducing spirits[30] came to root in this vineyard, but God so rated[31] them off that they have not prevailed much farther than the edges of our land. After this, we have had a continual blast upon some of our principal grain, annually diminishing a vast part of our ordinary food. Herewithal, wasting sicknesses, especially burning and mortal agues,[32] have shot the arrows of death in at our windows. Next, we have had many adversaries of our own language, who have been perpetually assaying to deprive us of those English liberties in the encouragement whereof these territories have been settled. As if this had not been enough, the Tawnies[33] among whom we came have watered our soil with the blood of many hundreds of our inhabitants. Desolating fires also have many times laid the chief

---

[29] Indian shamans or religious practitioners, whom Puritans believed to be in communion with the Devil.
[30] Heretics.
[31] Drove.
[32] Fevers.
[33] Indians.

Cotton Mather, *The Wonders of the Invisible World* (Boston, 1692), 41–43, 48.

treasure of the whole province in ashes. As for losses by sea, they have been multiplied upon us; and particularly in the present French War,[34] the whole English nation have observed that no part of the nation has proportionately had so many vessels taken as our poor New England. Besides all which, now at last the devils are (if I may so speak) in person come down upon us, with such a wrath as is justly much and will quickly be more the astonishment of the world. Alas, I may sigh over this wilderness, as Moses did over his, in Psalm 90.7, 9: "We are consumed by thine anger, and by thy wrath we are troubled: All our days are passed away in thy wrath." And I may add this unto it: the wrath of the Devil too has been troubling and spending of us all our days. . . .

Let us now make a good and a right use of the prodigious descent which the Devil in great wrath is at this day making upon our land. Upon the death of a great man once, an orator called the town together, crying out, "Concurrite cives, dilapsa sunt vestra moenia!" That is, "Come together neighbors, your town walls are fallen down!" But such is the descent of the Devil at this day upon our selves that I may truly tell you, the walls of the whole world are broken down! The usual walls of defense about mankind have such a gap made in them that the very devils are broke in upon us to seduce the souls, torment the bodies, sully the credits, and consume the estates of our neighbors, with impressions both as real and as furious as if the invisible world were becoming incarnate on purpose for the vexing of us. . . .

In as much as the devil is come down in great wrath, we had need labor, with all the care and speed we can, to divert the great wrath of Heaven from coming at the same time upon us. The God of Heaven has with long and loud admonitions been calling us to a reformation of our provoking evils as the only way to avoid that wrath of his which does not only threaten but consume us. It is because we have been deaf to those calls that we are now by a provoked God laid open to the wrath of the Devil himself.

[34] When James II's daughter Mary and her Dutch Protestant husband, William, became king and queen in 1689, France (which was already at war with the Dutch) declared war on England and its colonies.

2

Beginnings

The beginnings of the witch scare in Salem Village remain shrouded in mystery. But two accounts written by observers who arrived on the scene quite early in the crisis provide important clues. John Hale, the minister at nearby Beverly, Massachusetts, was almost certainly one of the ministers invited by Samuel Parris to join him in praying and fasting for the afflicted girls. Hale attended many of the subsequent examinations and trials, gave testimony against three of the accused women, and devoted many hours to praying in prison with those awaiting trial or execution. Yet by the fall of 1692, Hale had become increasingly doubtful about the legitimacy of the proceedings and the convictions they were producing. He would later write a book, published in 1702, about the challenges of prosecuting invisible crimes in a court of law. Hale included in that book a narrative of the events in early 1692 (Document 10). Even though Hale believed that mistakes had been made that year, he was eager to show why the accusations had seemed credible at the time.

Deodat Lawson, who had preceded Samuel Parris as minister in Salem Village, traveled out from Boston in mid-March to give his support and to preside over a service in the village church. Lawson wrote a detailed account of what he observed during his visit. That account (Document 11) was published several months later in Boston. Lawson clearly intended to convince his readers that witchcraft was responsible for the afflictions in Salem Village; there were, after all, other possible explanations such as natural illness or fraud. Not all readers would accept immediately that fits such as these were the result of witchcraft; throughout the seventeenth century, New Englanders had often been quite cautious about accepting such diagnoses. Therefore Lawson provided a detailed description of the symptoms and behavior exhibited by the afflicted girls, explaining carefully why he was convinced that they were under occult attack.

Samuel Parris provided his own commentary on the outbreak of witch accusations week by week from the pulpit; his notes for one of these sermons, delivered at the end of March, are excerpted in Document 12.

The minister's warning that "devils" may have infiltrated the church ended with an attack on "covetous" people who would "sell Christ to his enemies and their souls to the Devil" to fulfill their material "lusts" and acquire "a little pelf" (money). This was a none-too-subtle reference to villagers who identified with the commercial interests of nearby Salem Town. (See the introduction for a discussion of the tensions between Salem Village and Salem Town.) Parris also chronicled in the church records his response on discovering that Mary Sibley, a member of the congregation, had turned to an occult technique that involved baking a urine-cake in order to find out who was bewitching her niece (Document 13).

It is worth noting that Hale's description of youthful experiments with divination before the fits began makes no mention of Tituba (the Indian slave owned by Samuel Parris) being involved, though subsequent accounts have often claimed that she encouraged the girls to dabble in occult experiments and even that she was their teacher. Tituba and her husband, John, were clearly involved in the urine-cake experiment, though it was Mary Sibley who asked them to bake the cake.

10

John Hale's Account

1702

In the latter end of the year 1691,[1] Mr. Samuel Parris, pastor of the church in Salem Village, had a daughter of nine and a niece of about eleven years of age sadly afflicted of they knew not what distempers; and he made his application to physicians, yet still they grew worse. And at length one physician gave his opinion that they were under an evil hand. This the neighbors quickly took up and concluded they were bewitched. He had also an Indian man servant and his wife who afterwards confessed that, without the knowledge of their master or mistress, they had

---

[1] Hale was operating by the Julian calendar, according to which March was the first month of the year, so "the latter end of the year 1691" refers to what we would describe as early 1692. The fits seem to have begun in January; see Mary Beth Norton, *In the Devil's Snare: The Salem Witchcraft Crisis of 1692* (New York: Knopf, 2002), 333, n. 12.

John Hale, *A Modest Enquiry into the Nature of Witchcraft* (Boston, 1702), 23–27, 132–33.

taken some of the afflicted persons' urine and mixing it with meal[2] had made a cake and baked it, to find out the witch, as they said. After this, the afflicted persons cried out of the Indian woman, named Tituba, that she did pinch, prick, and grievously torment them, and that they saw her here and there, where nobody else could. Yea they could tell where she was and what she did when out of their human sight. These children were bitten and pinched by invisible agents, their arms, necks, and backs turned this way and that way, and returned back again, so as it was impossible for them to do of themselves, and beyond the power of any epileptic fits or natural disease to effect. Sometimes they were taken dumb, their mouths stopped, their throats choked, their limbs wracked and tormented, so as might move a heart of stone to sympathize with them, with bowels of compassion[3] for them. . . . Mr. Parris, seeing the distressed condition of his family, desired the presence of some worthy gentlemen of Salem and some neighbor[ing] ministers to consult together at his house; who when they came, and had enquired diligently into the sufferings of the afflicted, concluded [that] they were preternatural and feared the hand of Satan was in them.

The advice given to Mr. Parris by them was that he should sit still and wait upon the Providence of God to see what time might discover; and to be much in prayer for the discovery of what was yet secret. They also examined Tituba, who confessed the making [of] a cake, as is above mentioned, and said her mistress in her own country was a witch and had taught her some means to be used for the discovery of a witch and for the prevention of being bewitched, etc., but said that she herself was not a witch.

Soon after this, there were two or three private fasts at the minister's house, one of which was kept by sundry[4] neighbor[ing] ministers, and after this another in public at the village, and several days afterwards of public humiliation[5] during these molestations, not only there but in other congregations for them. And one general fast by order of the General Court, observed throughout the colony, to seek the Lord that he would rebuke Satan and be a light unto his people in this day of darkness.

---

[2] Edible grain, coarsely ground or powdered.

[3] A reference to 1 John 3.17, as translated in the King James Version of the Bible (published in 1611). In the seventeenth century, people associated tender feelings such as pity with the bowels rather than the heart.

[4] Several.

[5] Days set aside for collective acknowledgment and contemplation of the sinfulness that had prompted God to punish Salem Village and neighboring communities by allowing witches to assault the residents there.

But I return to the history of these troubles. In a short time after, other persons who were of age to be witnesses were molested by Satan and in their fits cried out upon Tituba and Goody [Sarah] O[sborne] and S[arah] G[ood], that they or specters in their shapes did grievously torment them; hereupon some of their village neighbors complained to the magistrates at Salem, desiring [that] they would come and examine the afflicted and accused together, the which they did; the effect of which examination was that Tituba confessed she was a witch and that she, with the two others accused, did torment and bewitch the complainers, and that these with two others whose names she knew not had their witch-meeting together, relating the times when and places where they met, with many other circumstances to be seen at large. Upon this the said Tituba and O[sborne] and S[arah] G[ood] were committed to prison upon suspicion of acting witchcraft. After this the said Tituba was again examined in prison and owned her first confession in all points, and then was herself afflicted and complained of her fellow witches tormenting of her for her confession and accusing them; and being searched by a woman, she was found to have upon her body the marks of the Devil's wounding of her.

Here were these things [that] rendered her confession credible. (1) That at this examination she answered every question just as she did at the first. And it was thought that if she had feigned her confession, she could not have remembered her answers so exactly. A liar, we say, had need of a good memory, but truth being always consistent with itself is the same today as it was yesterday. (2) She seemed very penitent for her sin in covenanting with the Devil. (3) She became a sufferer herself and, as she said, for her confession. (4) Her confession agreed exactly (which was afterwards verified in the other confessors) with the accusations of the afflicted.

Soon after, these afflicted persons complained of other persons afflicting of them in their fits, and the number of the afflicted and accused began to increase. And the success of Tituba's confession encouraged those in authority to examine others that were suspected, and the event was that more confessed themselves guilty of the crimes they were suspected for. And thus was this matter driven on. . . .

I fear some young persons, through a vain curiosity to know their future condition, have tampered with the Devil's tools so far that hereby one door was opened to Satan to play those pranks, anno[6] 1692. I knew one of the afflicted persons who (as I was credibly informed) did try with

---

[6] In the year.

an egg and a glass to find her future husband's calling;[7] till there came up a coffin, that is, a specter in likeness of a coffin. And she was afterward followed with diabolical molestation to her death; and so died a single person. A just warning to others, to take heed of handling the Devil's weapons, lest they get a wound thereby.

Another I was called to pray with, being under sore fits and vexations of Satan. And upon examination I found she had tried the same charm; and after her confession of it and manifestation of repentance for it, and our prayers to God for her, she was speedily released from those bonds of Satan. This iniquity, though I take it not to be the capital crime condemned [in] Exodus 22,[8] because such persons act ignorantly, not considering they thereby go to the Devil, yet borders very much upon it.

[7] Trade or profession.
[8] "Thou shalt not suffer a witch to live" (Exodus 22.18, King James Version).

11

Deodat Lawson's Account
1692

On March 19, I went to Salem Village and lodged at Nathaniel Ingersoll's [inn] near to the minister Mr. P[arris]'s house, and presently after I came into my lodging Captain Walcott's daughter Mary came to Lieutenant Ingersoll's[9] [inn] and spoke to me, but suddenly after, as she stood by the door, was bitten so that she cried out of her wrist, and looking on it with a candle, we saw apparently the marks of teeth, both upper and lower set, on each side of her wrist.

In the beginning of the evening, I went to give Mr. P[arris] a visit. When I was there, his kinswoman, Abigail Williams (about 12 years of age), had a grievous fit; she was at first hurried with violence to and fro in the room, though Mrs. Ingersoll endeavored to hold her, sometimes making as if she would fly, stretching up her arms as high as she could

[9] Captain Walcott and Lieutenant Ingersoll were officers in the local militia.

Deodat Lawson, *A Brief and True Narrative of Some Remarkable Passages Relating to Sundry Persons Afflicted by Witchcraft at Salem Village Which Happened from the Nineteenth of March to the Fifth of April 1692* (Boston, 1692).

and crying, "Whish, Whish, Whish!" several times. Presently after, she said [that] there was Goodwife [Rebecca] N[urse] and said, "Do you not see her? Why there she stands!" And the said Goodwife N[urse] offered her the book, but she was resolved she would not take it, saying often, "I won't, I won't, I won't take it. I do not know what book it is: I am sure it is none of God's book; it is the Devil's book, for ought I know."[10] After that, she ran to the fire and began to throw fire brands about the house; and ran against the back [of the fireplace], as if she would run up [the] chimney; and, as they said, she had attempted to go into the fire in other fits.

On Lords Day, March 20, there were sundry of the afflicted persons at meeting, as Mrs. Pope, and Goodwife Bibber, Abigail Williams, Mary Walcott, Mercy Lewis, and Doctor Griggs's maid.[11] There was also at meeting Goodwife [Martha] C[orey] (who was afterward examined on suspicion of being a witch). They had several sore fits in the time of public worship, which did something interrupt me in my first prayer, being so unusual. After psalm was sung, Abigail Williams said to me, "Now stand up, and name your text." And after it was read, she said, "It is a long text." In the beginning of sermon, Mrs. Pope, a woman afflicted, said to me, "Now there is enough of that." And in the afternoon, Abigail Williams, upon my referring to my doctrine, said to me, "I know no doctrine you had. If you did name one, I have forgot it."

In sermon time, when Goodwife C[orey] was present in the meeting house, Ab[igail] W[illiams] called out, "Look where Goodwife C[orey] sits on the beam, suckling her yellow bird betwixt her fingers!" Ann Putnam, another girl afflicted, said there was a yellow bird sat on my hat as it hung on the pin[12] in the pulpit; but those that were by restrained her from speaking loud about it.

On Monday, March 21, the magistrates of Salem appointed to come to examination of Goodwife C[orey]. And about twelve of the clock, they went into the meeting house, which was thronged with spectators. Mr. [Nicholas] Noyes began with a very pertinent and pathetic[13] prayer; and Goodwife C[orey] being called to answer to what was alleged against her, she desired to go to prayer, which was much wondered at in the presence of so many hundred people. The magistrates told her they would not admit it; they came not there to hear her pray, but to examine

[10] The afflicted girls and confessing witches claimed that those who entered the Devil's service had to sign a covenant (an agreement or contract) in "the Devil's book," which mimicked the holy covenant, so important to Puritan spirituality, by which believers committed to try to live in obedience to God's laws.

[11] Elizabeth Hubbard.

[12] Hook.

[13] Moving.

her in what was alleged against her. The worshipful Mr. Hathorne asked her why she afflicted those children. She said [that] she did not afflict them. He asked her, "Who did then?" She said, "I do not know. How should I know?" The number of the afflicted persons were about that time ten, viz. four married women, Mrs. Pope, Mrs. Putnam, Goodwife Bibber, and an ancient woman named Goodall; three maids, Mary Walcott, Mercy Lewis [who lived] at Thomas Putnam's, and a maid at Dr. Griggs's; there were three girls from nine to twelve years of age each of them, or thereabouts, viz. Elizabeth Parris, Abigail Williams, and Ann Putnam. These were most of them at Goodwife C[orey]'s examination and did vehemently accuse her in the assembly of afflicting them by biting, pinching, strangling, etc., and that they did in their fits see her likeness coming to them, and bringing a book to them. She said [that] she had no book. They affirmed [that] she had a yellow bird that used to suck betwixt her fingers. And being asked about it, if she had any familiar spirit that attended her, she said [that] she had no familiarity with any such thing: she was a gospel woman, which title she called herself by. And the afflicted persons told her, "Ah! She was a gospel witch." Ann Putnam did there affirm that one day, when Lieutenant Fuller was at prayer at her father's house, she saw the shape of Goodwife C[orey] and she thought Goodwife Nurse, praying at the same time to the Devil; she was not sure it was Goodwife N[urse], [though] she thought it was; but [was] very sure she saw the shape of Goodwife C[orey]. The said C[orey] said they were poor, distracted children, and no heed [was] to be given to what they said. Mr. Hathorne and Mr. Noyes replied, it was the judgment of all that were present [that] they were bewitched and only she, the accused person, said [that] they were distracted. It was observed several times that if she did but bite her underlip in time of examination the persons afflicted were bitten on their arms and wrists, and produced the marks before the magistrates, ministers, and others. And being watched for that, if she did but pinch her fingers or grasp one hand hard in another, they were pinched and produced the marks before the magistrates and spectators. After that, it was observed that if she did but lean her breast against the seat in the meeting house (being the bar at which she stood), they were afflicted. Particularly Mrs. Pope complained of grievous torment in her bowels as if they were torn out. She vehemently accused said C[orey] as the instrument, and first threw her muff[14] at her; but that flying not home, she got off her shoe and

---

[14] A cylindrical covering, usually made of fur, into which the hands are placed from either end to keep them warm.

hit Goodwife C[orey] on the head with it. After these postures were watched, if said C[orey] did but stir her feet, they were afflicted in their feet and stamped fearfully. The afflicted persons asked her why she did not go to the company of witches which were before the meeting house mustering?[15] Did she not hear the drum beat? They accused her of having familiarity with the Devil in the time of examination, in the shape of a black man whispering in her ear. They affirmed that her yellow bird sucked betwixt her fingers in the assembly; and order being given to see if there were any sign, the girl that saw it said [that] it was too late now; she [Corey] had removed a pin and put it on her head, which was found there sticking upright.[16]

They told her [that] she had covenanted with the Devil for ten years; six of them were gone and four more to come. She was required by the magistrates to answer that question in the catechism, "How many persons be there in the God-Head?" She answered it but oddly, yet was there no great thing to be gathered from it. She denied all that was charged upon her and said [that] they could not prove [her] a witch; she was that afternoon committed to Salem Prison; and after she was in custody, she did not so appear to them and afflict them as before. . . .

On Thursday, March 24 (being in course the Lecture[17] Day at the village), Goodwife N[urse] was brought before the magistrates, Mr. Hathorne and Mr. Corwin, about ten of [the] clock in the forenoon, to be examined in the meeting house. The Reverend Mr. Hale began with prayer, and the warrant being read, she was required to give answer why she afflicted those persons. She pleaded her own innocency with earnestness. Thomas Putnam's wife, Abigail Williams and Thomas Putnam's daughter accused her that she appeared to them and afflicted them in their fits; but some of the others said that they had seen her, but knew not that ever she had hurt them, amongst which was Mary Walcott, who was presently, after she had so declared, bitten and cried out of her in the meeting house, producing the marks of teeth on her wrist. It was so disposed that I had not leisure to attend the whole time of examination, but both magistrates and ministers told me that the things alleged by the afflicted and defenses made by her were much after the same manner as the former was. And her motions did produce like effects as to biting, pinching, bruising, tormenting at their

---

[15] Assembling for inspection or roll call, generally used in a military context.

[16] The afflicted girl was claiming that Corey had pricked the skin between her fingers with the pin so that the yellow bird, her demonic familiar, could feed on her blood.

[17] Ministers generally gave two public addresses each week: a "sermon" on Sunday and a "lecture" on a weekday.

breasts by her leaning, and when [she] bended back, [they] were as if their backs were broken. The afflicted persons said [that] the black man whispered to her in the assembly, and therefore she could not hear what the magistrates said unto her. They said also that she did then ride by the meeting house behind the black man. Thomas Putnam's wife had a grievous fit in the time of examination, to the very great impairing of her strength and wasting of her spirits, insomuch as she could hardly move hand or foot when she was carried out. Others also were there grievously afflicted, so that there was once such an hideous screech and noise (which I heard as I walked at a little distance from the meeting house) as did amaze me, and some that were within told me [that] the whole assembly was struck with consternation, and they were afraid that those that sat next to them were under the influence of witchcraft. This woman also was that day committed to Salem Prison. . . .

[On] March 31, there was a public fast kept at Salem on account of these afflicted persons. And Abigail Williams said that the witches had a sacrament that day at a house in the village, and that they had red bread and red drink. [On] April 1, Mercy Lewis, Thomas Putnam's maid, in her fit said [that] they did eat red bread like man's flesh and would have had her eat some, but she would not, but turned away her head, and spat at them, and said, "I will not eat, I will not drink, it is blood, etc." She said, "That is not the bread of life; that is not the water of life; Christ gives the bread of life; I will have none of it!" This first of April also Mercy Lewis aforesaid saw in her fit a white man and was with him in a glorious place, which had no candles nor sun, yet was full of light and brightness, where was a great multitude in white glittering robes, and they sung the song in the fifth [chapter] of Revelation the ninth verse, and the 110 Psalm, and the 149 Psalm; and said with herself, "How long shall I stay here? Let me be along with you." She was loath to leave this place and grieved that she could tarry no longer. This white man hath appeared several times to some of them, and given them notice how long it should be before they had another fit, which was sometimes a day, or day and half, or more or less: it hath fallen out accordingly.[18]

[On] April 3, the Lords Day, being sacrament day at the village, Goodwife [Sarah] C[loyce][19] upon Mr. Parris's naming his text, John 6:70, "One of them is a Devil," the said Goodwife C[loyce] went immediately out of the meeting house and flung the door after her violently, to the

---

[18] See number 6 of Lawson's remarks about the accused at the end of this document.
[19] Sarah Cloyce was sister to Rebecca Nurse.

amazement of the congregation. She was afterward seen by some in their fits, who said, "O Goodwife C[loyce], I did not think to see you here!" And [the witches] being at their red bread and drink, [the afflicted] said to her, "Is this a time to receive the sacrament? You ran away on the Lords Day, and scorned to receive it in the meeting house, and is this a time to receive it? I wonder at you!" This is the sum of what I either saw myself, or did receive information from persons of undoubted reputation and credit.

Remarks of things more than ordinary about the afflicted persons:

1. They are in their fits tempted to be witches, are showed the list of the names of others, and are tortured because they will not yield to, subscribe, or meddle with, or touch the book, and are promised to have present relief if they would do it.

2. They did in the assembly mutually cure each other, even with a touch of their hand, when strangled and otherwise tortured; and would endeavor to get their afflicted [companions] to relieve them.

3. They did also foretell when another's fit was a-coming and would say, "Look at her! She will have a fit presently," which fell out accordingly, as many can bear witness that heard and saw it.

4. That at the same time, when the accused person was present, the afflicted persons saw her likeness in other places of the meeting house, suckling her familiar, sometimes in one place and posture, and sometimes in another.

5. That their motions in their fits are preternatural, both as to the manner, which is so strange as a well person could not screw their body into; and as to the violence also it is preternatural, being much beyond the ordinary force of the same person when they are in their right mind.

6. The eyes of some of them in their fits are exceeding fast closed, and if you ask a question they can give no answer, and I do believe they cannot hear at that time, yet do they plainly converse with the appearances as if they did discourse with real persons.

7. They are utterly pressed against any persons praying with them, and told by the appearances they shall not go to prayer. So Tho[mas] Putnam's wife was told [that] I should not pray; but she said [that] I should. And after I had done [praying], [she]

reasoned with the appearance, "Did not I say he should go to prayer?"

8. The forementioned Mary W[alcott] being a little better at ease, the afflicted persons said she had signed the book and that was the reason she was better. Told me by Edward Putnam.

Remarks concerning the accused:

1. For introduction to the discovery of those that afflicted them, it is reported [that] Mr. Parris's Indian man and woman made a cake of rye meal and the children's water, baked it in the ashes, and gave it to a dog, since which they have discovered and seen particular persons hurting of them.

2. In time of examination, they seemed little affected, though all the spectators were much grieved to see it.

3. Natural actions in them produced preternatural actions in the afflicted, so that they are their own image without any poppets[20] of wax or otherwise.

4. That they are accused to have a company [of] about twenty-three or twenty-four and they did muster in arms, as it seemed to the afflicted persons.

5. Since they were confined, the persons have not been so much afflicted with their appearing to them, biting or pinching of them, etc.

6. They are reported by the afflicted persons to keep days of fast and days of thanksgiving and sacraments; Satan endeavors to transform himself to an angel of light, and to make his kingdom and administrations to resemble those of our Lord Jesus Christ.

7. Satan rages principally amongst the visible subjects of Christ's kingdom and makes use (at least in appearance) of some of them to afflict others, [so] that Christ's kingdom may be divided against itself and so be weakened.

8. Several things used in England at trial of witches, to the number of fourteen or fifteen, which are wont to pass instead of or in concurrence with witnesses, at least six or seven of them are found in these accused. . . .

---

[20] Dolls, often made of cloth. Witches were believed to injure their enemies by sticking pins into poppets that represented them.

9. Some of the most solid afflicted persons do affirm the same things concerning seeing the accused out of their fits as well as in them.

10. The witches had a fast and told one of the afflicted girls [that] she must not eat because it was fast day; she said [that] she would; they told her [that] they would choke her then; which, when she did eat, was endeavored.

12

Samuel Parris on the Outbreak of Witch Accusations in Salem Village

March 27, 1692

The following is an extract from Samuel Parris's notes for a sermon expounding on John 6.70, "Have not I chosen you twelve, and one of you is a devil" (King James Version).

Occasioned by dreadful witchcraft broke out here a few weeks past, and one member of this church and another of Salem upon public examination by civil authority vehemently suspected for she-witches, and upon it committed. . . .

Doctrine: Our Lord Jesus Christ knows how many devils there are in his church, and who they are. . . .

1st Proposition: There are devils as well as saints in the church of Christ. Here three things may be spoken to:

1. Show you what is meant here by devils.

2. That there are such devils in the church.

3. Last, that there are also true saints in such churches.

Rev. Samuel Parris Sermons, 1689–1695, Ms 100740, Connecticut Historical Society, Hartford, Connecticut.

1. What is meant here by devils [in] "One of you is a devil."

Answer: By devil is ordinarily meant any wicked angel or spirit. Sometimes it is put for the prince or head of the evil spirits, or fallen angels. Sometimes it is used for vile and wicked persons, the worst of such, who for their villainy and impiety do most resemble devils and wicked spirits. Thus Christ in our text calls Judas a devil, for his great likeness to the Devil . . . a devil for quality and disposition, not a devil for nature, for he was a man. . . .

2. There are such devils in the church. Not only sinners but notorious sinners; sinners more like to the Devil than others. So here in Christ's little church. This also Christ teacheth us in the parable of the tares,[21] Matthew 13.38, where Christ tells us that such are the children of the wicked one, i.e., of the Devil. . . .

3. Last, there are also true saints in the church. The church consists of good and bad, as a garden that has weeds as well as flowers, and as a field that has wheat as well as tares. . . . Here are good men to be found, yea, the very best; and here are bad men to be found, yea, the very worst; such as shall have the highest seat in glory, and such also as shall be cast into the lowest and fiercest flames of misery. . . .

2nd Proposition: Christ knows how many of these devils there are in his churches. As in our text there was one among the twelve. And so in our churches God knows how many devils there are, whether one, two, three, or four in twelve. . . .

3rd Proposition: Christ knows who these devils are. There is one among you, says Christ to the twelve: Well who is that? Why, it is Judas. Why, so Christ knows how many devils [there are] among us, whether one or ten, or twenty, and also who they are. He knows us perfectly; and he knows those of us that are in the church, that we are either saints or devils; true believers or hypocrites and dissembling Judases that would sell Christ and his kingdom to gratify a lust. . . .

1st Use. Let none then build their hopes of salvation merely upon this, that they are church members. This you and I may be, and yet devils for all that. . . .

2nd Use. Let none then be stumbled[22] at religion because too often there are devils found among the saints. You see here was a great church,

---

[21] Harmful weeds found in cornfields. "The field is the world; the good seed are the children of the Kingdom; but the tares are the children of the wicked one" (Matt. 13.38).

[22] Perplexed or troubled.

sincere converts and sound believers, and yet here was a devil among them. . . .

3rd Use. Terror to hypocrites who profess much love to Christ but indeed are in league with their lusts, which they prefer above Christ. Oh remember that you are devils in Christ's account. . . .

4th Use. Exhortation in two branches:

1. To be deeply humbled for the appearances of devils among our churches. If the church of Corinth were called to mourn because of one incestuous person among them, 1 Corinthians 5 initio,[23] how much more may New England churches mourn that such as work witchcraft, or are vehemently suspected so to do, should be found among them.

2. To be much in prayer that God would deliver our churches from devils. That God would not suffer devils in the guise of saints to associate with us. One sinner destroys much good; how much more one devil. Pray we also that not one true saint may suffer as a devil, either in name or body. The Devil would represent the best saints as devils if he could, but it is not easy to imagine that his power is of such extent, to the hazard of the church.

5th Use. Last: examine we ourselves well what we are, what we church members are. We are either saints or devils; the scripture gives us no medium. . . . Oh it is a dreadful thing to be a devil, and yet to sit down at the Lord's table. 1 Corinthians 10.21. Such incur the hottest of God's wrath, as follows. 22. v. Now if we would not be devils, we must give ourselves wholly up to Christ and not suffer the predominancy of one lust, and particularly that lust of covetousness, which is made so light of and which so sadly prevails in these perilous times; why this one lust made Judas a devil. John 12.6. Matthew 26.15. And no doubt it has made more devils than one. For a little pelf,[24] men sell Christ to his enemies and their souls to the Devil. . . .

None ought, nor is it possible that any should, maintain communion with Christ and yet keep up fellowship with devils.

---

[23] Beginning.

[24] Money or wealth; a negative term implying ill-gotten gains.

13

Samuel Parris's Statement to His Congregation about Mary Sibley's Use of Countermagic
March 27, 1692

It is altogether undeniable that our great and blessed God, for wise and holy ends, hath suffered many persons in several families of this little village to be grievously vexed and tortured in body, and to be deeply tempted to the endangering of the destruction of their souls; and all these amazing feats (well known to many of us) to be done by witchcraft and diabolical operations.

It is also well known that when these calamities first began, which was in my own family, the affliction was several weeks before such hellish operations as witchcraft was suspected. Nay, it never broke forth to any considerable light until diabolical means were used, by the making of a cake by my Indian man, who had his direction from this our sister, Mary Sibley; since which apparitions have been plenty, and exceeding much mischief hath followed. But by this means (it seems) the Devil hath been raised amongst us, and his rage is vehement and terrible, and when he shall be silenced, the Lord only knows.

But now that this our sister should be instrumental to such distress is a great grief to myself and our godly, honored, and reverend neighbors who have had the knowledge of it. Nevertheless, I do truly hope and believe that this our sister doth truly fear the Lord, and am well satisfied from her that what she did, she did it ignorantly, from what she had heard of this nature from other ignorant, or worse, persons. Yet we are in duty bound to protest against such actions, as being indeed a going to the Devil for help against the Devil. We having no such directions from nature or God's word, it must therefore be, and is accounted by godly Protestants who write or speak of such matters as, diabolical; and [we] therefore call this our sister to deep humiliation for what she has done; and all of us to be watchful against Satan's wiles and devices.

Therefore, as we in duty as a church of Christ are deeply bound to protest against it as most directly contrary to the Gospel, yet inasmuch as this our sister did it in ignorance, as she professeth and we believe,

---

Salem Village Ministers' Record Book, Courtesy Danvers Archival Center, Danvers, Massachusetts.

we can continue in our holy fellowship, upon her serious promise of future better advisedness and caution, and acknowledging that she is indeed sorrowful for her rashness herein.

Brethren, if this be your mind, that this iniquity be thus borne witness against, manifest it by your usual sign of lifting up your hands.

The brethren voted generally, or universally; none made any exceptions.

Sister Sibley, if you are convinced that you herein did sinfully and are sorry for it, let us hear it from your own mouth.

She did manifest to satisfaction her error and grief for it.

Brethren, if herein you have received satisfaction, testify it by lifting up of your hands.

A general vote passed; no exception made.

Note. March 25, 1692. I discoursed said sister in my study about the grand error above said and also then read to her what I had written as above to read to the church, and said sister Sibley assented to the same with tears and sorrowful confession.

3

Witches on Trial

Hundreds of legal documents have survived from the Salem witch hunt of 1692. These fall into three principal categories: (1) transcripts of preliminary examinations conducted by magistrates following the arrest of suspects; (2) depositions both for and against the accused; and (3) formal documents that mark the progress of individual cases. The formal documents include complaints against suspected individuals, arrest warrants, mittimus[1] warrants that ordered a prison keeper to hold prisoners in custody until delivered by due process of law, indictments (formal charges), subpoenas[2] summoning witnesses to court, and execution warrants. Many of the examination transcripts and depositions were recorded by individuals who were known to sympathize with the accusers, not least Samuel Parris—a sobering reminder that in 1692 our modern commitment to avoiding conflicts of interest had yet to become an established judicial principle. The official transcripts of examinations included not only questions and answers but also the observations and comments of the writer. The trial records themselves do not survive, but we do know from contemporary accounts that the magistrates and jurymen heard from three groups hostile to the accused: (1) the afflicted girls, who often experienced yet more torments in the courtroom; (2) those who had already confessed and who now accused other defendants of belonging to the witch conspiracy; and (3) neighbors who had witnessed incidents that seemed to incriminate the accused (such as arguments and angry curses followed by mysterious ailments or mishaps).

Magistrates John Hathorne and Jonathan Corwin began their preliminary examinations of witch suspects in Nathaniel Ingersoll's tavern, but they soon shifted them to the village meetinghouse, which would accommodate a larger crowd of observers. (Hathorne and Corwin had decided to disregard the usual practice of questioning suspects in private.)

---

[1] Latin for "we send."
[2] Latin for "under penalty."

The meetinghouse was the largest building in the village, a wooden structure of thirty-four feet by twenty-eight feet, with rows of benches on the ground floor and two galleries above. The magistrates sat behind a large communion table; the accused stood before them. This was the same space in which Samuel Parris continued in his sermons to denounce the servants of Satan who were, he claimed, conspiring against God and his own ministry. The actual trials took place in Salem Town at the courthouse there.

This section contains documents from six cases targeting Sarah Good (Documents 14–27), Tituba (Documents 28–32), John Proctor (Documents 33–41), Bridget Bishop (Documents 42–51), Dorcas Hoar (Documents 52–61), and George Burroughs (Documents 62–75). The cases are arranged in order of arrest; the documents for each case appear in chronological order. Due to limitations of space, some of the more repetitive depositions have been omitted, along with most of the procedural documents. A sample arrest warrant, indictment, and death warrant are included for Sarah Good; these are almost identical to the procedural documents that survive from other witch prosecutions that year.[3]

SARAH GOOD

Sarah Good was one of the first three individuals to be accused, the other two being Sarah Osborne and Tituba. Warrants went out for their arrest on February 29, 1692. After several days of examination, magistrates Jonathan Corwin and John Hathorne gave orders for all three women to be committed to the jail in Boston. Osborne, who was ill at the time of her arrest, died of natural causes in prison on May 10 and so never stood trial; she had maintained her innocence throughout the

[3] Many of these documents were first published in an 1864 two-volume compilation. A fuller and more accurate version of the surviving legal records emerged from a project undertaken in the late 1930s that was funded by the Works Progress Administration (a New Deal work relief agency). Almost forty years later, historians Paul Boyer and Stephen Nissenbaum prepared a new and improved version of that WPA transcript for publication in a three-volume work, published in 1977. That edition became the authoritative source for scholars working on Salem until the publication in 2009 of an ambitious new compilation, edited by Bernard Rosenthal. This latest version contains new documents and corrects many errors that crept into previous editions of the transcripts. Instead of organizing the documents case by case, Rosenthal presents the documents chronologically, which helps us to understand the crisis as it unfolded in ways that older editions inadvertently obscured. Yet some historians have pointed out that presenting the documents case by case best enables us to understand the individual stories and tragedies that lie at the center of the witch hunt. I share that concern and have accordingly organized the documents below as a series of case studies.

examinations. Sarah Good also denied that she was a witch, but she was brought to trial on June 28, convicted, and hanged on July 19.

Sarah Good's father had been a prosperous innkeeper. At his death he left a substantial estate, but the man whom her mother subsequently married never handed over Sarah's rightful share of that estate. Her first husband, Daniel Poole, was a former indentured servant; he died only a few years after they married, leaving Sarah nothing but his debts. Her second husband, William Good, was described in the records sometimes as a weaver and sometimes as a laborer. William and Sarah ended up homeless, destitute, and reliant upon local residents for food and shelter.

Sarah Good did not hold back her feelings of bitterness and resentment in the face of her declining fortunes. Her reluctance to accept God's will doubtless shocked pious neighbors, and such outspokenness was particularly disturbing when coming from a woman. Good also had a reputation for holding a grudge and for muttering curses against those who crossed her, which would have alarmed her neighbors, not least because many people believed that such curses could work. The depositions against Good illustrate vividly how interpersonal conflicts could accumulate and fester in tiny communities like Salem Village. They also show how easily people could become convinced that hostile neighbors were wielding occult forces against them. Personal animosity, inexplicable misfortunes, and belief in witchcraft combined in a lethal cocktail to bring about Sarah Good's death.

14

Arrest Warrant for Sarah Good

February 29, 1692

To Constable George Locker

Whereas Masters Joseph Hutcheson, Thomas Putnam, Edward Putnam, and Thomas Preston, yeomen[4] of Salem Village in the county

---

[4]A yeoman owned and cultivated a small piece of land; he was of respectable standing but not affluent.

Essex County Court Archives, vol. 1, no. 4, from the Records of the Court of Oyer and Terminer, 1692, Property of the Supreme Judicial Court, Division of Archives and Records Preservation, on deposit at the Peabody Essex Museum, Salem, Massachusetts.

of Essex, personally appeared before us and made complaint on behalf of their Majesties against Sarah Good, the wife of William Good of Salem Village abovesaid, for suspicion of witchcraft by her committed, and thereby much injury done to Elizabeth Parris, Abigail Williams, Ann Putnam, and Elizabeth Hubbard, all of Salem Village aforesaid, sundry times within this two months and lately also done at Salem Village, contrary to the peace of our Sovereign Lord and Lady, William and Mary, King and Queen of England, etc., you are therefore in their Majesties' names hereby required to apprehend and bring before us the said Sarah Good, tomorrow about ten of the clock in the forenoon at the house of Lieutenant Nathaniel Ingersoll in Salem Village, or as soon as may be, then and there to be examined relating to the abovesaid premises. And hereof you are not to fail at your peril.

John Hathorne
Jonathan Corwin

15

Examination of Sarah Good (as Recorded by Ezekiel Cheever)
March 1, 1692

Hathorne: Sarah Good, what evil spirit have you familiarity with?
Good: None.
Hathorne: Have you made no contract with the Devil?
Good: No.
Hathorne: Why do you hurt these children?
Good: I do not hurt them. I scorn it.
Hathorne: Who do you employ, then, to do it?
Good: I employ nobody.
Hathorne: What creature do you employ, then?
Good: No creature, but I am falsely accused.
Hathorne: Why did you go away muttering from Mr. Parris's house?
Good: I did not mutter, but I thanked him for what he gave my child.

Essex County Court Archives, vol. 1, no. 11, from the Records of the Court of Oyer and Terminer, 1692, Property of the Supreme Judicial Court, Division of Archives and Records Preservation, on deposit at the Peabody Essex Museum, Salem, Massachusetts.

Hathorne: Have you made no contract with the Devil?
Good: No.

Mr. Hathorne desired the children, all of them, to look upon her and see if this were the person that had hurt them and so they all did look upon her and said this was one of the persons that did torment them. Presently they were all tormented.

Hathorne: Sarah Good, do you not see now what you have done? Why do you not tell us the truth? Why do you thus torment these poor children?
Good: I do not torment them.
Hathorne: Who do you employ, then?
Good: I employ nobody. I scorn it.
Hathorne: How came they thus tormented?
Good: What do I know? You bring others here and now you charge me with it.
Hathorne: Why, who was it?
Good: I do not know, but it was some you brought into the meeting house with you.
Hathorne: We brought you into the meeting house.
Good: But you brought in two more.
Hathorne: Who was it, then, that tormented the children?
Good: It was Osborne.
Hathorne: What is it that you say when you go muttering away from persons' houses?
Good: If I must tell, I will tell.
Hathorne: Do tell us, then.
Good: If I must tell, I will tell: it is the commandments. I may say my commandments, I hope.
Hathorne: What commandment is it?
Good: If I must tell you, I will tell: it is a psalm.
Hathorne: What psalm?

After a long time she muttered over some part of a psalm.

Hathorne: Who do you serve?
Good: I serve God.
Hathorne: What God do you serve?
Good: The God that made heaven and earth (though she was not willing to mention the word God).

Her answers were in a very wicked, spiteful manner, reflecting and retorting against the authority with base and abusive words, and many lies she was taken in. It was here said that her husband had said that he was afraid that she either was a witch or would be one very quickly the worse. Mr. Hathorne asked him his reason why he said so of her, whether he had ever seen anything by her.[5] He answered no, not in this nature, but it was her bad carriage to him. "And indeed," said he, "I may say with tears that she is an enemy to all good."

[5] In other words, had he seen her do anything that might lead him to believe that she was a witch?

16

Elizabeth Hubbard against Sarah Good
March 1, 1692

The deposition of Elizabeth Hubbard, aged about seventeen years, who testifieth and saith that on February 26, 1692 I saw the apparition of Sarah Good who did most grievously afflict me by pinching and pricking me and so she continued hurting of me till March 1, being the day of her examination, and then she did also most grievously afflict and torture me also during the time of her examination. And also several times since she hath afflicted me and urged me to write in her book. Also on the day of her examination, I saw the apparition of Sarah Good go and hurt and afflict the bodies of Elizabeth Parris, Abigail Williams, and Ann Putnam, Jr., and also I have seen the apparition of Sarah Good afflicting the body of Sarah Bibber.

Also in the night after Sarah Good's examination, Sarah Good came to me bare foot and bare legged[6] and did most grievously torment me by pricking and pinching me; and I verily believe that Sarah Good hath bewitched me. Also that night, Samuel Sibley that was then attending me struck Sarah Good on her arm.

[6] Many Puritans would have considered such a state of undress to be indecent. According to Document 26, Elizabeth Hubbard claimed that Good's breasts were also uncovered and called her "nasty slut."

Essex County Court Archives, vol. 1, no. 20, from the Records of the Court of Oyer and Terminer, 1692, Property of the Supreme Judicial Court, Division of Archives and Records Preservation, on deposit at the Peabody Essex Museum, Salem, Massachusetts.

Ann Putnam Jr. against Sarah Good

March 1, 1692

The deposition of Ann Putnam, Jr., who testifieth and saith that on February 25, 1692 I saw the apparition of Sarah Good which did torture me most grievously, but I did not know her name till February 27, and then she told me her name was Sarah Good and then she did prick me and pinch me most grievously, and also since several times, urging me vehemently to write in her book. And also on March 1, being the day of her examination, Sarah Good did most grievously torture me and also several times since. And also on March 1, 1692 I saw the apparition of Sarah Good go and afflict and torture the bodies of Elizabeth Parris, Abigail Williams, and Elizabeth Hubbard. Also I have seen the apparition of Sarah Good afflicting the body of Sarah Bibber.

Essex County Court Archives, vol. 1, no. 19, from the Records of the Court of Oyer and Terminer, 1692, Property of the Supreme Judicial Court, Division of Archives and Records Preservation, on deposit at the Peabody Essex Museum, Salem, Massachusetts.

William Allen, John Hughes, William Good, and Samuel Braybrook against Sarah Good, Sarah Osborne, and Tituba

March 5, 1692

William Allen saith that on March 1 at night he heard a strange noise not usually heard, and so [it] continued for many times so that he was affrighted, and coming nearer to it he there saw a strange and unusual beast lying on the ground, so that going up to it the said beast vanished

Essex County Court Archives, vol. 1, no. 29, from the Records of the Court of Oyer and Terminer, 1692, Property of the Supreme Judicial Court, Division of Archives and Records Preservation, on deposit at the Peabody Essex Museum, Salem, Massachusetts.

away and in the said place started up two or three women and flew from me, not after the manner of other women, but swiftly vanished away out of our sight, which women we took to be Sarah Good, Sarah Osborne, and Tituba. The time was about an hour within night and I, John Hughes, saith the same, being in company then with said Allen, as witness our hands.

William Allen further saith that on March 2 the said Sarah Good visibly appeared to him in his chamber, said Allen being in bed, and [she] brought an unusual light in with her. The said Sarah came and sat upon his foot; the said Allen went to kick at her, upon which she vanished and the light with her.

William Good saith that the night before his said wife was examined, he saw a wart or teat a little below her right shoulder which he never saw before and asked Goodwife Ingersoll whether she did not see it when she searched her.

John Hughes further saith that on March 2, coming from Goodman Sibley's about eight of the clock in the night, he saw a great white dog whom he came up to, but he [the dog] would not stir, but when he [Hughes] was past, he, the said dog, followed him about four or five poles[7] and so disappeared. The same night, the said John Hughes being in bed in a closed room and the door being fast so that no cat nor dog could come in, the said John saw a great light appear in the said chamber, and rising up in his bed he saw a large grey cat at his bed's foot.

[On] March 2 Samuel Braybrook saith that, carrying Sarah Good to Ipswich, the said Sarah leapt off her horse three times, which was between twelve and three of the clock of the same day [on] which the daughter of Thomas Putnam declared the same at her father's house. The said Braybrook further saith that said Sarah Good told him that she would not own herself to be a witch unless she is proved one; she saith that there is but one evidence, and that's an Indian, and therefore she fears not, and so continued railing against the magistrates and she endeavored to kill herself.

[7] One pole equaled 5½ yards.

19

Abigail Williams against Sarah Good, Sarah Osborne, and Tituba

May 23, 1692

Abigail Williams testifieth and saith that several times last February she hath been much afflicted with pains in her head and other parts and often pinched by the apparition of Sarah Good, Sarah Osborne, and Tituba Indian, all of Salem Village, and also excessively afflicted by the said apparition of said Good, Osborne, and Tituba at their examination before authority [on] March 1, 1692. Further the said Abigail Williams testifieth that she saw the apparition of said Sarah Good at her examination pinch Elizabeth Hubbard and set her into fits and also Elizabeth Parris and Ann Putnam.

Essex County Court Archives, vol. 1, no. 31, from the Records of the Court of Oyer and Terminer, 1692, Property of the Supreme Judicial Court, Division of Archives and Records Preservation, on deposit at the Peabody Essex Museum, Salem, Massachusetts.

20

Indictment against Sarah Good for Afflicting Sarah Bibber[8]

June 28, 1692

Anno [Regni] Regis et Reginae Willm et Mariae nunc Angliae etc. Quarto [in the fourth year of the reign of William and Mary, King and Queen of England, etc.]
[In] Essex [County]

[8] Almost identical indictments accused Sarah Good of using witchcraft to afflict Elizabeth Hubbard and Ann Putnam Jr.

Essex County Court Archives, vol. 1, no. 3, from the Records of the Court of Oyer and Terminer, 1692, Property of the Supreme Judicial Court, Division of Archives and Records Preservation, on deposit at the Peabody Essex Museum, Salem, Massachusetts.

The Jurors for our Sovereign Lord and Lady, the King and Queen, present that Sarah Good, wife of William Good of Salem Village in the county of Essex, husbandman,[9] [on] May 2 in the fourth year of the reign of our Sovereign Lord and Lady, William and Mary, by the grace of God of England, Scotland, France, and Ireland King and Queen, Defenders of the Faith, etc., and [on] diverse other days and times as well before as after, certain detestable arts called witchcrafts and sorceries wickedly and feloniously hath used, practiced, and exercised at and within the township of Salem in the county of Essex aforesaid, in, upon, and against one Sarah Bibber, wife of John Bibber of Salem aforesaid, husbandman, by which said wicked arts she, the said Sarah Bibber, [on] the said May 2 in the fourth year abovesaid and diverse other days and times as well before as after, was and is tortured, afflicted, pined, consumed, wasted, and tormented, and also for sundry other acts of witchcraft by said Sarah Good committed and done before and since that time against the peace of our Sovereign Lord and Lady, the King and Queen, their crown and dignity, and against the form of the Statute in that case made and provided.

[9] Farmer.

21

Sarah Bibber against Sarah Good
June 28, 1692

The deposition of Sarah Bibber, aged about thirty-six years, who testifieth and saith that since I have been afflicted I have often seen the apparition of Sarah Good, but she did not hurt me till May 2, 1692, though I saw her apparition most grievously torture Mercy Lewis and John Indian at Salem on April 11, 1692. But on May 2, 1692 the apparition of Sarah Good did most grievously torment me by pressing my breath almost out of my body; and also she did immediately afflict my child by pinching of it [so] that I could hardly hold it, and my husband seeing of it took hold

Essex County Court Archives, vol. 1, no. 26, from the Records of the Court of Oyer and Terminer, 1692, Property of the Supreme Judicial Court, Division of Archives and Records Preservation, on deposit at the Peabody Essex Museum, Salem, Massachusetts.

of the child, but it cried out and twisted so dreadfully by reason of the torture that the apparition of Sarah Good did afflict it withal that it got out of its father's arms too. Also several times since, the apparition of Sarah Good has most grievously tormented me by beating and pinching me, and almost choking me to death, and pricking me with pins after a most dreadful manner.

22

Sarah Gadge and Thomas Gadge against Sarah Good

June 28, 1692

The deposition of Sarah Gadge, the wife of Thomas Gadge, aged about forty years: this deponent testifieth and saith that about two years and a half ago Sarah Good came to her house and would have come into the house, but said Sarah Gadge told her she should not come in for she was afraid she had been with them that had the smallpox, and with that she [Good] fell to muttering and scolding extremely, and so told said Gadge [that] if she would not let her in she should give her something; and she answered she would not have anything to do with her; and the next morning after, to said deponent's best remembrance, one of said Gadge's cows died in a sudden, terrible, and strange, unusual manner, so that some of the neighbors and said deponent did think it to be done by witchcraft, and [she] farther saith not.

And Thomas Gadge, husband of said Sarah, testifieth that he had a cow so died about the time above mentioned, and though he and some neighbors opened the cow, yet they could find no natural cause of said cow's death, and [he] farther saith not.

Essex County Court Archives, vol. 1, no. 15, from the Records of the Court of Oyer and Terminer, 1692, Property of the Supreme Judicial Court, Division of Archives and Records Preservation, on deposit at the Peabody Essex Museum, Salem, Massachusetts.

Joseph Herrick Sr. and Mary Herrick
against Sarah Good

June 28, 1692

The deposition of Joseph Herrick, Sr., who testifieth and saith that on March 1, 1692, I being then Constable for Salem, there was delivered to me by warrant from the worshipful John Hathorne and Jonathan Corwin, Esquires, Sarah Good for me to carry to their Majesties' jail at Ipswich. And that night I set a guard to watch her at my own house, namely Samuel Braybrook, Michael Dunell, [and] Jonathan Baker. And the aforenamed persons informed me in the morning that that night Sarah Good was gone for some time from them, both bare foot and bare legged. And I was also informed that that night Elizabeth Hubbard, one of the afflicted persons, complained that Sarah Good came and afflicted her, being bare foot and bare legged, and Samuel Sibley, that was one that was attending of Elizabeth Hubbard, struck Good on the arm, as Elizabeth Hubbard said, and Mary Herrick, wife of the above said Joseph Herrick, testifieth that on March 2, 1692 in the morning, I took notice of Sarah Good in the morning and one of her arms was bloody from a little below the elbow to the wrist, and I also took notice of her arms on the night before and there was no sign of blood on them.

Essex County Court Archives, vol. 1, no. 16, from the Records of the Court of Oyer and Terminer, 1692, Property of the Supreme Judicial Court, Division of Archives and Records Preservation, on deposit at the Peabody Essex Museum, Salem, Massachusetts.

Samuel Abbey and Mary Abbey against Sarah Good
June 29, 1692

Samuel Abbey of Salem Village, aged forty-five years or thereabouts, and Mary Abbey, his wife, aged thirty-eight years or thereabouts, deposeth and saith that about this time three years past, William Good and his wife Sarah Good, being destitute of a house to dwell in, these deponents, out of charity, they being poor, let them live in theirs some time, until that the said Sarah Good was of so turbulent a spirit, spiteful, and so maliciously bent that these deponents could not suffer her to live in their house any longer and was forced for quietness sake to turn she, the said Sarah, with her husband, out of their house. Ever since, which is about two years and an half ago, the said Sarah Good hath carried it very spitefully and maliciously towards them. The winter following after the said Sarah was gone from our house, we began to lose cattle and lost several after an unusual manner, in a drooping condition, and yet they would eat, and your deponents have lost after that manner seventeen head of cattle within two years, besides sheep and hogs, and both do believe they died by witchcraft. The said William Good on the last of May, [that] was twelve months [ago], went home to his wife the said Sarah Good, and told her what a sad accident had fallen out. She asked what. He answered that his neighbor Abbey had lost two cows, both dying within half an hour of one another. The said Sarah Good said she did not care if he, the said Abbey, had lost all the cattle he had, as the said John Good told us. Just that very day that the said Sarah Good was taken up,[10] we, your deponents, had a cow that could not rise alone, but since presently after she [Good] was taken up, the said cow was well and could rise so well as if she had ailed nothing. She, the said Sarah Good, ever since these deponents turned her out of their house, hath behaved herself very crossly and maliciously to them and their children, calling their children vile names and hath threatened them often.

[10] Arrested.

Essex County Court Archives, vol. 1, no. 18, from the Records of the Court of Oyer and Terminer, 1692, Property of the Supreme Judicial Court, Division of Archives and Records Preservation, on deposit at the Peabody Essex Museum, Salem, Massachusetts.

Henry Herrick and Jonathan Batchelor against Sarah Good

June 29, 1692

The deposition of Henry Herrick, aged about twenty-one years: this deponent testifieth and saith that in last March, [that] was two years [ago], Sarah Good came to his father's house and desired to lodge there, and his father forbid it, and she went away grumbling and my father bid us follow her and see that she went away clear, lest she should lie in the barn and by smoking of her pipe should fire the barn. And said deponent with Jonathan Batchelor seeing her make a stop near the barn, bid her be gone, or he would set her further off, to which she replied that then it should cost his father Zachariah Herrick one or two of the best cows which he had.

And Jonathan Batchelor, aged fourteen years, testifieth the same above written, and doth farther testify that about a week after, two of his grandfather's master cattle were removed from their places and other younger cattle put in their rooms and since that several of their cattle have been set loose in a strange manner.

Essex County Court Archives, vol. 1, no. 21, from the Records of the Court of Oyer and Terminer, 1692, Property of the Supreme Judicial Court, Division of Archives and Records Preservation, on deposit at the Peabody Essex Museum, Salem, Massachusetts.

26

Samuel Sibley against Sarah Good
June 29, 1692

Samuel Sibley, aged about thirty-four years, testifieth and saith that I being at the house of Doctor Griggs that night after that Sarah Good was examined, and Elizabeth Hubbard said, "There stands Sarah Good upon the table by you with all her naked breast and bare footed [and] bare legged," and said, "O nasty slut! If I had something I would kill her!" Then I struck with my staff where she, said Sarah Good, stood and Elizabeth Hubbard cried out, "You have hit her right across the back, you have almost killed her." If anybody was there they may see it.

Essex Institute Collection, vol. 1, no. 30, from the Records of the Court of Oyer and Terminer, 1692, Property of the Supreme Judicial Court, Division of Archives and Records Preservation, on deposit at the Peabody Essex Museum, Salem, Massachusetts.

27

Death Warrant for Sarah Good, Rebecca Nurse, Susannah Martin, Elizabeth How, and Sarah Wilds and Officer's Return
July 12, 1692, and July 19, 1692

To George Corwin, Gentleman, High Sheriff of the County of Essex Greeting:

Whereas Sarah Good, wife of William Good of Salem Village, Rebecca Nurse, wife of Francis Nurse of Salem Village, Susannah Martin of Amesbury, widow, Elizabeth How, wife of James How of Ipswich, [and] Sarah Wilds, wife of John Wilds of Topsfield, all of the county of Essex in their Majesties' province of the Massachusetts Bay in New England, at a Court of Oyer and Terminer held by adjournment for our Sovereign

Ms.Am.48, Rare Books and Manuscripts, Boston Public Library, Boston, Massachusetts, Courtesy of the Trustees of the Boston Public Library.

Lord and Lady, King William and Queen Mary, for the said county of Essex at Salem in the said county on June 29 were severally arraigned on several indictments for the horrible crime of witchcraft by them practiced and committed on several persons, and pleading not guilty did for their trial put themselves on God and their country, whereupon they were each of them found and brought in guilty by the jury that passed on them according to their respective indictments and sentence of death did then pass upon them as the law directs execution, whereof yet remains to be done.

These are therefore in their Majesties' names, William and Mary, now King and Queen over England, etc., to will and command you that upon Tuesday next, being July 19, between the hours of eight and twelve in the forenoon [of] the same day, you safely conduct the said Sarah Good, Rebecca Nurse, Susannah Martin, Elizabeth How, and Sarah Wilds from their Majesties' jail in Salem aforesaid to the place of execution, and there cause them and every of them to be hanged by the necks until they be dead, and of the doings herein make return to the clerk of the said court and this precept. And hereof you are not to fail at your peril. And this shall be your sufficient warrant, given under my hand and seal at Boston July 12 in the fourth year of the reign of our Sovereign Lord and Lady, William and Mary, King and Queen, etc.

William Stoughton

July 19, 1692

I caused the within mentioned persons to be executed according to the tenor of the within warrant.

George Corwin, Sheriff

TITUBA

Tituba, described in the seventeenth-century records as an "Indian woman," was a slave in the household of Salem Village's minister, Samuel Parris. Parris had purchased Tituba, along with her husband John (also characterized in the records as an "Indian"), during his residence in Barbados during the 1670s. Almost no information survives regarding Tituba's personal or family history, either before or after the Salem crisis, though she would become a central figure in the popular mythology surrounding 1692. We do know that she had a reputation for supernatural knowledge and in early 1692 was commissioned by the aunt of one of the afflicted girls to bake a urine-cake, the purpose of which was to identify the witch responsible for the girl's affliction. Tituba's initial role in the crisis was, then, as an ally of those who believed that their relatives were bewitched. But given her association with the occult, along with the Puritan belief that Indians worshipped the Devil, it is hardly surprising that the afflicted girls proceeded to name her as one of their tormentors. It is also surely no coincidence that several of the afflicted girls were refugees from communities recently attacked by Indians.

Tituba at first denied the charges against her, but she then changed her mind and confessed (the first of the accused to do so). She proceeded to give a detailed, lurid account of her temptation by a mysterious man and four women, two of whom she named as Sarah Good and Sarah Osborne (the two women who had been arrested alongside her, which made her story more plausible). She did not name anyone else as a fellow witch. Tituba's rapid surrender under interrogation, her subsequent eagerness to provide the judges with the detailed narrative that they evidently wanted, and her attempts to present herself as a victim even as she confessed provide insight into her personal ordeal as well as the dynamics at work as the trials got under way. In the fall of 1692, Tituba recanted her confession. When the trials were suspended, Samuel Parris refused to pay her jail fees; she remained in prison until someone whose identity is unknown paid them and took her away in April 1693. Her fate thereafter is a mystery, as is that of her husband, John.

28

First Examination of Tituba (as Recorded by Jonathan Corwin)

March 1, 1692

Q. Why do you hurt these poor children? What harm have they done unto you?

Ans. They do no harm to me. I no hurt them at all.

Q. Why have you done it?

Ans. I have done nothing. I can't tell when the Devil works.

Q. What doth the Devil tell you? That he hurts them?

Miscellaneous Collections, U.S. States and Territories, Massachusetts, Manuscripts and Archives Division, The New York Public Library, Astor, Lenox and Tilden Foundations.

Ans. No. He tells me nothing.

Q. Do you never see something appear in some shape?

Ans. No. [I] never see anything.

Q. What familiarity have you with the Devil? Or what is it that you converse withal? Tell the truth, who is it that hurts them?

Ans. The Devil, for ought I know.

Q. What appearance [has he], or how doth he appear when he hurts them? With what shape or what is he like that hurts them?

Ans. Like a man, I think. Yesterday, I being in the lean-to chamber,[11] I saw a thing like a man, that told me [to] serve him and I told him, no, I would not do such thing. She charges Goody Osborne and Sarah Good as those that hurt the children, and [they] would have had her done it.[12] She saith she hath seen four, two of which she knew not. She saw them last night as she was washing the room. They told me [to] hurt the children and would have had me gone to Boston. There was five of them with the man. They told me, if I would not go and hurt them, they would do so to me. At first I did agree with them, but afterward I told them I do so no more.

Q. Would they have had you hurt the children the last night?

Ans. Yes, but I was sorry and I said [that] I would do so no more, but told [them] I would fear God.

Q. But why did not you do so before?

Ans. Why, they tell me I had done so before and therefore I must go on. These were the four women and the man, but she knew none but Osborne and Good only. The others were of Boston.

Q. At first beginning with them, what then appeared to you? What was it like that got you to do it?

Ans. One like a man, just as I was going to sleep, came to me. This was when the children was first hurt. He said [that] he would kill the children and she[13] would never be well, and he said, if I would not serve him, he would do so to me.

Q. Is that the same man that appeared before to you that appeared the last night and told you this?

Ans. Yes.

Q. What other likenesses besides a man hath appeared to you?

---

[11] This would have been a room added onto the Parrises' house that had a sloping roof (a "lean-to"), the upper end of which was attached to the preexisting structure.

[12] At this point, the person recording Tituba's words, Jonathan Corwin, shifted into the third person.

[13] Probably Elizabeth Parris, the daughter of Tituba's master and therefore of particular concern to Tituba. The household slave declared in her second examination (Document 29) that she "loved Betty."

Ans. Sometimes like a hog, sometimes like a great black dog, four times.

Q. But what did they say unto you?

Ans. They told me [to] serve him and that was a good way; that was the black dog. I told him I was afraid. He told me he would be worse then to me.

Q. What did you say to him then after that?

Ans. I answer, "I will serve you no longer." He told me he would do me hurt then.

Q. What other creatures have you seen?

Ans. A bird.

Q. What bird?

Ans. A little yellow bird.

Q. Where doth it keep?

Ans. With the man who hath pretty things here besides.

Q. What other pretty things?

Ans. He hath not showed them yet unto me, but he said he would show them [to] me tomorrow, and he told me, if I would serve him, I should have the bird.

Q. What other creatures did you see?

Ans. I saw two cats, one red, another black [and] as big as a little dog.

Q. What did these cats do?

Ans. I don't know. I have seen them two times.

Q. What did they say?

Ans. They say [to] serve them.

Q. When did you see them?

Ans. I saw them last night.

Q. Did they do any hurt to you or threaten you?

Ans. They did scratch me.

Q. When?

Ans. After prayer, and scratched me because I would not serve them, and when they went away I could not see, but they stood before the fire.

Q. What service do they expect from you?

Ans. They say [to do] more hurt to the children.

Q. How did you pinch them when you hurt them?

Ans. The other[s] pull me and haul me to pinch the children, and I am very sorry for it.

Q. What made you hold your arm when you were searched? What had you there?

Ans. I had nothing.

Q. Do not those cats suck you?

Ans. No, never yet. I would not let them, but they had almost thrust me into the fire.

Q. How do you hurt those that you pinch? Do you get those cats or other things to do it for you? Tell us, how is it done?

Ans. The man sends the cats to me and bids me pinch them, and I think I went over to Mr. Griggs' and have pinched her this day in the morning. The man brought Mr. Griggs' maid to me and made me pinch her.

Q. Did you ever go with these women?

Ans. They are very strong and pull me and make me go with them.

Q. Where did you go?

Ans. Up to Mr. Putnam's and [they] make me hurt the child.

Q. Who did make you go?

Ans. A man that is very strong and these two women, Good and Osborne, but I am sorry.

Q. How did you go? What do you ride upon?

Ans. I ride upon a stick or pole, and Good and Osborne behind me. We ride taking hold of one another, and [I] don't know how we go for I saw no trees nor path, but was presently there when we were up.

Q. How long [is it] since you began to pinch Mr. Parris's children?

Ans. I did not pinch them at the first, but he make me afterward.

Q. Have you seen Good and Osborne ride upon a pole?

Ans. Yes, and [they] have held fast by me. I was not at Mr. Griggs' but once, but it may be [they] send something like me; neither would I have gone, but that they tell me they will hurt me. Last night they tell me I must kill somebody with the knife.

Q. Who were they that told you so?

Ans. Sarah Good and Osborne and they would have had me killed Thomas Putnam's child last night.

The child also affirmed that at the same time they would have had her cut off her own head, for if she would not, they told her Tituba would cut it off; and then she complained at the same time of a knife cutting of her. When her master hath asked her [Tituba] about these things, she saith [that] they will not let her tell, but tell her [that] if she tells her head will be cut off.

Q. Who tells you so?

Ans. The man, Good, and Osborne's wife. Goody Good came to her last night when her master was at prayer and would not let her hear and she could not hear a good while. Good hath one of these birds, the yellow bird, and would have given me it, but I would not have it, and in prayer time she stopped my ears and would not let me hear.

Q. What should you have done with it?

Ans. Give it to the children (which yellow bird hath been several times seen by the children). I saw Sarah Good have it on her hand when she came to her [Tituba] when Mr. Parris was at prayer. I saw the bird suck Good between the forefinger and long finger upon the right hand.

Q. Did you never practice witchcraft in your own country?

Ans. No, never before now.

Q. Did you see them do it now?

Ans. Yes, today, but that was in the morning.

Q. But did you see them do it now while you are examining?[14]

Ans. No, I did not see them, but I saw them hurt at other times. I saw Good have a cat beside the yellow bird which was with her.

Q. What hath Osborne got to go with her?

Ans. Something. I don't know what it is. I can't name it. I don't know how it looks. She hath two of them. One of them hath wings and two legs and a head like a woman.

The children saw the same but yesterday, which afterward turned into a woman.

Q. What is the other thing that Goody Osborne hath?

Ans. A thing all over hairy, all the face hairy and a long nose, and I don't know how to tell how the face looks, with two legs; it goeth upright and is about two or three foot high, and goeth upright like a man, and last night it stood before the fire in Mr. Parris's hall.

Q. Who was [it] that appeared like a wolf to Hubbard as she was going from Proctor's?

Ans. It was Sarah Good and I saw her send the wolf to her.

Q. What clothes doth the man appear unto you in?

Ans. Black clothes sometimes, sometimes [a] serge[15] coat of other color. [He is] a tall man with white hair, I think.

Q. What apparel do the women wear?

Ans. I don't know what color.

Q. What kind of clothes hath she?

---

[14] Being examined.

[15] A strong fabric woven with a double thread so as to have parallel diagonal ribs.

Ans. A black silk hood with a white silk hood under it, with top knots, which woman I know not, but [I] have seen her in Boston when I lived there.

Q. What clothes [hath] the little woman?

Ans. A serge coat with a white cap, as I think.

The children having fits at this very time, she was asked who hurt them. She answered, "Goody Good," and the children affirmed the same, but Hubbard being taken in an extreme fit, after[ward] she [Tituba] was asked who hurt her, and she said she could not tell, but said they blinded her, and would not let her see, and after that was once or twice taken dumb herself.

29

Second Examination of Tituba (as Recorded by Jonathan Corwin)

March 2, 1692

Q. What covenant did you make with that man that came to you? What did he tell you?

Ans. He tell me he God, and I must believe him and serve him six years and he would give me many fine things.

Q. How long ago was this?

Ans. About six weeks and a little more, the Friday night before Abigail was ill.

Q. What did he say you must do more? Did he say [that] you must write anything? Did he offer you any paper?

Ans. Yes, the next time he come to see me and showed me some fine things, something like creatures, a little bird, something like green and white.

Q. Did you promise him then when he spoke to you then? What did you answer him?

Miscellaneous Collections, U.S. States and Territories, Massachusetts, Manuscripts and Archives Division, The New York Public Library, Astor, Lenox and Tilden Foundations.

Ans. I then said this: I told him I could not believe him God. I told him I [would] ask my master and would have gone up,[16] but he stopped me and would not let me.

Q. What did you promise him?

Ans. The first time I believe him [to be] God and then he was glad.

Q. What did he say to you then? What did he say you must do?

Ans. This he tell me, they must meet together.

Q. When did he say you must meet together?

Ans. He tell me Wednesday next at my master's house, and then they all meet together, and that night I saw them all stand in the corner, all four of them, and the man stand behind me and take hold of me to make me stand still in the hall.

Q. [What] time of night?

Ans. A little before prayer time.

Q. What did this man say to you when he took hold of you?

Ans. He say, "Go into the other room and see the children and do hurt to them and pinch them," and then I went in, and would not hurt them a good while. I would not hurt Betty, I loved Betty, but they haul me and make me pinch Betty, and the next Abigail, and then quickly went away altogether after I had pinched them.

Q. Did they pinch?

Ans. No, but they all looked on and see me pinch them.

Q. Did you go into that room in your own person and all the rest?

Ans. Yes, and my master did not see us, for they would not let my master see.

Q. Did you go with the company?

Ans. No, I stayed and the man stayed with me.

Q. What did he then [say] to you?

Ans. He tell me my master go to prayer and he [would] read in book and he [Parris] [would] ask me what I remember, but [the man said,] don't you remember anything.

Q. Did he ask you no more but the first time to serve him or [did he also ask] the second time?

Ans. Yes, he ask me again, and that I serve him six years, and he come the next time and show me a book.

Q. And when would he come then?

Ans. The next Friday and showed me a book, in the daytime, betimes[17] in the morning.

---

[16] Upstairs to speak with her master.
[17] Early.

Q. And what book did he bring? A great or little book?

Ans. He did not show it me, nor would not, but had it in his pocket.

Q. Did not he make you write your name?

Ans. No, not yet, for [my] mistress called me into the other room.

Q. What did he say you must do in that book?

Ans. He said [to] write and set my name to it.

Q. Did you write?

Ans. Yes, once I made a mark in the book and made it with red like blood.

Q. Did he get it out of your body?

Ans. He said he must get it out the next time he come again; he give me a pin tied in a stick to do it with, but he no let me blood with it as yet, but intended another time when he come again.

Q. Did you see any other marks in his book?

Ans. Yes, a great many; some marks red, some yellow; he opened his book [and there were] a great many marks in it.

Q. Did he tell you the names of them?

Ans. Yes, of two, no more, Good and Osborne, and he say they make them marks in that book and he showed them me.

Q. How many marks do you think there was?

Ans. Nine.

Q. Did they write their names?

Ans. They made marks. Goody Good said she made her mark, but Goody Osborne would not tell; she was cross to me.

Q. When did Good tell you she set her hand to the book?

Ans. The same day I came hither to prison.

Q. Did you see the man that morning?

Ans. Yes, a little in the morning, and he tell me the magistrates come up to examine me.

Q. What did he say you must say?

Ans. He tell me [to] tell nothing; if I did, he would cut my head off.

Q. Tell us true: how many women do use to come when you ride abroad?

Ans. Four of them: these two, Osborne and Good, and those two strangers.

Q. You say that there was nine. Did he tell you who they were?

Ans. No, he no let me see, but he tell me I should see them the next time.

Q. What sights did you see?

Ans. I see a man, a dog, a hog, and two cats, a black and red, and the strange monster [that] was Osborne's that I mentioned before; this was the hairy imp. The man would give it to me, but I would not have it.

Q. Did he show you in the book which was Osborne's and which was Good's mark?

Ans. Yes, I see their marks.

Q. But did he tell [you] the names of the others?

Ans. No, sir.

Q. And what did he say to you when you made your mark?

Ans. He said, "Serve me, and always serve me," the man with the two women [who] came from Boston.

Q. How many times did you go to Boston?

Ans. I was going and then came back again; I was never at Boston.

Q. Who came back with you again?

Ans. The man came back with me and the women go away; I was not willing to go.

Q. How far did you go? To what town?

Ans. I never went to any town; I see no trees, no town.

Q. Did he tell you where the nine lived?

Ans. Yes, some in Boston, and some here in this town, but he would not tell me who they were.

30

Elizabeth Hubbard against Tituba
March 1, 1692

The deposition of Elizabeth Hubbard, aged about seventeen years, who testifieth that on February 25, 1692 I saw the apparition of Tituba Indian, which did immediately most grievously torment me by pricking, pinching, and almost choking me; and so continued hurting me most grievously betimes till the day of her examination, being March 1, and then also at the beginning of her examination, but as soon as she began to confess she left off hurting me and has hurt me but little since.

Essex County Court Archives, vol. 1, no. 32, from the Records of the Court of Oyer and Terminer, 1692, Property of the Supreme Judicial Court, Division of Archives and Records Preservation, on deposit at the Peabody Essex Museum, Salem, Massachusetts.

Ann Putnam Jr. against Tituba
March 1, 1692

The deposition of Ann Putnam, who testifieth and saith that on February 25, 1692 I saw the apparition of Tituba, Mr. Parris's Indian woman, which did torture me most grievously by pricking and pinching me most dreadfully till March 1, being the day of her examination, and then also most grievously also at the beginning of her examination, but since she confessed she has hurt me but little.[18]

---

[18] See also Document 19, Abigail Williams against Good, Osborne, and Tituba.

Essex County Court Archives, vol. 1, no. 35, from the Records of the Court of Oyer and Terminer, 1692, Property of the Supreme Judicial Court, Division of Archives and Records Preservation, on deposit at the Peabody Essex Museum, Salem, Massachusetts.

Indictment against Tituba for Covenanting with the Devil
May 9, 1693

Province of the Massachusetts Bay in New England
[In] Essex [County]
At a Court of Assize and General Jail Delivery, held in Ipswich for the County of Essex aforesaid [on] May 9, 1693, in the fifth year of their Majesties' reign

The Jurors for our Sovereign Lord and Lady, the King and Queen, present that Tituba, an Indian woman, servant to Mr. Samuel Parris of Salem Village in the county of Essex aforesaid, upon or about the latter

---

Suffolk Court Files, vol. 32, docket 2760, p. 102, Massachusetts Supreme Judicial Court Archives, Boston, Massachusetts.

end of the year 1691 in the town of Salem Village aforesaid wickedly, maliciously, and feloniously a covenant with the Devil did make and signed the Devil's book with a mark like A:C, by which wicked covenanting with the Devil she, the said Tituba, is become a detestable witch, against the peace of our Sovereign Lord and Lady, the King and Queen, their crown and dignity, and the laws in that case made and provided.

Returned Ignoramus[19]

JOHN PROCTOR

On both sides of the Atlantic, women were much more vulnerable than men to accusations of witchcraft, and the Salem witch hunt was no exception to this. Yet over three dozen men were charged in 1692, and five of the nineteen individuals hanged that year were male. Some of these men were targeted because of their association with the divisions and tensions within Salem Village described in the introduction. John Proctor had flourished as a farmer and had engaged in a range of successful commercial dealings. He ran a tavern on the Ipswich Road, which divided Salem Village from Salem Town, and he seems to have had much closer relations with residents of Ipswich and Salem Town than with those who lived in Salem Village. He worshipped in Salem Town, not in the village church. Proctor's success and his identification with the town made him a likely suspect in the minds of villagers who feared Salem Town and what they saw as its malign impact on their lives.

Equally significant was Proctor's vocal opposition to the trials. One of the afflicted girls worked as a servant in his household, and Proctor made no secret of his skepticism about her alleged fits. The depositions against Proctor show just how dangerous it was to criticize the accusers or the court's handling of the crisis: anyone who did not support the witch hunt could be suspected of belonging to the witch confederacy. Yet some of Proctor's neighbors were willing to speak out on his behalf, whatever the risks involved. John Proctor's arrest and trial, along with that of his wife, Elizabeth, prompted dozens of local residents to sign petitions of protest (Documents 40 and 41). The petitioners depicted Proctor's plight as a judgment from God for his sins, though witchcraft, they insisted, was not one of them (Document 40).

---

[19] Rejected by the Grand Jury.

John Proctor was arrested on April 11 (there is no surviving transcript of his examination). He was tried and convicted on August 5 and hanged on August 19. Elizabeth Proctor was also convicted, but because she was pregnant, the court granted her a reprieve.

Two and a half centuries after his death, Proctor would become the central character in Arthur Miller's *The Crucible*, a veiled attack on Senator Joseph McCarthy's "witch hunt" of the 1950s (the purpose of which was to root out alleged Communists threatening the security and moral fiber of the nation). Miller's play is a gripping piece of theater and a powerful commentary on the deadly impact of fear, suspicion, and malice. Yet the Proctor of Miller's imagination bears little resemblance to the man revealed by surviving records. There is, for example, not a shred of evidence to suggest that Proctor was attracted to eleven-year-old Abigail Williams.

33

Elizabeth Booth against John Proctor
April 11, 1692

The deposition of Elizabeth Booth, aged eighteen years, who testifieth and saith that since I have been afflicted I have been most grievously tormented by my neighbor John Proctor, Sr., or his appearance. Also I have seen John Proctor, Sr., or his appearance most grievously torment and afflict Mary Walcott, Mercy Lewis, and Ann Putnam, Jr., by pinching, twisting, and almost choking them.

Essex County Court Archives, vol. 1, no. 51, from the Records of the Court of Oyer and Terminer, 1692, Property of the Supreme Judicial Court, Division of Archives and Records Preservation, on deposit at the Peabody Essex Museum, Salem, Massachusetts.

<h1 style="text-align:center">34</h1>

Abigail Williams against John Proctor

May 31, 1692

The testimony of Abigail Williams, [who] witnesseth and saith that diverse times in the month of April past and particularly on the fourth, sixth, eleventh, and thirteenth days of the same month, she the said Abigail hath been much vexed with the apparition of John Proctor, Sr., of Salem, husbandman, by which apparition she, the said Abigail, hath been often pinched and otherwise tortured.

Essex County Court Archives, vol. 1, no. 54, from the Records of the Court of Oyer and Terminer, 1692, Property of the Supreme Judicial Court, Division of Archives and Records Preservation, on deposit at the Peabody Essex Museum, Salem, Massachusetts.

<h1 style="text-align:center">35</h1>

Physical Examination of John Proctor and John Willard

June 2, 1692

We whose names [are] underwritten, having searched the bodies of John Proctor, Sr., and John Willard, now in the jail, do not find any thing to further suspect them.

	J. Barton, surgeon
John Rogers	John Giles
Joshua Rea Jr.	William Hine
John Cook	Ezekiel Cheever

Essex County Court Archives, vol. 1, no. 50, from the Records of the Court of Oyer and Terminer, 1692, Property of the Supreme Judicial Court, Division of Archives and Records Preservation, on deposit at the Peabody Essex Museum, Salem, Massachusetts.

Mary Warren against John Proctor[20]
June 30, 1692

The deposition of Mary Warren, aged twenty years, who testifieth, I have seen the apparition of John Proctor, Sr., among the witches and he hath often tortured me by pinching me and biting me and choking me and pressing me on my stomach till the blood came out of my mouth. And also I saw him torture Mistress Pope and Mercy Lewis and John Indian upon the day of his examination. And he hath also tempted me to write in his book and to eat bread which he brought to me, which I refusing to do, John Proctor did most grievously torture me with variety of tortures, almost ready to kill me.

[20]Sarah Bibber, Elizabeth Hubbard, Ann Putnam Jr., Susannah Sheldon, and Mary Walcott also testified that John Proctor had tormented them.

Essex County Court Archives, vol. 1, no. 59, from the Records of the Court of Oyer and Terminer, 1692, Property of the Supreme Judicial Court, Division of Archives and Records Preservation, on deposit at the Peabody Essex Museum, Salem, Massachusetts.

37

Petition of John Proctor
July 23, 1692

[From] Salem Prison
[To] Mr. Mather, Mr. Allen, Mr. Moody, Mr. Willard, and Mr. Bailey

Reverend Gentlemen,
The innocency of our case with the enmity of our accusers and our judges and jury, whom nothing but our innocent blood will serve their turn, having condemned us already before our trials, being so much incensed and engaged against us by the Devil, makes us bold to beg

Robert Calef, *More Wonders of the Invisible World* (London, 1700), 104–5.

and implore your favorable assistance of this our humble petition to his Excellency, that if it be possible our innocent blood may be spared, which undoubtedly otherwise will be shed, if the Lord doth not mercifully step in. The magistrates, ministers, juries, and all the people in general being so much enraged and incensed against us by the delusion of the Devil, which we can term no other, by reason we know in our own consciences [that] we are all innocent persons. Here are five persons who have lately confessed themselves to be witches, and do accuse some of us of being along with them at a sacrament since we were committed into close prison, which we know to be lies. Two of the five are Carrier's sons, young men who would not confess anything till they tied them neck and heels till the blood was ready to come out of their noses, and 'tis credibly believed and reported [that] this was the occasion of making them confess that [which] they never did, by [which] reason they said one had been a witch a month, and another five weeks, and that their mother had made them so, who has been confined here this nine weeks. My son, William Proctor, when he was examined, because he would not confess that he was guilty when he was innocent, they tied him neck and heels till the blood gushed out at his nose, and would have kept him so twenty-four hours, if one more merciful than the rest had not taken pity on him and caused him to be unbound. These actions are very like the Popish cruelties.[21] They have already undone us in our estates, and that will not serve their turns, without our innocent bloods. If it cannot be granted that we can have our trials at Boston, we humbly beg that you would endeavor to have these magistrates changed and others in their rooms,[22] begging also and beseeching you would be pleased to be here, if not all, some of you at our trials, hoping [that] thereby you may be the means of saving the shedding [of] our innocent bloods. Desiring your prayers to the Lord in our behalf, we rest your poor afflicted servants,

John Proctor, etc.

---

[21] Proctor was referring to the Catholic Inquisition, infamous for its use of torture to extract confessions.
[22] Place.

John DeRich against John Proctor and Others

August 4, 1692

John DeRich, aged sixteen years or thereabouts, testifieth and saith that John Small and his wife Ann, both deceased and formerly of the town of Salem, doth both appear to this deponent and told him that they would tear him to pieces if he did not go and declare to Mr. Hathorne that George Jacobs Sr. did kill them; and likewise that Mary Warren's mother did appear to this deponent this day with a white man and told him that Goodwife Parker[23] and [Bridget] Oliver[24] did kill her; and likewise Corey,[25] Proctor and his wife [Elizabeth], Sarah Proctor, Joseph Proctor, and John Proctor did all afflict this deponent and do continually every day since he hath begun to be afflicted, and would have him this deponent to set his hand to a book, but this deponent told them he would not. Likewise Phillip English and his wife Mary doth appear to this deponent and afflict him, and all the abovesaid persons threaten to tear this deponent in pieces if he doth not sign to a book. Likewise Goodwife [Sarah] Pease and [Deliverance] Hobbs and her [step]daughter Abigail doth afflict him and threaten the same. And likewise a woman appears to this deponent who lives at Boston at the upper end of the town, whose name is Mary: she goes in black clothes, hath but one eye, with a crooked neck, and she saith there is none in Boston like her. She did afflict this deponent, but saith she will not any more, nor tell him her name.

---

[23] DeRich could have been referring to Alice or Mary Parker, both of whom were convicted and executed.

[24] Bridget Oliver had remarried following the death of her husband, Thomas Oliver. Her new husband was Edward Bishop; she was convicted and executed in 1692 as Bridget Bishop (see Documents 42–51).

[25] This could have been a reference to Giles or Martha Corey. Both were arrested. Giles was pressed to death under interrogation; Martha was hanged.

Essex County Court Archives, vol. 1, no. 127, from the Records of the Court of Oyer and Terminer, 1692, Property of the Supreme Judicial Court, Division of Archives and Records Preservation, on deposit at the Peabody Essex Museum, Salem, Massachusetts.

Samuel Sibley against John Proctor
August 5, 1692

The morning after the examination of Goody Nurse, Samuel Sibley met John Proctor about Mr. Phillips['s house] who called to said Sibley as he was going to said Phillips and asked how the folks did at the village. He answered he heard they were very bad last night but he had heard nothing this morning. Proctor replied he was going to fetch home his jade.[26] He left her there last night and had rather given 40s [shillings] than let her come up. Said Sibley asked why he talked so. Proctor replied, if they were let alone, so we should all be devils and witches quickly; they should rather be had to the whipping post, but he would fetch his jade home and thrash the Devil out of her, and more to the like purpose, crying, hang them, hang them. And also added that when she was first taken with fits, he kept her close to the wheel and threatened to thrash her, and then she had no more fits till the next day he was gone forth, and then she must have her fits again, forsooth, etc.

Proctor owns [that] he meant Mary Warren.

[26] An insolent, saucy, or disreputable young woman.

Essex County Court Archives, vol. 1, no. 52, from the Records of the Court of Oyer and Terminer, 1692, Property of the Supreme Judicial Court, Division of Archives and Records Preservation, on deposit at the Peabody Essex Museum, Salem, Massachusetts.

Petition for John Proctor and Elizabeth Proctor
August 5, 1692

The humble and sincere declaration of us subscribers, inhabitants in Ipswich, on the behalf of our neighbors John Proctor and his wife, now in trouble and under suspicion of witchcraft

To the Honorable Court of Assistants now sitting in Boston:
Honored and Right Worshipful:
   The foresaid John Proctor may have great reason to justify the divine sovereignty of God under these severe remarks of Providence upon his peace and honor under a due reflection upon his life past. And so the best of us have reason to adore the great pity and indulgence of God's Providence, that we are not as exposed to the utmost shame that the Devil can invent under the permissions of sovereignty, though not for that sin forenamed, yet for our many transgressions; for we do at present suppose that it may be a method within the severer but just transaction of the infinite majesty of God that he sometimes may permit Satan to [im]personate, dissemble, and thereby abuse innocents and such as do in the fear of God defy the Devil and all his works. The great rage he is permitted to attempt holy Job with, the abuse he does the famous Samuel, in disquieting his silent dust, by shadowing his venerable person in answer to the charms of witchcraft, and other instances from good hands may be argued, besides the unsearchable footsteps of God's judgments that are brought to light every morning that astonish our weaker reasons, to teach us adoration, trembling, and dependence, etc. But—
   We must not trouble your honors by being tedious. Therefore, we being smitten with the notice of what hath happened, we reckon it within the duties of our charity that teacheth us to do as we would be done by to offer thus much for the clearing of our neighbor's innocence, viz:[27] that

---

[27] That is.

Essex County Court Archives, vol. 1, no. 60, from the Records of the Court of Oyer and Terminer, 1692, Property of the Supreme Judicial Court, Division of Archives and Records Preservation, on deposit at the Peabody Essex Museum, Salem, Massachusetts.

we never had the least knowledge of such a nefandous[28] wickedness in our said neighbors since they have been within our acquaintance; neither do we remember any such thoughts in us concerning them, or any action by them or either of them directly tending that way, no more than might be in the lives of any other persons of the clearest reputation as to any such evils. What[ever] God may have left them to, we cannot go into God's pavilions clothed with clouds of darkness round about.[29]

But as to what we have ever seen or heard of them, upon our consciences we judge them innocent of the crime objected. His breeding hath been amongst us and was of religious parents in our place; and by reason of relations and properties within our town hath had constant intercourse with us.

We speak upon our personal acquaintance and observations, and so leave our neighbors, and this our testimony on their behalf, to the wise thoughts of your honors, and subscribe, etc.

John Wise	Nathaniel Perkins	Benjamin Marshall
William Story, Sr.	Thomas Lovkin	John Andrews, Jr.
Reginald Foster	William Cogswell	William Butler
Thomas Choate	Thomas Varney	William Andrews
John Burnham, Sr.	John Fellows	John Andrews
William Thomson	William Cogswell, Sr.	John Choate, Sr.
Thomas Low, Sr.	Jonathan Cogswell	Joseph Proctor
Isaac Foster	John Cogswell, Jr.	Samuel Gidding
John Burnham, Jr.	John Cogswell	Joseph Euleth
William Goodhugh	Thomas Andrews	James White
Isaac Perkins	Joseph Andrews	

---

[28] Unmentionable, abominable.

[29] In other words, whatever they have done as a result of God's judgment upon them, we are not able to penetrate the mysteries of Providence.

Petition for John Proctor and Elizabeth Proctor
August 5, 1692

We whose names are underwritten, having several years known John Proctor and his wife, do testify that we never heard or understood that they were ever suspected to be guilty of the crime now charged upon them; and several of us, being their near neighbors, do testify that to our apprehension they lived Christian life in their family and were ever ready to help such as stood in need of their help.

Nathaniel Felton Sr. and Mary, his wife	Samuel Frail and Ann, his wife
Samuel Marsh and Priscilla, his wife	Samuel Endicott and Hannah, his wife
James Holton and Ruth, his wife	Samuel Stone
John Felton	George Locker
Samuel Gaskell and Provided, his wife	George Smith
Nathaniel Felton Jr.	Edward Gaskell
	Zachariah Marsh and Mary, his wife

Essex County Court Archives, vol. 1, no. 110, from the Records of the Court of Oyer and Terminer, 1692, Property of the Supreme Judicial Court, Division of Archives and Records Preservation, on deposit at the Peabody Essex Museum, Salem, Massachusetts.

BRIDGET BISHOP

Bridget Bishop lived in Salem Town with her third husband, Edward Bishop. She had been accused of witchcraft once before, in the winter of 1679–1680, shortly after the death of her second husband, Thomas Oliver. (Some of the witnesses still thought of her as Goodwife Oliver and referred to her as such in their depositions.) A striking number of female witch suspects were accused within a few years of their becoming widows. No longer under the authority of a father or husband, widows could own land in their own right or control it on behalf of children who had not yet reached adulthood. They represented an aberration in a culture that assumed land would rest in male hands, and they were often the objects of suspicion and hostility. Oliver was acquitted in 1680, but her association with witchcraft clearly lived on in the minds of her neighbors.

The former Goodwife Oliver, now Goodwife Bishop, was in several respects a likely witch suspect. She was self-confident and sometimes argumentative, qualities considered inappropriate in a woman. She also seems to have been a physically attractive woman who captured the imagination of some of her male neighbors. Given that Puritans associated female allure with Eve's temptation of Adam into sin, this would have made Bishop as frightening as she was appealing.

Some of Bishop's neighbors believed that she had been using image magic against her enemies. Two workmen claimed that they had found "poppets" (small dolls) hidden in her cellar with pins stuck in them (Document 47). In another deposition Samuel Shattuck described her as having shown him pieces of lace that she wanted him to dye; these were so small that he "could not judge them fit for any use" (Document 50). The implication was that she had been using them to dress the dolls. Given how difficult it was to prove witchcraft, descriptions of hard evidence such as poppets would have been invaluable to those in favor of conviction. The magistrates issued a warrant for Bridget Bishop's arrest on April 18 and examined her the following day. Bishop was the first of the accused to be tried, on June 2. She was convicted and hanged on June 10.[30]

[30] Bridget Bishop has sometimes been confused with Sarah Bishop (also married to an Edward Bishop), who ran an unlicensed tavern. Some locals alleged that Sarah Bishop's tavern was attracting young people, who "were in danger to be corrupted" (Bernard Rosenthal et al., eds., *Records of the Salem Witch-Hunt* [New York: Cambridge University Press, 2009], 300).

42

Examination of Bridget Bishop (as Recorded by Ezekiel Cheever)

April 19, 1692

Bridget Bishop being now coming in to be examined relating to her accusation of suspicion of sundry acts of witchcrafts, the afflicted persons are now dreadfully afflicted by her, as they do say.

Essex County Court Archives, vol. 1, no. 137, from the Records of the Court of Oyer and Terminer, 1692, Property of the Supreme Judicial Court, Division of Archives and Records Preservation, on deposit at the Peabody Essex Museum, Salem, Massachusetts.

Mr. Hathorne: Bishop, what do you say? You here stand charged with sundry acts of witchcraft by you done or committed upon the bodies of Mercy Lewis and Ann Putnam and others.

Bishop: I am innocent. I know nothing of it. I have done no witchcraft.

Mr. Hathorne: Look upon this woman [speaking to the afflicted] and see if this be the woman that you have seen hurting you.

Mercy Lewis and Ann Putnam and others do now charge her to her face with hurting of them.

Mr. Hathorne: What do you say? Now you see they charge you to your face.

Bishop: I never did hurt them in my life. I did never see these persons before. I am as innocent as the child unborn.

Mr. Hathorne: Is not your coat cut?

Bishop answers "No," but her garment being looked upon, they find it cut or torn two ways. Jonathan Walcott saith that the sword that he struck at Goody Bishop with was not naked but was within the scabbard,[31] so that the rent may very probably be the very same that Mary Walcott did tell that she [Bridget Bishop] had in her coat by Jonathan's striking at her appearance. The afflicted persons charge her with having hurt them many ways and by tempting them to sign to the Devil's book, at which charge she seemed to be very angry and shaking her head at them, saying it was false. They are all greatly tormented (as I conceive) by the shaking of her head.

Mr. Hathorne: Goody Bishop, what contract have you made with the Devil?

Bishop: I have made no contract with the Devil. I never saw him in my life.

Ann Putnam sayeth that she calls the Devil her God.

Mr. Hathorne: What say you to all this that you are charged with? Can you not find in your heart to tell the truth?

Bishop: I do tell the truth. I never hurt these persons in my life. I never saw them before.

---

[31] A sheath or case that holds the blade of a sword or dagger.

Mercy Lewis: Oh, Goody Bishop, did you not come to our house last night and did you not tell me that your master made you tell more than you were willing to tell?

Mr. Hathorne: Tell us the truth in this matter. How come these persons to be thus tormented and to charge you with doing?

Bishop: I am not come here to say I am a witch to take away my life.

Mr. Hathorne: Who is it that doth it if you do not? They say it is your likeness that comes and torments them and tempts them to write in the book. What book is [it] that you tempt them with?

Bishop: I know nothing of it. I am innocent.

Mr. Hathorne: Do you not see how they are tormented? You are acting witchcraft before us. What do you say to this? Why, have you not a heart to confess the truth?

Bishop: I am innocent. I know nothing of it. I am no witch. I know not what a witch is.

Mr. Hathorne: Have you not given consent that some evil spirit should do this in your likeness?

Bishop: No. I am innocent of being a witch. I know no man, woman, or child here.

Marshall Herrick: How came you into my bedchamber one morning, then, and asked me whether I had any curtains to sell?

She is by some of the afflicted persons charged with murder.

Mr. Hathorne: What do you say to these murders you are charged with?

Bishop: I am innocent. I know nothing of it.

Now she lifts up her eyes and they are greatly tormented.

Mr. Hathorne: What do you say to these things here, [these] horrible acts of witchcraft?

Bishop: I know nothing of it. I do not know whether [there] be any witches or no.

Mr. Hathorne: No? Have you not heard that some have confessed?

Bishop: No. I did not.

Two men told her to her face that they had told her. Here she is taken in a plain lie. Now she is going away, they are dreadfully afflicted. Five afflicted persons do charge this woman to be the very woman that hurts them.

This is a true account of what I have taken down at her examination according to [my] best understanding and observation. I have also in her examination taken notice that all her actions have great influence upon the afflicted persons and that [they] have been tortured by her.

Ezekiel Cheever.

43

William Stacy against Bridget Bishop
May 30, 1692

William Stacy of the town of Salem, aged thirty-six years or thereabouts, deposeth and saith that about fourteen years ago this deponent was visited with the smallpox. Then Bridget Bishop did give him a visit and withal professed a great love for this deponent in his affliction, more than ordinary, at which this deponent admired.[32] Some time after this deponent was well, the said Bishop got him to do some work for her, for which she gave him three pence, which seemed to this deponent as if it had been good money; but he had not gone above three or four rods[33] before he looked in his pocket, where he put it, for it, but could not find any. Some time after, this deponent met the said Bishop in the street going to [the] mill; she asking this deponent whether his father would grind her grist,[34] he put it to the said Bishop why she asked. She answered because folks counted her a witch. This deponent made answer [that] he did not question but that his father would grind it; but being gone about six rods from her, the said Bishop, with a small load in his cart, suddenly the off wheel[35] slumped or sunk down into a hole upon plain ground, that this deponent was forced to get one to help him get

---

[32] Was astonished.
[33] One rod was equivalent to five and a half yards.
[34] Grain.
[35] The wheel on the right, as opposed to that on the near or left side, where the driver walked.

Essex County Court Archives, vol. 1, no. 138 and 139, from the Records of the Court of Oyer and Terminer, 1692, Property of the Supreme Judicial Court, Division of Archives and Records Preservation, on deposit at the Peabody Essex Museum, Salem, Massachusetts.

the wheel out. Afterwards this deponent went back to look for said hole where his wheel sunk in, but could not find any hole. Some time after, in the winter about midnight, this deponent felt something between his lips pressing hard against his teeth and withal was very cold insomuch that it did awake him, so that he got up and sat upon his bed, he at the same time seeing the said Bridget Bishop sitting at the foot of his bed, being to his seeming it was then as light as if it had been day, or one in the said Bishop's shape, she having then a black cap and a black hat, and a red coat with two eakes[36] of two colors. Then she, the said Bishop, or her shape, clapped her coat close to her legs and hopped upon the bed and about the room and then went out, and then it was dark again. Some time after, the said Bishop went to this deponent and asked him whether that which he had reported was true that he had told to several. He answered that [it] was true and that it was she, and bid her deny it if she dare. The said Bishop did not deny it and went away very angry and said that this deponent did her more mischief than any other body. He asked, "Why?" She answered, because folks would believe him before anybody else. Some time after, the said Bishop threatened this deponent and told him [that] he was the occasion of bringing her out about the brass she stole. Some time after, this deponent in a dark night was going to the barn and was suddenly taken or hoisted from the ground and thrown against a stone wall, after that taken up again and thrown down a bank at the end of his house. Some time after, this deponent met the said Bishop by Isaac Stearns' brick kiln;[37] after he had passed by her, this deponent's horse stood still with a small load going up the hill so that the horse striving to draw, all his gears and tacking flew in pieces and the cart fell down. Afterward this deponent went to lift a bag of corn of about two bushels, but could not budge it with all his might. This deponent hath met with several other of her pranks at several times, which would take up a great time to tell of.

This deponent doth verily believe that the said Bridget Bishop was instrumental to his daughter Priscilla's death about two years ago; the child was a likely thriving child, and suddenly screeched out and so continued in an unusual manner for about a fortnight and so died in that lamentable manner.

---

[36] This may be an idiosyncratic spelling of *eke*, which meant a piece added on.
[37] A furnace or oven for baking bricks.

Sarah Churchill and Mary Warren against
Bridget Bishop and Others

June 1, 1692

Sarah Churchill confesseth that Goody Pudeator brought the book to this examinant and she signed it, but [she] did not know her at that time, but when she saw her she knew her to be the same, and that Goody Bishop, alias Oliver, appeared to this examinant and told her [that] she had killed John Trask's child (whose child died about that time), and said Bishop, alias Oliver, afflicted her, as also did old George Jacobs, and before that time this examinant, being afflicted, could not do her service[38] as formerly and her said master Jacobs called her "bitch witch" and ill names and then afflicted her as above, and that Pudeator brought three images like Mercy Lewis, Ann Putnam, and Elizabeth Hubbard, and they brought her thorns and she stuck them in the images and [they] told her [that] the persons whose likeness they were would be afflicted, and the other day [she] saw Goody Oliver sat upon her knee.

Mary Warren, aged twenty years or thereabouts, testifieth and saith that several times after April 19 when Bridget Bishop, alias Oliver, was in the jail at Salem, she did appear to this deponent tempting her to sign the book and oft times during her being there, as aforesaid, the said Bridget did torture and afflict this deponent and, being in chains, said [that] though she could not do it, she would bring one that should do it, which now she knows to be Mr. Corey that then came and afflicted her.

[38] Her work as a servant.

Essex County Court Archives, vol. 1, no. 262, from the Records of the Court of Oyer and Terminer, 1692, Property of the Supreme Judicial Court, Division of Archives and Records Preservation, on deposit at the Peabody Essex Museum, Salem, Massachusetts.

Physical Examinations of
Bridget Bishop and Others
June 2, 1692

Salem, June 2, 1692, about ten in [the] morning

We whose names are underwritten, being commanded by Captain George Corwin, Esquire, Sheriff of the county of Essex, this June 2, 1692, for to view the bodies of Bridget Bishop, alias Oliver, Rebecca Nurse, Elizabeth Proctor, Alice Parker, Susannah Martin, [and] Sarah Good.

[On] the first three, namely Bishop, Nurse, [and] Proctor, by diligent search [we] have discovered a preternatural excrescence of flesh between the pudendum[39] and anus much like to teats and not usual in women and much unlike to the other three that hath been searched by us and that they were in all the three women near the same place.

Salem, June 2, 1692, about four [in the] afternoon

We whose names are subscribed to the within mentioned, upon a second search about three or four hours distance, did find the said Bridget Bishop, alias Oliver, in a clear and free state from any preternatural excrescence as formerly seen by us, also Rebecca Nurse, instead of that excrescence within mentioned it appears only as a dry skin without sense,[40] and as for Elizabeth Proctor which excrescence [was] like a teat red and fresh, not anything appears, but only a proper procedentia ani,[41] and as for Susannah Martin, whose breast in the morning search appeared to us very full, the nipples fresh and starting, now at this searching [they are] all lank and pendant, which is all at present from the within mentioned subscribers, [and] that that piece of flesh of

[39] A woman's external genitals or vulva.
[40] Insensitive to touch.
[41] The opening of the anus.

Essex County Court Archives, vol. 1, no. 136, from the Records of the Court of Oyer and Terminer, 1692, Property of the Supreme Judicial Court, Division of Archives and Records Preservation, on deposit at the Peabody Essex Museum, Salem, Massachusetts.

Goodwife Nurse's formerly seen is gone and only a dry skin nearer to the anus in another place.

		J Barton, surgeon
Eleanor Henderson	Alice Pickering	Anna Stephens
Elizabeth Hill	Lydia Pickman	Marjory Williams
Hannah Kezer	Rebecca Sharpe	Jane Woolings

46

John Bly Sr. and Rebecca Bly against Bridget Bishop

June 2, 1692

John Bly, Sr. and Rebecca Bly, his wife, of Salem, both testify and say that said John Bly bought a sow of Edward Bishop of Salem, sawyer,[42] and by agreement with said Bishop was to pay the price agreed upon unto Lieutenant Jeremiah Neale of Salem. And Bridget, the wife of said Edward Bishop, because she could not have the money or value agreed for paid unto her, she [came] to the house of the deponents in Salem and quarreled with them about it. Soon after which, the sow having pigged,[43] she was taken with strange fits, jumping up and knocking her head against the fence and seemed blind and deaf and would not eat, neither let her pigs suck, but foamed at the mouth, which Goody Henderson hearing of said she believed she was over-looked,[44] and that they had their cattle ill in such a manner at the eastward when she lived there, and [they] used to cure them by giving of them red ocher[45] and milk, which we also gave the sow, quickly after eating of which she grew better, and then for the space of near two hours together she getting into the street did set of jumping and running between the house of said

---

[42] Carpenter.
[43] Having given birth to piglets.
[44] Bewitched.
[45] An earthy clay containing iron oxide, usually yellow or reddish brown, often used as a pigment.

Essex County Court Archives, vol. 1, no. 150, from the Records of the Court of Oyer and Terminer, 1692, Property of the Supreme Judicial Court, Division of Archives and Records Preservation, on deposit at the Peabody Essex Museum, Salem, Massachusetts.

deponents and said Bishops as if she were stark mad, and after that was well again; and we did then apprehend, or judge, and do still, that said Bishop had bewitched said sow.

47

John Bly Sr. and William Bly against Bridget Bishop
June 2, 1692

John Bly, Sr., aged about fifty-seven years, and William Bly, aged about fifteen years, both of Salem, testifieth and saith that being employed by Bridget Bishop, alias Oliver, of Salem to help take down the cellar wall of the old house she formerly lived in, we the said deponents in holes of the said old wall belonging to the said cellar found several poppets made up of rags and hogs' bristles with headless pins in them with the points outward, and this was about seven years last past.

Essex County Court Archives, vol. 1, no. 147, from the Records of the Court of Oyer and Terminer, 1692, Property of the Supreme Judicial Court, Division of Archives and Records Preservation, on deposit at the Peabody Essex Museum, Salem, Massachusetts.

48

Richard Coman against Bridget Bishop
June 2, 1692

Richard Coman, aged about thirty-two years, testifieth that some time about eight years since, I then being in bed with my wife at Salem, one fifth day of the week at night, either in the latter end of May or the beginning of June, and a light burning in our room, I being awake did then

Essex County Court Archives, vol. 1, no. 146, from the Records of the Court of Oyer and Terminer, 1692, Property of the Supreme Judicial Court, Division of Archives and Records Preservation, on deposit at the Peabody Essex Museum, Salem, Massachusetts.

see Bridget Bishop of Salem, alias Oliver, come into the room we lay in and two women more with her, which two women were strangers to me; I knew them not. But said Bishop came in her red paragon bodice[46] and the rest of her clothing that she then usually did wear, and I knowing of her well, also the garb she did use to go in, did clearly and plainly know her, and testifieth that as he locked the door of the house when he went to bed, so he found it afterwards when he did rise. And quickly after they appeared the light was out, and the curtains at the foot of the bed opened, where I did see her, and presently [she] came and lay upon my breast or body and so oppressed him that he could not speak nor stir, no, not so much as to awake his wife, although he endeavored much so to do it. The next night they all appeared again in like manner and she, said Bishop, alias Oliver, took hold of him by the throat and almost hauled him out of the bed. The Saturday night following, I having been that day telling of what I had seen and how I suffered the two nights before, my kinsman William Coman told me [that] he would stay with me and lodge with me and see if they would come again and advised me to lay my sword athwart[47] my body. Quickly after we went to bed that said night and [we] both well awake and discoursing together, in came all the three women again and said Bishop was the first, as she had been the other two nights. So I told him, "William, here they be all come again," and he was immediately struck speechless and could not move, hand or foot, and immediately they got hold of my sword and strived to take it from me but I held so fast as they did not get it away. And I had then liberty of speech and called William, also my wife and Sarah Phillips that lay with my wife, who all told me afterwards [that] they heard me, but had not power to speak or stir. And the first that spoke was Sarah Phillips and [she] said, "In the name of God, Goodman Coman, what is the matter with you," [and] so they all vanished away.

---

[46] A tight-fitting outer vest; paragon was a shiny fabric made of silk and wool or goat's hair.

[47] Across.

John Louder against Bridget Bishop
June 2, 1692

John Louder of Salem, aged about thirty-two years, testifieth and saith that about seven or eight years since, I then living with Mr. John Gedney in Salem and having had some controversy with Bridget Bishop, the wife of Edward Bishop of Salem, sawyer, about her fowls that used to come into our orchard or garden, some little time after which, I going well to bed, about the dead of the night felt a great weight upon my breast and awakening looked and it being bright moonlight did clearly see said Bridget Bishop, or her likeness, sitting upon my stomach; and putting my arms off of the bed to free myself from that great oppression, she presently laid hold of my throat and almost choked me, and I had no strength or power in my hands to resist or help myself; and in this condition she held me to almost day. Some time after this, my mistress, Susannah Gedney, was in our orchard and I was then with her, and said Bridget Bishop, being then in her orchard, which was next adjoining to ours, my mistress told said Bridget that I said or affirmed that she came one night and sat upon my breast as aforesaid, which she denied and I affirmed to her face to be true and that I did plainly see her, upon which discourse with her she threatened me. And some time after that, I, being not very well, stayed at home on a Lord's Day and on the afternoon of said day, the doors being shut, I did see a black pig in the room coming towards me, so I went towards it to kick it and it vanished away. Immediately after I sat down on a narrow bar and did see a black thing jump into the window and [it] came and stood just before my face upon the bar. The body of it looked like a monkey, only the feet were like a cock's feet with claws and the face somewhat more like a man's than a monkey. And I being greatly affrighted, not being able to speak or help myself by reason of fear, I suppose, so the thing spake to me and said, "I am a messenger sent to you, for I understand you are troubled in mind, and if you will be ruled by me, you shall want for nothing in this world," upon which I endeavored to clap my hands upon it, and said, "You Devil! I will kill you!" But [I] could feel no substance and it jumped out of the window

Essex County Court Archives, vol. 1, no. 145, from the Records of the Court of Oyer and Terminer, 1692, Property of the Supreme Judicial Court, Division of Archives and Records Preservation, on deposit at the Peabody Essex Museum, Salem, Massachusetts.

again and immediately came in by the porch, although the doors were shut, and said, "You had better take my counsel," whereupon I struck at it with a stick but struck the groundsill[48] and broke the stick, but felt no substance, and that arm with which I struck was presently disenabled. Then it vanished away and I opened the back door and went out and going towards the house end I espied said Bridget Bishop in her orchard going towards her house, and seeing her [I] had no power to set one foot forward but returned in again, and going to shut the door I again did see that or the like creature that I before did see within doors, in such a posture as it seemed to be going to fly at me, upon which I cried out, "The whole armor of God be between me and you!" So it sprang back and flew over the apple tree, flinging the dust with its feet against my stomach, upon which I was struck dumb and so continued for about three days time, and [it] also shook many of the apples off from the tree which it flew over.

On her trial Bridget Bishop, alias Oliver, denied that she knew this deponent, though the orchard of this deponent and the orchard of said Bishop joined and they often had difference for some years together.

[48]The lowest horizontal timber in the framework of a building, or the base of a door frame or threshold.

50

Samuel Shattuck and Sarah Shattuck against Bridget Bishop

June 2, 1692

Samuel Shattuck, aged forty-one years, testifieth that in the year 1680 Bridget Oliver, formerly wife to old Goodman Oliver, now wife to Edward Bishop, did come to my house pretending to buy an old hogshead[49] which, though I asked very little for [it] and for all her pretended

[49]A large barrel.

Essex County Court Archives, vol. 1, no. 144, from the Records of the Court of Oyer and Terminer, 1692, Property of the Supreme Judicial Court, Division of Archives and Records Preservation, on deposit at the Peabody Essex Museum, Salem, Massachusetts.

want, she went away without it; and sundry other times she came in a smooth flattering manner on very slight errands, we have thought since on purpose to work mischief. At or very near this time, our eldest child, who promised as much health and understanding both by countenance and actions as any other children of his years, was taken in a very drooping condition; and as she came oftener to the house, he grew worse and worse, as he would be standing at the door [and] would fall out and bruise his face upon a great step[ping] stone as if he had been thrust out by an invisible hand, oftentimes falling and hitting his face against the sides of the house, bruising his face in a very miserable manner. After this the abovesaid Oliver brought me a pair of sleeves to dye and after that sundry pieces of lace, some of which were so short that I could not judge them fit for any use; she paid me two pence for dying them, which two pence I gave to Henry Williams who lived with me [and] he told me [that] he put it in a purse among some other money which he locked up in a box and that the purse and money was [since then] gone out of the box, he could not tell how, and never found it after. Just after the dying of these things, this child was taken in a terrible fit, his mouth and eyes drawn aside, and [he] gasped in such a manner as if he was upon the point of death; after this he grew worse in his fits, and out of them would be almost always crying, that for many months he would be crying till nature's strength was spent and then would fall asleep and then awake and fall to crying and moaning, that his very countenance did bespeak compassion; and at length we perceived his understanding decayed so that we feared (as it has since proved) that he would be quite bereft of his wits, for ever since he has been stupefied and void of reason, his fits still following of him. After he had been in this kind of sickness, sometimes he has gone into the garden and has got upon a board of an inch thick which lay flat upon the ground and we have called him. He would come to the edge of the board and hold out his hand and make as if he would come but could not till he was helped off the board. [At] other times when he has got upon a board as aforesaid, my wife has said she has offered him a cake and money to come to her and he has held out his hand and reached after it but could not come till he has been helped off the board, by which I judge some enchantment kept him on. About seventeen or eighteen months after the first of this illness, there came a stranger to my house and pitied this child and said, among other words, we are all born, some to one thing and some to another. I asked him, "And what do you say this child is born to?" He replied, "He is born to be bewitched and is bewitched." I told him [that] he did not know. He said he did know and said to me, "You have a neighbor that lives not far off that is a witch." I told him [that] we had no neighbor but what was honest folk. He replied, "You have a neighbor that is a witch, and she has had a falling out with your wife and said, 'In her heart, your wife is a proud woman,' and [that] she would bring down her pride in this child." I paused in myself and did remember that my wife had told me that Goodwife Oliver had been at the house and spoke to her to beat Henry Williams that lived with us and that she went away muttering and, she thought, threatening, but little before our child was taken ill. I told the aforesaid stranger that there was such a woman as [he] spoke of. He asked where she lived, for he would go and see her if he knew how. I gave him money and bid him ask her for a pot of cider. Away he went and I sent my boy with him, who after a short time both returned, the boy's face bleeding, and I asked what was the matter. They told me the man knocked at the door and Goody Oliver came to the door and asked the stranger what he would have; he told her a pot of cider. She said he should have none and bid him get out and took up a spade and made him go out. She followed him and when she came without the porch she saw my boy and ran to him and scratched his face and made it bleed, saying to him, "Thou rogue, what, dost thou bring this fellow here to plague me?" Now this man did say before he went that he would fetch blood of her. And ever since this child hath been followed with grievous fits as if he would never recover more, his head and eyes drawn aside so as if they would never come to rights more, lying as if he were in a manner dead, falling anywhere, either into fire or water, if he be not constantly looked to, and generally in such an uneasy and restless frame, almost always running to and fro, acting so strange that I cannot judge otherwise but that he is bewitched, and by these circumstances do believe that the aforesaid Bridget Oliver, now called Bishop, is the cause of it, and it has been the judgment of doctors such as lived here and foreigners that he is under an evil hand of witchcraft.

51

Susannah Sheldon against Bridget Bishop and Others

June 3, 1692

The deposition of Susannah Sheldon, aged about eighteen years, who testifieth and said that on June 2, 1692 I saw the apparition of Bridget Bishop and immediately appeared two little children and [they] said that they were Thomas Green's two twins and told Bridget Bishop to her face that she had murdered them in setting them into fits whereof they died.

Essex County Court Archives, vol. 1, no. 149, from the Records of the Court of Oyer and Terminer, 1692, Property of the Supreme Judicial Court, Division of Archives and Records Preservation, on deposit at the Peabody Essex Museum, Salem, Massachusetts.

DORCAS HOAR

Dorcas Hoar of Beverly was known as a cunning woman and had apparently boasted of her ability to predict future events. The position of cunning folk within their communities was ambiguous and potentially dangerous because they could be suspected of using their powers for malevolent as well as benign purposes. And where did that power come from? Puritan theologians argued that magic required the Devil's assistance. Hoar's minister, John Hale, had clear opinions on the subject. He became very concerned when he heard about her interest in fortune-telling and wanted her "to renounce or reject all such practices" (Document 58). Hoar seems to have been unable or unwilling to do so, for which she almost paid with her life. Some neighbors suspected that she had also used occult means to murder her husband.

Dorcas Hoar was arrested at the end of April and examined on May 2. She was tried and convicted on September 6; but later that month she was granted a reprieve after she confessed to her guilt and asked for time to repent, "for the salvation of her soul" (Document 61). This saved her life: in October the trials and executions were suspended.

Dorcas Hoar was not the only accused witch in 1692 to have a reputation for magical skill. Samuel Wardwell was also "much addicted" to fortune-telling, and his predictions often turned out to be accurate. Wardwell did not survive the trials. At first he was reprieved because he had confessed, but then he withdrew his confession, and the court sentenced him to death.[50]

[50] Bernard Rosenthal et al., eds., *Records of the Salem Witch-Hunt* (New York: Cambridge University Press, 2009), 644.

52

Examination of Dorcas Hoar (as Recorded by Samuel Parris)

May 2, 1692

Several of the afflicted fell into fits as soon as she was brought in.

Elizabeth Hubbard said, "This woman hath afflicted me ever since last sabbath [which] was seven night[s] [ago], and hurt me ever since, and she choked her own husband."

Mary Walcott said, "She told me the same."

Abigail Williams saith [that] this is the woman that she saw first, before Tituba Indian or any else.

Ann Putnam said [that] this is the woman that hurts her and the first time she was hurt by her was the Sabbath, [which] was seven night[s] [ago].

Susan Sheldon accused her of hurting her last Monday night.

Abigail Williams and Ann Putnam said [that] she told them that she had choked a woman lately at Boston.

Elizabeth Hubbard cried, "Why do you pinch me?" The mark was visible to the standers by. The Marshall said [that] she [Hoar] pinched her fingers at that time.

Q. Dorcas Hoar, why do you hurt these?
Ans. I never hurt any child in my life.
Q. It is you, or your appearance.
Ans. How can I help it?
Q. What is it from you that hurts these?

Ans. I never saw worse than myself.

Q. You need not see worse. They charge you with killing your husband.

Ans. I never did, nor never saw you before.

Q. You sent for Goody Gale to cut your head off. What do you say to that?

Ans. I never sent for her upon that account.

Q. What do you say about killing your husband?

Susan Sheldon also charged her that she came in with two cats, and brought me [Susan] the book, and fell into a fit and told me your [Hoar's] name was Goody Buckley.

Ans. No, I never did. I never saw thee before.

Q. What black cats were those you had?

Ans. I had none.

Mary Walcott, Susan Sheldon, and Abigail Williams said [that] they saw a black man whispering in her ears.

Ans. Oh! you are liars, and God will stop the mouth of liars.

Q. You are not to speak after this manner in the court.

Ans. I will speak the truth as long as I live.

Mary Walcott and Susan Sheldon and Elizabeth Hubbard said again [that] there was a man whispering in her ear, and said she should never confess. Goody Bibber, free from fits hitherto, said there was a black man with her and fell into a fit.

Q. What do you say to those cats that sucked your breast? What are they?

Ans. I had no cats.

Q. You do not call them cats. What are they that suck you?

Ans. I never sucked none, but my child.

Q. Why do you say [that] you never saw Goody Buckley?

Ans. I never knew her.

Goodman Buckley testified that she had been at the house often.

Ans. I know you, but not the woman.

Q. You said you did not know the name.

Many by-standers testified [that] she disowned that she knew the name.

Ans. I did not know the name so as to go to the woman.

Susan Sheldon and Abigail Williams cried [that] there was a blue bird gone into her back. The Marshall struck, and several of the by-standers testified that they saw a fly like a miller.[51]

Q. What did you see, Goody Bibber (who was looking up)?

Goody Bibber was taken dumb.

Q. What, can you have no heart to confess?
Ans. I have nothing to do with witchcraft.
Q. They say the Devil is whispering in your ear.
Ans. I cannot help it if they do see it.
Q. Cannot you confess what you think of these things?
Ans. Why should I confess that [which] I do not know.

Susan Sheldon cried, "O Goody Hoar, do not kill me," and fell into a fit, and when she came to herself she said she saw a black man whispering in her [Hoar's] ear, and she brought me the book.

Ans. I have no book, but the Lord's book.
Q. What Lord's book.
Ans. The Lord's book.

"Oh," said some of the afflicted, "there is one whispering in her ears." "There is somebody will rub your ears shortly," said the examinant. Immediately they were afflicted, and among others Mercy Lewis.

Q. Why do you threaten they should be rubbed?
Ans. I did not speak a word of rubbing.

Many testified she did.

Ans. My meaning was [that] God would bring things to light.

---

[51] A moth with dusty-looking wings that resembled a miller's clothing.

Q. Your meaning for God to bring the thing to light would be to deliver these poor afflicted ones; that would not rub them. This is unusual impudence to threaten before authority. Who hurts them now?

Ans. I know not.

Q. They were rubbed after you had threatened them.

Mary Walcott, Abigail Williams, and Elizabeth Hubbard were carried towards her, but they could not come near her.

Q. What is the reason these cannot come near you?

Ans. I cannot help it. I do them no wrong. They may come if they will.

Q. Why you see, they cannot come near you.

Ans. I do them no wrong.

Note. The afflicted were much distressed during her examination. This is a true account of the examination of Dorcas Hoar without wrong to any party, according to my original from characters at the moments thereof. Witness my hand, Samuel Parris.

53

Sarah Bibber against Dorcas Hoar
July 2, 1692

The deposition of Sarah Bibber, aged about thirty-six years, who testifieth and saith that Dorcas Hoar of Beverly has most grievously tormented me a great many times with variety of tortures. Also, on May 2, 1692, being the day of her examination, I saw Dorcas Hoar or her appearance most grievously torment Mary Walcott, Elizabeth Hubbard, Abigail Williams, Ann Putnam, Jr., and Susannah Sheldon by biting, pinching, and almost choking them, and I verily believe in my heart that Dorcas Hoar is a witch, for since she went to prison she has most dreadfully tortured me with variety of tortures, which I believe if she were [not] a witch she could not do.

Essex County Court Archives, vol. 1, no. 209, from the Records of the Court of Oyer and Terminer, 1692, Property of the Supreme Judicial Court, Division of Archives and Records Preservation, on deposit at the Peabody Essex Museum, Salem, Massachusetts.

Elizabeth Hubbard against Dorcas Hoar

July 2, 1692

The deposition of Elizabeth Hubbard, aged about seventeen years, who testifieth and saith, I have been a long time afflicted by a woman that told me her name was Hoar, but on May 2, 1692 Dorcas Hoar of Beverly did most grievously torment me during the time of her examination and then I saw that it was the very same woman that told me her name was Hoar and if she did but look upon me she would strike me down or almost choke me. Also, on the day of her examination, I saw Dorcas Hoar or her appearance most grievously torment and afflict the bodies of Mary Walcott, Abigail Williams, [and] Ann Putnam by biting, pinching, and almost choking them to death. Also several times since, Dorcas Hoar or her appearance has most grievously tormented me with variety of tortures and I verily believe that Dorcas Hoar, the prisoner at the bar, is a witch for since she has been in prison she or her appearance has come to me and most dreadfully tormented [me] with variety of tortures, which I believe she could not do without she were a witch.

Essex County Court Archives, vol. 1, no. 210, from the Records of the Court of Oyer and Terminer, 1692, Property of the Supreme Judicial Court, Division of Archives and Records Preservation, on deposit at the Peabody Essex Museum, Salem, Massachusetts.

Ann Putnam Jr. against Dorcas Hoar

July 2, 1692

The deposition of Ann Putnam, Jr., who testifieth and saith that on the latter end of April 1692 there came an old woman and did most grievously torment me and told me her name was Hoar, but on May 2, 1692 Dorcas Hoar did most dreadfully torment me during the time of her

Essex County Court Archives, vol. 1, no. 213, from the Records of the Court of Oyer and Terminer, 1692, Property of the Supreme Judicial Court, Division of Archives and Records Preservation, on deposit at the Peabody Essex Museum, Salem, Massachusetts.

examination and then I saw that it was the very same woman that told me her name was Hoar. Also, on the day of her examination, I saw Dorcas Hoar or her appearance most grievously torment and afflict Mary Walcott, Elizabeth Hubbard, Sarah Bibber, [and] Abigail Williams, and I verily believe in my heart that Dorcas Hoar is a witch, for since she went to prison she or her appearance has come to me and most grievously tormented me by biting, pinching, and almost choking me to death.

56

Mary Walcott against Dorcas Hoar

July 2, 1692

The deposition of Mary Walcott, aged about seventeen years, who testifieth and saith, I have been a long time afflicted by a woman that told me her name was Hoar, but on May 2, 1692 Dorcas Hoar of Beverly did most grievously torment me during the time of her examination, for if she did but look personally upon me she would strike me down or almost choke me to death. Also, on the day of the examination of Dorcas Hoar, I saw her or her appearance most grievously torment and afflict the bodies of Elizabeth Hubbard, Abigail Williams, Ann Putnam, and Susannah Sheldon. Also several times since, the aforesaid Dorcas Hoar or her appearance has most grievously tormented me by biting, pinching, and almost choking me to death, and I verily believe in my heart that Dorcas Hoar is a most dreadful witch, for she or her appearance has come and most dreadfully tormented me since she was put in prison, which I believe she could not do if she were not a witch.

Essex County Court Archives, vol. 1, no. 212, from the Records of the Court of Oyer and Terminer, 1692, Property of the Supreme Judicial Court, Division of Archives and Records Preservation, on deposit at the Peabody Essex Museum, Salem, Massachusetts.

Mary Gage against Dorcas Hoar and Others
September 6, 1692

The deposition of Mary Gage, aged about forty-eight years: this deponent testifieth and saith that about nine years ago said deponent and her son Josiah Wood being at the house of John Giles in Beverly and Dorcas Hoar being there also, the said Hoar told her that her child was not long lived, and said deponent asked her how she knew, the child being well then. Said Hoar replied [that] it would not live long and bade her mark the end of it; and about a month after that time her said child was taken sick and died suddenly. And about half a year after [this] said deponent asked said Hoar how she could foretell the death of the child. Her answer was she had acquaintance with a doctor that taught her to know and had a doctor's book by her. And said deponent saith further that about two years ago said deponent, being often concerned at the house of Benjamin Balch, Sr., with his son David being then sick, she heard said David Balch often complain that he was tormented by witches. Said deponent asked him whether he knew who they were, and said David Balch answered [that] it was Goody Wilds and her daughter and Goody Hoar and one of Marblehead [whom] he knew not by name, saying also there was a confederacy of them and they were then whispering together at his bed's feet, and desired Gabriel Hood to strike them. And when he did strike at the place where said Balch said they sat, said Balch said that he had struck Goody Wilds and she was gone presently, and at several other times said Balch cried out of Goody Hoar's tormenting him and prayed earnestly to the Lord to bring them out and discover them, and farther saith not.

Essex County Court Archives, vol. 1, no. 217, from the Records of the Court of Oyer and Terminer, 1692, Property of the Supreme Judicial Court, Division of Archives and Records Preservation, on deposit at the Peabody Essex Museum, Salem, Massachusetts.

John Hale against Dorcas Hoar
September 6, 1692

John Hale, aged fifty-six years, testifieth [on] September 6, 1692 that for several years ago formerly were stories told concerning Dorcas Hoar, her being a fortune teller. And that she had told her own fortune, viz. that she should live poorly so long as her husband William Hoar did live, but the said William should die before her, and after that she should live better, also the fortune of Ensign Corning and his wife, who should die first, and that she had a book of fortune telling. About twenty-two years ago the said Dorcas manifested to me great repentance for the sins of her former life and that she had borrowed a book of palmistry,[52] and there were rules to know what should come to pass. But I telling her that it was an evil book and evil art, she seemed to me to renounce or reject all such practices, whereupon I had great charity for her [over] several years. But fourteen years ago last spring I discovered an evil practice [that] had been between a servant of mine and some of said Hoar's children in conveying goods out of my house to the said Hoar's [house], and I had a daughter Rebecca, then between eleven and twelve years old, whom I asked if she knew of the Hoars stealing. She told me yea, but durst not reveal it to me, and one reason was, she was threatened that Goody Hoar was a witch and had a book by which she could tell what said Rebecca did tell me in my house and if the said Rebecca told me of the stealing, the said Hoar would raise the Devil to kill her, or bewitch her, or words to that effect (but whether she said that Dorcas herself or her children told Rebecca those words I remember not). I asked Rebecca if she saw the book. She said yea, she was showed the book and there were many streaks and pictures in it by which (as she was told) the said Hoar could reveal secrets and work witchcrafts. I asked her how big the book was. She said it was like a grammar [book] that lay on the table. And said she, "Now I have told you of the stealing, Goody Hoar will bewitch me." I persuaded my daughter not to think so

---

[52] Palmistry is the art of predicting a person's fortune by examining the lines and marks on the palm of the person's hand.

Essex County Court Archives, vol. 1, no. 211, from the Records of the Court of Oyer and Terminer, 1692, Property of the Supreme Judicial Court, Division of Archives and Records Preservation, on deposit at the Peabody Essex Museum, Salem, Massachusetts.

hardly of Goody Hoar. But she replied, "I know Goody Hoar is a witch" (or to that effect), and then told stories of strange things that had been acted in or about my house when I and my wife were abroad to fright said Rebecca into silence about the theft, which said Rebecca judged to be acts of said Hoar's witchcraft; the particulars I have now forgotten. I called to mind that the said Hoar had told me of a book of palmistry she had, but not the bigness of it. Therefore, that I might be better satisfied, I asked Thomas Tuck if he knew Goody Hoar to have a book of fortune telling and he said yea, she had such a kind of book, which he had seen with streaks and pictures in it and that it was about the bigness of such a book pointing to a grammar, or book of like magnitude. This confirmed me in the opinion that my daughter had seen such a book. And after my daughter's death a friend told me that my daughter said to her [that] she went in fear of her life by the Hoars till quieted by the scripture, "Fear not them which can kill the body, etc."

About those times other things were spoken of the said Hoar [regarding] suspicions of her witchcraft, whereupon a friend of mine did, as I was informed, acquaint Major Denison with them for his consideration and, as I was informed, Major Denison took an opportunity to examine said William Hoar about a fortune book [that] his wife had and William Hoar answered [that] the book was John Samson's and [that] his wife had returned the book long ago and so the matter was left for that time. When discourses arose about witchcrafts at the village [in 1692], then I heard discourses revived of Goody Hoar's fortune telling of later times, and she being committed to Boston, I did last May speak with her of many things that I had known and heard of her. She told me that her own fortune that she spoke of she was told by a shipmaster when she was first married, and Ensign Corning's fortune, viz. that his first wife should die before him (which is since come to pass), she spoke it from observing a certain streak under the eye of said Corning or his wife, but as I take it, it was his wife had the streak. And [as] for seeing the Devil (which was one thing I spake to her of), she said [that] she never saw the Devil, or any spirit but once, and that was soon after old Thomas Tuck died (which I take to be about ten years since) and that she took it to be the ghost of Thomas Tuck coming to speak with her about some land [that] said Tuck had told her of before his death, but that she fled from the ghost and got away.

The fortune book, she said, was about the bigness of a child's psalter[53] (which agrees with that of a grammar), but [she] owned no other

---

[53] A version of the Psalms for use in religious services or devotional exercises.

but that of John Samson's which he had [back] from her, as she said,
above twenty years ago, and [she said] that she had not told fortunes
since the time I had laid before her the evil of it, which is about twenty
or twenty-two years since.

I lately spoke with John Samson and he told me that he had a book of
palmistry when he lived at Goody Hoar's which she had seen, but that
it was a book in quarto[54] and he sold it at Casco Bay about thirty years
since and had not seen it since.

[54] A book about nine by twelve inches in size, so named because a standard sheet of
paper was folded twice to form four leaves.

59

Joseph Morgan and Deborah Morgan against Dorcas Hoar

September 6, 1692

The deposition of Joseph Morgan, aged about forty-six years or thereabouts, testifieth and saith that Goody Hoar being at my house did pre-
tend something of fortune telling and there said that I should die before
my wife and that my oldest daughter should not live to be a woman;
and further saith that myself being called to sit on the jury to search
the body of Goodman Hoar, he dying very suddenly, that then on [our]
desiring to have his body stripped there, said Goody Hoar did fly out
in a great passion and said, "What do you think that I have killed my
husband, you wretches?"

The deposition of Deborah Morgan, aged forty-three years or thereabouts, testifieth and saith that Goody Hoar being at our house said that
my oldest daughter should never live to be a woman; and I asking her
how she knew, she told me that she observed some veins about her eyes
by which she knew, and further saith not.

Essex County Court Archives, vol. 1, no. 214, from the Records of the Court of Oyer
and Terminer, 1692, Property of the Supreme Judicial Court, Division of Archives and
Records Preservation, on deposit at the Peabody Essex Museum, Salem, Massachusetts.

60

John Tuck against Dorcas Hoar
September 6, 1692

The deposition of John Tuck, aged about eighteen years: this deponent doth testify and say that I the said deponent, being at the house of Dorcas Hoar about three years ago with John Neal who was then Thomas Whitredge's servant, then the said Neal brought a hen of the said Hoar's which he the said Neal had killed doing damage in his said master's corn, and I the said deponent being there when the said Neal presented the hen to her, the said Hoar did then break out in great passion and told the said John Neal that it should be the worst week's work that ever he did, [and he] further saith not.

Essex County Court Archives, vol. 1, no. 216, from the Records of the Court of Oyer and Terminer, 1692, Property of the Supreme Judicial Court, Division of Archives and Records Preservation, on deposit at the Peabody Essex Museum, Salem, Massachusetts.

61

Petition of John Hale, Nicholas Noyes,
Daniel Epes, and John Emerson Jr.
September 21, 1692

To his Excellency Sir William Phips, Governor of the Province of the Massachusetts Colony in New England, or, in his absence, to the Honorable William Stoughton, Esquire, Lieutenant Governor:[55]

The petition of the subscribers humbly showeth that it hath pleased the Lord, we hope in mercy to the soul of Dorcas Hoar of Beverly, to open her

---

[55] Stoughton was also serving as chief justice on the special court handling the Salem trials.

Miscellaneous Collections, U.S. States and Territories, Massachusetts, Manuscripts and Archives Division, The New York Public Library, Astor, Lenox and Tilden Foundations.

heart out of distress of conscience, as she professeth, to confess herself guilty of the heinous crime of witchcraft for which she is condemned, and how and when she was taken in the snare of the Devil, and that she signed his book with the forefinger of her right hand etc. Also she gives account of some other persons that she hath known to be guilty of the same crime. And being in great distress of conscience, [she] earnestly craves a little longer time of life to realize and perfect her repentance for the salvation of her soul.

These are therefore humbly to petition in her behalf that there may be granted her one month's time or more to prepare for death and eternity, unless by her relapse or afflicting others she shall give grounds to hasten her execution. And this we conceive, if the Lord sanctify, it may tend to save a soul, and to give opportunity for her making some discovery of these mysteries of iniquity, and be providential to the encouraging others to confess and give glory to God.

And the petitioners shall pray etc.
The humble servants

John Hale
Nicholas Noyes
Daniel Epes
John Emerson, Jr.

September 21, 1692: Having heard and taken the confession of Dorcas Hoar, [we] do consent that her execution be respited until further order.

Bartholemew Gedney[56]

GEORGE BURROUGHS

George Burroughs, alleged leader of the witch conspiracy, was the second of three men who had tried and failed to establish a successful ministry in Salem Village prior to the appointment of Samuel Parris. Burroughs was born in Virginia but spent most of his childhood in Roxbury, Massachusetts. After graduating from Harvard in 1670, he preached in Maine at Falmouth, a settlement on Casco Bay. Following the Indian attacks on Falmouth in 1676, Burroughs sought refuge in Massachusetts. He was subsequently hired by Salem Village as its min-

------

[56] Gedney was another of the judges presiding over the Salem trials.

ister, but his time there would prove frustrating and galling. Following his departure from that community, Burroughs returned to Maine. In 1690 Burroughs relocated within Maine just before Indians attacked the community in which he had been living; in retrospect, this struck some people as all too convenient. In 1692 he was brought back to Salem as an accused witch. The afflicted girls claimed that he had conspired with French Canadians and Indians against New England.

Burroughs's link to the Indian wars and his implication in Salem Village's internal conflict made him a likely focus for the fears and antagonisms that exploded as witch accusations that year. But his own personality and behavior contributed to his vulnerability. Scholars have pointed out that women who seemed to contravene gendered expectations and hierarchies were especially vulnerable to accusations of witchcraft. The depositions against Burroughs suggest that this could also apply to men who violated masculine codes, in his case by failing in his duty to be a caring and protective husband. (John Willard, another male suspect in 1692, had apparently mistreated his wife.) Burroughs was also suspiciously strong and so in another sense could be seen as a distortion of normal manhood; neighbors suspected that he used occult means to lift heavy objects, such as a barrel of molasses.

The documents in which afflicted girls denounced Burroughs, a minister of God, for becoming an emissary of the Devil remind us that this was a world in which the forces of good and evil were never entirely distinct. His transformation into the leader of a witch conspiracy would have horrified Puritans in part because it was so plausible: even the most committed of believers was tainted by inherited depravity and might at any moment succumb to temptation, then becoming a tempter to others. The magistrates issued a warrant for George Burroughs's arrest on April 30. He was examined just over a week later on May 9. Burroughs was tried on August 5, convicted, and hanged on August 19.

Benjamin Hutchinson against George Burroughs and Others

April 22, 1692

Benjamin Hutchinson said that on April 21, 1692 Abigail Williams said that there was a little black minister that lived at Casco Bay, he told me so [she said], and [then she] said that he had killed three wives, two for himself and one for Mr. Lawson, and that he had made nine witches in this place, and said that he could hold out the heaviest gun that is in Casco Bay with one hand, [which] no man can, [even with the] case held out with both hands. This [was] about eleven o'clock and I ask[ed] her whereabouts this little man stood. Said she, "Just where the cart wheel went along." I had a three graned irne fork[57] in my hand and I threw it where she said he stood and she presently fell in a little fit and when it was over, said she, "You have torn his coat, for I heard it tear." "Whereabouts?" said I. "On one side," said she. Then we came into the house of Lieutenant Ingersoll and I went into the great room and Abigail came in and said, "There he stands." I said, "Where? Where?" And presently [I] drawed my rapier, but he immediately was gone, as she said. Then said she, "There is a gray cat." Then I said, "Whereabouts doth she stand?" "There," said she. There then I struck with my rapier; then she fell in a fit and when it was over she said, "You killed her," and immediately, [Abigail told us,] Sarah Good came and carried her[58] away. This was about twelve o'clock. The same day, after lecture in the said Ingersoll's chamber, Abigail Williams [and] Mary Walcott said that Goody Hobbs of Topsfield bit Mary Walcott by the foot, then both falling into a fit. As soon as it was over, the said William Hobbs and his wife [went] both of them along the table; the said Hutchinson took his rapier [and] stabbed Goody Hobbs on the side, as Abigail Williams and Mary Walcott said. The said Abigail and Mary said the room was full of them. Then the said Hutchinson and Ely Putnam stabbed with their rapiers at

---

[57] Probably a farming tool of some kind.
[58] The dead witch.

Essex County Court Archives, vol. 2, no. 35, from the Records of the Court of Oyer and Terminer, 1692, Property of the Supreme Judicial Court, Division of Archives and Records Preservation, on deposit at the Peabody Essex Museum, Salem, Massachusetts.

a venture.[59] Then said Mary and Abigail, "You have killed a great black woman of Stoningtown and an Indian that comes with her, for the floor is all covered with blood." Then the said Mary and Abigail looked out of doors and said they saw a great company of them on a hill and there was three of them lay dead, the black woman and the Indian and one more that they knew not, this being about four o'clock in the afternoon.

[59] At random.

63

Examination of George Burroughs (as Recorded by Samuel Parris)
May 9, 1692

Being asked when he partook of the Lord's Supper, he being (as he said) in full communion at Roxbury, he answered it was so long since [that] he could not tell, yet he owned he was at meeting one Sabbath at Boston part of the day, and the other at Charlestown part of a Sabbath when that sacrament happened to be at both, yet did not partake of either. He denied that his house at Casco was haunted, yet he owned there were toads. He denied that he made his wife swear that she should not write to her father Ruck without his approbation of her letter to her father. He owned that none of his children but the eldest was baptized. The above said was in private, none of the bewitched being present.

At his entry into the room, many if not all of the bewitched were grievously tortured.

Susannah Sheldon testified that Burroughs' two wives appeared in their winding sheets[60] and said [that] that man killed them. He was bid to look upon Susannah Sheldon. He looked back and knocked down all or most of the afflicted who stood behind him. Mercy Lewis's deposition going to be read, he looked upon her and she fell into a dreadful

[60] The sheets in which a corpse was wrapped for burial.

Samuel Parris, "Examination of George Burroughs 1692 May 9–11," Photostats Collection, Massachusetts Historical Society, Boston, Massachusetts.

and tedious[61] fit. Mary Walcott, Elizabeth Hubbard, [and] Susannah Sheldon's testimony going to be read, they all fell into fits. Susannah Sheldon [and] Ann Putnam, Jr. affirmed each of them that he brought the book and would have them write.

Being asked what he thought of these things, he answered it was an amazing and humbling providence, but he understood nothing of it and he said, "Some of you may observe, that when they begin to name my name, they cannot name it."

Ann Putnam, Jr. and Susannah Sheldon testified that his two wives and two children did accuse him. The bewitched were so tortured that authority ordered them to be taken away, [or] some of them. Sarah Bibber testified that he had hurt her, though she had not seen him personally before as she knew.

[61] Long and exhausting.

64

Elizar Keyser against George Burroughs
May 9, 1692

Elizar Keyser, aged about forty-five years, saith that on Thursday last past, being May 5, I was at the house of Thomas Beadle in Salem, and Captain Daniel King being there also at the same time and in the same room, said Captain Daniel King asked me whether I would not go up and see Mr. Burroughs and discourse with him, he being then in one of the chambers in said house. I told him it did not belong to me, and I was not willing to meddle or make with it. Then said King said, "Are you not a Christian? If you are a Christian, go see him and discourse with him." But I told him [that] I did believe it did not belong to such as I was to discourse [with] him, he being a learned man. Then said King said, "I believe he is a child of God, a choice child of God, and that God would clear up his innocency." So I told him [that] my opinion or fear was that he was the chief of all the persons accused for witchcraft, or the ring leader of them all, and told him also that I believed [that] if he was such an one, his master, meaning the Devil, had told him before

Miscellaneous Collections, U.S. States and Territories, Massachusetts, Manuscripts and Archives Division, The New York Public Library, Astor, Lenox and Tilden Foundations.

now what I said of him. And said King seeming to me to be in a passion, I did afterwards forbear. The same afternoon, I having occasion to be at the said Beadle's house and being in the chamber where Mr. George Burroughs kept, I observed that said Burroughs did steadfastly fix his eyes upon me. The same evening, being in my own house, in a room without any light, I did see very strange things appear in the chimney, I suppose a dozen of them, which seemed to me to be something like jelly that used to be in the water and quiver with a strange motion, and then quickly disappeared, soon after which I did see a light up in the chimney about the bigness of my hand, something above the bar which quivered and shook and seemed to have a motion upward, upon which I called the maid, and she looking up into the chimney saw the same, and my wife looking up could not see any thing; so I did and do consider it was some diabolical apparition.

65

Mercy Lewis against George Burroughs
May 9, 1692

The deposition of Mercy Lewis, who testifieth and saith that on May 7, 1692 at evening I saw the apparition of Mr. George Burroughs, whom I very well knew, which did grievously torture me and urged me to write in his book. And then he brought to me a new fashion book which he did not use to bring and told me I might write in that book, for that was a book that was in his study when I lived with him. But I told him I did not believe him, for I had been often in his study but I never saw that book there. But he told me that he had several books in his study which I never saw and he could raise the Devil and now had bewitched Mr. Sheppard's daughter, and I asked him how he could go to bewitch her now [that] he was kept at Salem, and he told me that the Devil was his servant and he sent him in his shape to do it. Then he again tortured me most dreadfully and threatened to kill me, for he said I should not witness against him. Also he told me that he had made Abigail Hobbs a witch and several more. Then again he did most dreadfully torture me

Essex County Court Archives, vol. 2, no. 25, from the Records of the Court of Oyer and Terminer, 1692, Property of the Supreme Judicial Court, Division of Archives and Records Preservation, on deposit at the Peabody Essex Museum, Salem, Massachusetts.

as if he would have racked me all to pieces and urged me to write in his
book, or else he would kill me, but I told him I hoped my life was not
in the power of his hands and that I would not write, though he did kill
me. The next night he told me [that] I should not see his two wives if he
could help it because I should not witness against him. [On] May 9 Mr.
Burroughs carried me up to an exceeding high mountain and showed
me all the kingdoms of the earth and told me that he would give them
all to me if I would write in his book and if I would not he would throw
me down and break my neck, but I told him [that] they were none of
his to give and [that] I would not write if he threw me down on a hundred pitchforks. Also on May 9, being the time of his examination, Mr.
George Burroughs did most dreadfully torment me, and also several
times since.

66

John Putnam Sr. and Rebecca Putnam against George Burroughs

May 9, 1692

The deposition of John Putnam and Rebecca, his wife, testifieth and
saith that in the year 1680 Mr. Burroughs lived in our house [for] nine
months, there being a great difference betwixt said Burroughs and his
wife, the difference was so great that they did desire us, the deponents,
to come into their room to hear their difference. The controversy that
was betwixt them was that the aforesaid Burroughs did require his wife
to give him a written covenant under her hand and seal that she would
never reveal his secrets. Our answer was that they had once made a
covenant before God and men, which covenant, we did conceive, did
bind each other to keep their lawful secrets. And further saith that all
the time that said Burroughs did live at our house he was a very sharp
man to his wife, notwithstanding [that] to our observation she was a
very good and dutiful wife to him.

Essex Institute Collection, vol. 2, no. 25, from the Records of the Court of Oyer and Terminer, 1692, Property of the Supreme Judicial Court, Division of Archives and Records
Preservation, on deposit at the Peabody Essex Museum, Salem, Massachusetts.

Mary Walcott against George Burroughs
May 9, 1692

The deposition of Mary Walcott, aged about seventeen years, who testifieth and saith that on the latter end of April 1692 Mr. George Burroughs or his appearance came to me, whom I formerly well knew, and he did immediately most grievously torment me by biting, pinching, and almost choking me, urging me to write in his book, which I refusing he did again most grievously torment me and told me [that] if I would but touch his book I should be well. But I told him I would not for all the world, and then he threatened to kill me and said I should never witness against him, but he continued torturing and tempting me till May 8, and then he told me he would have killed his first wife and child when his wife was in travail[62] but he had not the power, but he kept her in the kitchen till he gave her her death's wound, but he charged me in the name of his God I should not tell of it. But immediately there appeared to me Mr. Burroughs' two first wives in their winding sheets, whom I formerly well knew, and [they] told me that Mr. Burroughs had murdered them and that their blood did cry for vengeance against him. Also on May 9, being the day of his examination, he did most grievously torment me during the time of his examination, for if he did but look on me he would strike me down or almost choke me. Also during his examination, I saw Mr. George Burroughs or his appearance most grievously torment Mercy Lewis, Elizabeth Hubbard, Abigail Williams, and Ann Putnam, and I believe in my heart that Mr. George Burroughs is a dreadful wizard and that he had often afflicted and tormented me and the aforementioned persons by his acts of witchcraft.

[62] In the pains of childbirth.

Salem Witchcraft Papers, Massachusetts Historical Society, Boston, Massachusetts.

68

Simon Willard and William Wormall against George Burroughs

May 9, 1692

The deposition of Simon Willard, aged about forty-two years, saith [that] I being at the house of Mr. Robert Lawrence at Falmouth in Casco Bay in September 1689, said Mr. Lawrence was commending Mr. George Burroughs' strength, saying that we none of us could do what he could do, for said he Mr. Burroughs can hold out this gun with one hand. Mr. Burroughs being there said, "I held my hand here behind the lock," and took it up and held it out. I, said deponent, saw Mr. Burroughs put his hand on the gun to show us how he held it and where he held his hand, and saying "There," he held his hand when he held said gun out, but I saw him not hold it out then. Said gun was about or near seven foot barrel and very heavy. I then tried to hold out said gun with both hands, but could not do it long enough to take sight.[63]

Captain William Wormall sworn to the above and that he saw him raise it from the ground himself.

[63] To take aim.

Essex County Court Archives, vol. 2, no. 28, from the Records of the Court of Oyer and Terminer, 1692, Property of the Supreme Judicial Court, Division of Archives and Records Preservation, on deposit at the Peabody Essex Museum, Salem, Massachusetts.

Abigail Hobbs, Deliverance Hobbs, and Mary Warren against George Burroughs and Others

June 1, 1692

Abigail Hobbs then confessed before John Hathorne and Jonathan Corwin, Esquires, that at the general meeting of the witches in the field near Mr. Parris's house she saw Mr. George Burroughs, Sarah Good, Sarah Osborne, Bridget Bishop, alias Oliver, and Giles Corey. Two or three nights ago, Mr. Burroughs came and sat at the window and told her [that] he would terribly afflict her for saying so much against him and then [he] pinched her. Deliverance Hobbs then saw said Burroughs and he would have tempted her to set her hand to the book and almost shook her to pieces because she would not do it.

Mary Warren testifieth that when she was in prison in Salem about a fortnight ago Mr. George Burroughs, Goody Nurse, Goody Proctor, Goody Parker, Goody Pudeator, Abigail Soames, Goodman Proctor, Goody Dowing, and others unknown came to this deponent and Mr. Burroughs had a trumpet and sounded it, and they would have had this deponent to have gone up with them to a feast at Mr. Parris's, and Goody Nurse and Goody Proctor told her, this deponent, [that] they were deacons and would have had her eat some of their sweet bread and wine, and she asking them what wine that was, one of them said it was blood and better than our wine, but this deponent refused to eat or drink with them, and they then dreadfully afflicted her at that time.

Salem Witchcraft Papers, Massachusetts Historical Society, Boston, Massachusetts.

70

Mary Webber against George Burroughs
August 2, 1692

Mary Webber, widow, aged about fifty-three years, testifieth and saith that she, living at Casco Bay about six or seven years ago, when George Burroughs was minister at said place and [she] living a near neighbor to said Burroughs, was well acquainted with his wife, which was daughter to Mr. John Ruck of Salem. She hath heard her tell much of her husband's unkindness to her and that she dare not write to her father to acquaint him how it was with her, and so desired me to write to her father that he would be pleased to send for her, and told me she had been much affrighted, and that something in the night made a noise in the chamber where she lay, as if one went about the chamber, and she calling up the negro to come to her, the negro not coming said that she could not come [because] something stopped her; then her husband being called, he came up; something jumped down from between the chimney and the side of the house and ran down the stairs and said Burroughs followed it down, and the negro then said it was something like a white calf. Another time, lying with her husband, something came into the house and stood by her bedside and breathed on her, and she being much affrighted at it, would have awakened her husband but could not for a considerable time, but as soon as he did awake it went away; but this I heard her say and know nothing of it myself otherwise, except by common report of others also concerning such things.

Salem Witchcraft Papers, Massachusetts Historical Society, Boston, Massachusetts.

Ann Putnam Jr. against George Burroughs
August 3, 1692

The deposition of Ann Putnam, who testifieth and saith that on April 20, 1692 at evening she saw the apparition of a minister, at which she was grievously affrighted and cried out, "Oh dreadful! Dreadful! Here is a minister come! What, are ministers witches too? Whence come you? And what is your name? For I will complain of you, though you be a minister, if you be a wizard." And immediately I was tortured by him, being racked and almost choked by him, and he tempted me to write in his book, which I refused with loud outcries and said I would not write in his book though he tore me all to pieces, but told him that it was a dreadful thing that he which was a minister, that should teach children to fear God, should come to persuade poor creatures to give their souls to the Devil: "Oh dreadful! Dreadful! Tell me your name that I may know who you are." Then again he tortured me and urged me to write in his book, which I refused, and then presently he told me that his name was George Burroughs and that he had had three wives and that he had bewitched the two first of them to death, and that he killed Mistress Lawson because she was so unwilling to go from the village and also killed Mr. Lawson's child because he went to the eastward with Sir Edmund [Andros] and preached so to the soldiers, and that he had bewitched a great many soldiers to death at the eastward when Sir Edmund was there, and that he had made Abigail Hobbs a witch and several witches more, and he has continued ever since, by times tempting me to write in his book and grievously torturing me by beating, pinching, and almost choking me several times a day, and he also told me that he was above a witch for he was a conjuror.

Essex County Court Archives, vol. 2, no. 24, from the Records of the Court of Oyer and Terminer, 1692, Property of the Supreme Judicial Court, Division of Archives and Records Preservation, on deposit at the Peabody Essex Museum, Salem, Massachusetts.

72

Physical Examination of George Burroughs and George Jacobs Jr.

August 4, 1692

We whose names are underwritten, having received an order from the sheriff for to search the bodies of George Burroughs and George Jacobs, we find nothing upon the body of the above said Burroughs but what is natural, but upon the body of George Jacobs we find three teats which according to the best of our judgments we think is not natural, for we ran a pin through two of them and he was not sensible of it,[64] one of them being within his mouth upon the inside, and [the] second upon his right shoulder blade, and a third upon his right hip.

Ed Weld	Zeb Hill
Tom Flint	Sam Morgan
Will Gill	John Bare
Tom West	

[64] He could not feel it.

Essex County Court Archives, vol. 2, no. 23, from the Records of the Court of Oyer and Terminer, 1692, Property of the Supreme Judicial Court, Division of Archives and Records Preservation, on deposit at the Peabody Essex Museum, Salem, Massachusetts.

73

Hannah Harris against George Burroughs

August 5, 1692

The deposition of Hannah Harris, aged twenty-seven years or thereabouts, testifieth and saith that she lived at the house of George Burroughs at Falmouth and the abovesaid Hannah Harris many times hath

Essex County Court Archives, vol. 2, no. 32, from the Records of the Court of Oyer and Terminer, 1692, Property of the Supreme Judicial Court, Division of Archives and Records Preservation, on deposit at the Peabody Essex Museum, Salem, Massachusetts.

taken notice that when she hath had any discourse with the abovesaid Burroughs' wife, when the abovesaid Burroughs was from home, that upon his return he hath often scolded [his] wife and told her that he knew what they said when he was abroad. And further saith that upon a time when his wife had lain in[65] not above one week, that he fell out with his wife and kept her by discourse[66] at the door till she fell sick in the place and grew worse at night so that the abovesaid Hannah Harris was afraid she would die, and they called in their neighbors and the abovesaid Burroughs' daughter told one of the women that was there the cause of her mother's illness; and the abovesaid Burroughs chid[67] his daughter for telling and the abovesaid Burroughs came to the abovesaid Hannah Harris and told her [that] if his wife did otherwise than well she should not tell of it, and the abovesaid Hannah Harris told him that she would not be confined to any such thing.

[65] Lying-in was the period following childbirth during which a new mother convalesced in bed. See Laurel Thatcher Ulrich, *A Midwife's Tale: The Life of Martha Ballard* (New York: Knopf, 1990), 188–93.
[66] Talking.
[67] Scolded.

74

Thomas Greenslit against George Burroughs
September 15, 1692

Thomas Greenslit, aged about forty years, being deposed, testifieth that about the first breaking out of the last Indian war, being at the house of Captain Scottow's at Black Point, he saw Mr. George Burroughs lift and hold out a gun of six foot barrel or thereabouts, putting the forefinger of his right hand into the muzzle of said gun and that he held it out at arm's end only with that finger; and further this deponent testifieth that at the same time he saw the said Burroughs take up a full barrel of molasses

Essex County Court Archives, vol. 2, no. 33, from the Records of the Court of Oyer and Terminer, 1692, Property of the Supreme Judicial Court, Division of Archives and Records Preservation, on deposit at the Peabody Essex Museum, Salem, Massachusetts.

with but two fingers of one of his hands in the bung[68] and carry it from the stage head to the door at the end of the stage without letting it down and that Lieutenant Richard Hunniwell and John Greenslit were then present, and some other persons that are dead.

[68] A stopper for the mouth of a cask or barrel.

75

Sarah Wilson and Martha Tyler against George Burroughs
September 15, 1692

Sarah Wilson confessed that the night before Mr. Burroughs was executed there was a great meeting of the witches nigh Sergeant Chandler's, that Mr. Burroughs was there, and [that] they had the sacrament, and after they had done he took leave and bid them stand to their faith and not own anything. Martha Tyler saith the same with Sarah Wilson and several others.

Essex County Court Archives, vol. 2, no. 36, from the Records of the Court of Oyer and Terminer, 1692, Property of the Supreme Judicial Court, Division of Archives and Records Preservation, on deposit at the Peabody Essex Museum, Salem, Massachusetts.

4

The Witch Court under Attack

By early September, eleven people had been convicted and hanged as witches. Another eight would be executed on September 22. These convictions were made possible by seemingly plentiful evidence of a Satanic conspiracy to undermine God's kingdom in New England. Most of that evidence came from confessing witches and the afflicted girls. At witch trials prior to 1692 there had often been little or no evidence of the Devil's involvement (the basic requirement for conviction under New England's laws against witchcraft), and so most cases resulted in acquittal.

In sharp contrast, over fifty of those accused during the Salem witch hunt confessed to having covenanted with the Devil, sometimes in graphic detail (Document 76). The confessors often incriminated other individuals who they claimed were fellow disciples of the Devil. Yet during the summer and early fall a growing number of these women and men withdrew their confessions and explained why they had lied (Documents 77–80). In renouncing their confessions, they not only denied that they were guilty as charged, but also brought into question the testimony that they had provided against others.

Meanwhile, a growing chorus of observers questioned the court's use of depositions in which the afflicted girls claimed that specters in the shape of accused witches had assaulted them. The court assumed that specters could not assume someone's likeness without that person's approval and so treated their appearance as proof that the person represented was a witch, but others had their doubts. When Bridget Bishop was condemned to death in June and one of the judges resigned in protest, Governor Phips asked leading ministers to advise him on how to proceed. In a brief but forthright document, submitted to the governor and his council five days after Bishop's execution, the twelve ministers rejected spectral evidence as a reliable basis even for committing suspects to prison, let alone convicting them of witchcraft (Document 81). Cotton Mather, who composed that statement, subsequently wrote a letter to one of the judges, John Foster, in which his doubts about spectral evidence clearly battled with his eagerness for the court to make the most of whatever evidence was available and his desire to support the magistrates, most of whom were his neighbors and friends (Document 82). In the closing months of 1692, Cotton Mather would give an object lesson in how the torments of the girls and women in Salem Village might have been handled very differently when he took into his care an afflicted seventeen-year-old named Mercy Short. He refused to reveal the names of those supposedly assailing her and focused on prayer and fasting instead of accusation. Short recovered and was admitted into Mather's church.[1] Robert Pike, a magistrate who lived in nearby Salisbury, also voiced concerns about the evidence being admitted by the court in a letter to Jonathan Corwin. Like Mather he expressed his reservations in respectful language that avoided any explicit condemnation of the court (Document 83).

Other critics were less conciliatory. Thomas Brattle, a Boston merchant, was openly hostile and sarcastic in his remarks about the judges and those who supported their efforts (Document 84). Among his many allegations, he claimed that the court had used physical torture as well as psychological pressure to extract confessions, a claim seconded by John Proctor in the petition that he wrote prior to his own execution (see Document 37). Brattle poured scorn on the magistrates' use of current scientific theories to validate the touch test and their eagerness to find unusual lumps or marks on the bodies of the accused on the grounds that these might be teats from which demonic familiars fed on the blood of the accused. He also noted a basic discrepancy between the wording of the indictments and much of the evidence presented in court. While a considerable number of prominent citizens were now openly opposed to any further legal proceedings against the witch suspects, the witch hunt still had many supporters. The governor had to decide how to respond to this highly charged situation and how to justify his

---

[1] See Cotton Mather, "A Brand Pluck'd Out of the Burning," in George Lincoln Burr, ed., *Narratives of the Witchcraft Cases, 1648–1706* (New York: Charles Scribner's Sons, 1914), 259–87.

role in the witch hunt, which he attempted to do in a letter to William Blathwayt, Clerk of the Privy Council in London (Document 85).[2]

[2] Several other attacks on the court, omitted here due to space limitations, deserve close attention. Cotton Mather's father, Increase Mather, asked what evidence was admissible in a legal prosecution for witchcraft and urged caution in *Cases of Conscience Concerning Evil Spirits Personating Men* (Boston, 1692; deliberately misdated as 1693 on the title page to evade the governor's ban on publications relating to the witch panic, for which see Document 85). Samuel Willard, a respected Boston minister, published his thoughts on the crisis anonymously in *Some Miscellany Observations on Our Present Debates Respecting Witchcrafts* (Philadelphia, 1692; place of publication actually Boston, another ploy to evade the ban). Quaker Thomas Maule's *Truth Held Forth and Maintained* (New York, 1695) provided yet another indictment of the court's proceedings. Despite his reservations about the evidence admitted by the court, Cotton Mather defended the beleaguered magistrates in *Wonders of the Invisible World* (Boston, 1692; deliberately misdated as 1693 on the title page to evade the ban). This prompted a virulent attack on Mather himself in Robert Calef's *More Wonders of the Invisible World* (London, 1700); Calef claimed that Mather had committed sexual improprieties while caring for another young woman suffering from fits, Margaret Rule. (Mather sued Calef for libel, but subsequently dropped the suit.)

76

Confession of William Barker Sr.
August 29, 1692

He confesses he has been in the snare of the Devil three years, that the Devil first appeared to him like a black man and [he] perceived he had a cloven foot. That the Devil demanded of him to give up himself soul and body unto him, which he promised to do. He said he had a great family, the world went hard with him, and [he] was willing to pay every man his own.[3] And the Devil told him he would pay all his debts and he should live comfortably. He confesses he has afflicted said [Martha] Sprague, [Rose] Foster, and [Abigail] Martin, his three accusers. That he did sign the Devil's book with blood brought to him in a thing like an ink horn, that he dipped his fingers therein and made a blot in the book, which was a confirmation of the covenant with the Devil.

[3] Pay each man what he owed him.

SC1/Series 45X, Massachusetts Archives Collection, vol. 135, page 39, Massachusetts Archives at Columbia Point, Boston, Massachusetts.

He confesses he was at a meeting of witches at Salem Village, where he judges there was about a hundred of them, that the meeting was upon a green piece of ground near the minister's house. He said they met there to destroy that place by reason of the peoples being divided and their differing with their ministers.

Satan's design was to set up his own worship, abolish all the churches in the land, to fall next upon Salem, and so go through the country. He saith the Devil promised that all his people should live bravely, that all persons should be equal, that there should be no day of resurrection or of judgment, and neither punishment nor shame for sin. He saith there was a sacrament at that meeting; there was also bread and wine. Mr. Burroughs was a ringleader in that meeting and named several persons that were there at the meeting. It was proposed at the meeting to make as many witches as they could, and they were all by Mr. Burroughs and the black man exhorted to pull down the kingdom of Christ and set up the kingdom of the Devil. He said he knew Mr. Burroughs and Goody How to be such persons. And that he heard a trumpet sounded at the meeting and thinks it was Burroughs that did it; the sound is heard many miles off and then they all come one after another. In the spring of the year [1692] the witches came from Connecticut to afflict at Salem Village, but now they have left it off. And that he has been informed by some of the grandees[4] that there are about 307 witches in the country. He saith the witches are much disturbed with the afflicted persons because they are discovered[5] by them. They curse the judges because their society is brought under. They would have the afflicted persons counted as witches, but he thinks the afflicted persons are innocent and that they do God good service. And that he has not known or heard of one innocent person taken up and put in prison. He saith he is heartily sorry for what he has done and for hurting the afflicted persons, his accusers, prays their forgiveness, desires prayers for himself, promises to renounce the Devil and all his works, and then [following his confession] he could take them all by the hand without any harm by his eye or any otherwise.

---

[4] A person of high rank, in this context within the "society" of witches that Barker was describing.
[5] Exposed.

77

Recantation of Margaret Jacobs
Undated

The humble declaration of Margaret Jacobs unto the Honoured Court now sitting at Salem, showeth:

That whereas your poor and humble declarant being closely confined here in Salem jail for the crime of witchcraft, which crime thanks be to the Lord I am altogether ignorant of, as will appear at the great Day of Judgment, may it please the honored court, I was cried out upon by some of the possessed persons as afflicting them; whereupon I was brought to my examination, which persons at the sight of me fell down, which did very much startle and affright me. The Lord above knows I knew nothing, in the least measure, how or who afflicted them; [but] they told me [that] without doubt I did, or else they would not fall down at me; they told me [that] if I would not confess I should be put down into the dungeon and would be hanged; but if I would confess I should have my life; the which did so affright me, with my own vile wicked heart, [hoping] to save my life; [that it] made me make the like confession I did, which confession, may it please the honored court, is altogether false and untrue. The very first night after I had made confession, I was in such horror of conscience that I could not sleep for fear the Devil should carry me away for telling such horrid lies. I was, may it please the honored court, sworn to my confession, as I understand since, but then at that time was ignorant of it, not knowing what an oath did mean. The Lord, I hope, in whom I trust, out of the abundance of his mercy will forgive me my false forswearing myself. What I said was altogether false against my grandfather and Mr. Burroughs, which I did to save my life and to have my liberty; but the Lord, charging it to my conscience, made me in so much horror that I could not contain myself before I had denied my confession, which I did though I saw nothing but death before me, choosing rather death with a quiet conscience than to live in such horror, which I could not suffer. Whereupon my denying my confession, I

Thomas Hutchinson, *History of the Province of Massachusetts Bay from the Charter of King William and Queen Mary in 1691 until the Year 1750* (Boston, 1767), 38–40.

was committed to close prison, where I have enjoyed more felicity in spirit, a thousand times, than I did before in my enlargement.[6]

And now, may it please your honors, your declarant, having in part given your honors a description of my condition, do leave it to your honors' pious and judicious discretions to take pity and compassion on my young and tender years, to act and do with me as the Lord above and your honors shall see good, having no friend but the Lord to plead my cause for me; not being guilty in the least measure of the crime of witchcraft, nor any other sin that deserves death from man. And your poor and humble declarant shall forever pray, as she is bound in duty, for your honors' happiness in this life and eternal felicity in the world to come. So prays your honors' declarant,

Margaret Jacobs.

[6] Freedom from confinement.

78

Declaration of Mary Osgood, Mary Tyler, Deliverance Dane, Abigail Barker, Sarah Wilson, and Hannah Tyler

Undated

We whose names are underwritten, inhabitants of Andover:

When as that horrible and tremendous judgment beginning at Salem Village in the year 1692, by some called witchcraft, first breaking forth at Mr. Parris's house, several young persons, being seemingly afflicted, did accuse several persons for afflicting them, and many there believing it so to be, we being informed that if a person was sick, the afflicted person could tell what or who was the cause of that sickness, Joseph Ballard of Andover, his wife being sick at the same time, he, either from himself or by the advice of others, fetched two of the persons, called the afflicted persons, from Salem Village to Andover, which was the beginning

Thomas Hutchinson, *History of the Province of Massachusetts Bay from the Charter of King William and Queen Mary in 1691 until the Year 1750* (Boston, 1767), 40–41.

of that dreadful calamity that befell us in Andover. Believing the said accusations to be true, [those in authority] sent for the said [accused] persons to come together to the meeting house in Andover, the afflicted persons being there. After Mr. [Thomas] Barnard[7] had been at prayer, we were blindfolded and our hands were laid upon the afflicted persons, they being in their fits and falling into their fits at our coming into their presence, as they said; and some led us and laid our hands upon them, and then they said they were well and that we were guilty of afflicting them. Whereupon we were all seized as prisoners by a warrant from the Justice of the Peace and forthwith carried to Salem. And, by reason of that sudden surprisal,[8] we knowing ourselves altogether innocent of that crime, we were all exceedingly astonished and amazed, and consternated[9] and affrighted even out of our reason. And our nearest and dearest relations, seeing us in that dreadful condition and knowing our great danger, apprehended there was no other way to save our lives, as the case was then circumstanced, but by our confessing ourselves to be such and such persons as the afflicted represented us to be; they out of tenderness and pity persuaded us to confess what we did confess. And indeed that confession that it is said we made was no other than what was suggested to us by some gentlemen, they telling us that we were witches, and they knew it, and we knew it, which made us think that it was so; and our understandings, our reason, our faculties almost gone, we were not capable of judging of our condition; as also the hard measures they used with us rendered us incapable of making our defense, but [we] said anything and everything which they desired, and most of what we said was but, in effect, a consenting to what they said. Some time after, when we were better composed, they telling us what we had confessed, we did profess that we were innocent and ignorant of such things; and we hearing that Samuel Wardwell had renounced his confession and quickly after [was] condemned and executed, some of us were told we were going after Wardwell.

Mary Osgood	Deliverance Dane	Sarah Wilson
Mary Tyler	Abigail Barker	Hannah Tyler

[7] A young pastor hired to assist the town's elderly minister, Francis Dane.
[8] Surprise.
[9] Filled with dismay.

Increase Mather's Conversation in Prison with Mary Tyler

Undated

Goodwife Tyler did say that when she was first apprehended she had no fears upon her and did think that nothing could have made her confess against herself. But since [then] she had found to her great grief that she had wronged the truth and falsely accused herself. She said that when she was brought to Salem her brother Bridges rode with her; and that all along the way from Andover to Salem, her brother kept telling her that she must needs be a witch, since the afflicted accused her and at her touch were raised out of their fits, and urging her to confess herself a witch. She as constantly told him that she was no witch, that she knew nothing of witchcraft, and begged him not to urge her to confess. However, when she came to Salem, she was carried to a room where her brother on one side and Mr. John Emerson[10] on the other side did tell her that she was certainly a witch and that she saw the Devil before her eyes at that time (and accordingly the said Emerson would attempt with his hand to beat him away from her eyes); and they so urged her to confess that she wished herself in any dungeon rather than be so treated. Mr. Emerson told her once and again, "Well, I see you will not confess! Well, I will now leave you; and then you are undone, body and soul, for ever." Her brother urged her to confess and told her that in so doing she could not lie, to which she answered, "Good brother, do not say so; for I shall lie if I confess, and then who shall answer unto God for my lie?" He still asserted it and said that God would not suffer so many good men to be in such an error about it, and that she would be hanged if she did not confess; and continued so long and so violently to urge and press her to confess that she thought, verily, that her life would have gone from her and became so terrified in her mind that she owned, at length, almost anything that they propounded to her; that she had wronged her conscience in so doing; she was guilty of a great sin in belying[11] of herself and desired to mourn for it so long as she

[10] The minister in Gloucester.
[11] Telling lies about something or someone.

Charles W. Upham, *Salem Witchcraft*, 2 vols. (Boston: Wiggin and Lunt, 1867), 2:404–5.

lived. This she said and a great deal more of the like nature; and all with such affection, sorrow, relenting, grief, and mourning as that it exceeds any pen to describe and express the same.

80

Sarah Ingersoll for Sarah Churchill
Undated

The deposition of Sarah Ingersoll, aged about thirty years: [she] saith that seeing Sarah Churchill after her examination, she came to me crying and wringing her hands, seeming to be much troubled in spirit. I asked her what she ailed.[12] She answered [that] she had undone herself. I asked her in what. She said in belying herself and others in saying [that] she had set her hand to the Devil's book, whereas, she said, she never did. I told her [that] I believed she had set her hand to the book. She answered crying and said, "No! No! No! I never! I never did!" I asked then what had made her say she did. She answered because they threatened her and told her they would put her into the dungeon and put her along with Mr. Burroughs; and thus several times she followed me up and down, telling me that she had undone herself in belying herself and others. I asked her why she did not right it. She told me because she had stood out so long in it that now she darst[13] not. She said also that if she told Mr. Noyes[14] but once [that] she had set her hand to the book he would believe her; but if she told the truth and said she had not set her hand to the book a hundred times he would not believe her.

[12] What troubled her.
[13] Dared.
[14] The minister in Salem Town.

Essex County Court Archives, vol. 2, no. 113, from the Records of the Court of Oyer and Terminer, 1692, Property of the Supreme Judicial Court, Division of Archives and Records Preservation, on deposit at the Peabody Essex Museum, Salem, Massachusetts.

The Return of Several Ministers Consulted by His Excellency and the Honorable Council upon the Present Witchcrafts in Salem Village

June 15, 1692

I.   The afflicted state of our poor neighbors, that are now suffering by molestations from the invisible world, we apprehend so deplorable that we think their condition calls for the utmost help of all persons in their several capacities.

II.   We cannot but with all thankfulness acknowledge the success which the merciful God has given unto the sedulous and assiduous[15] endeavors of our honorable rulers to detect the abominable witchcrafts which have been committed in the country, humbly praying that the discovery of these mysterious and mischievous wickednesses may be perfected.

III.   We judge that in the prosecution of these and all such witchcrafts, there is need of a very critical and exquisite[16] caution, lest by too much credulity for things received only upon the Devil's authority, there be a door opened for a long train of miserable consequences and Satan get an advantage over us, for we should not be ignorant of his devices.

IV.   As in complaints upon witchcrafts there may be matters of enquiry which do not amount unto matters of presumption, and there may be matters of presumption which yet may not be reckoned matters of conviction; so 'tis necessary that all proceedings thereabout be managed with an exceeding tenderness towards those that may be complained of, especially if they have been persons formerly of unblemished reputation.

V.   When the first enquiry is made into the circumstances of such as may lie under any just suspicion of witchcrafts, we could

[15] Diligent and persistent.
[16] Careful, exact.

"The Return of Several Ministers," in Increase Mather, *Cases of Conscience Concerning Evil Spirits Personating Men* (Boston, 1692), postscript, pages not numbered.

wish that there may be admitted as little as is possible of such noise, company, and openness as may too hastily expose them that are examined; and that there may nothing be used as a test for the trial of the suspected, the lawfulness whereof may be doubted among the people of God; but that the directions given by such judicious writers as [William] Perkins and [Richard] Bernard[17] be consulted in such a case.

VI.   Presumptions whereupon persons may be committed, and much more convictions whereupon persons may be condemned as guilty of witchcrafts, ought certainly to be more considerable than barely the accused person being represented by a specter unto the afflicted; inasmuch as 'tis an undoubted and a notorious thing that a demon may, by God's permission, appear even to ill purposes in the shape of an innocent, yea, and a virtuous man. Nor can we esteem alterations made in the sufferers by a look or touch of the accused to be an infallible evidence of guilt, but frequently liable to be abused by the Devil's legerdemains.[18]

VII.   We know not whether some remarkable affronts given to the devils by our disbelieving of those testimonies, whose whole force and strength is from them alone, may not put a period[19] unto the progress of the dreadful calamity begun upon us in the accusation of so many persons, whereof we hope some are yet clear from the great transgression laid unto their charge.

VIII.   Nevertheless, we cannot but humbly recommend unto the government the speedy and vigorous prosecution of such as have rendered themselves obnoxious, according to the direction given in the laws of God and the wholesome statutes of the English nation for the detection of witchcraft.

---

[17] These two men wrote influential books about the legal challenges involved in trying witches: William Perkins, *A Discourse on the Damned Art of Witchcraft* (1608) and Richard Bernard, *A Guide to Grand-Jury Men* (1627). Their perspective on this problem is discussed in the introduction.

[18] Trickery.

[19] End.

Letter from Cotton Mather to John Foster
August 17, 1692

Sir:

You would know whether I still retain my opinion about the horrible witchcrafts among us, and I acknowledge that I do.

I do still think that when there is no further evidence against a person but only this, that a specter in their shape does afflict a neighbor, that evidence is not enough to convict the [person] of witchcraft.

That the devils have a natural power which makes them capable of exhibiting what shape they please, I suppose nobody doubts, and I have no absolute promise of God that they shall not exhibit mine.

It is the opinion generally of all Protestant writers that the Devil may thus abuse the innocent; yea, 'tis the confession of some Popish[20] ones. And our honorable judges are so eminent for their justice, wisdom, and goodness that, whatever their own particular sense may be, yet they will not proceed capitally against any upon a principle contested with great odds on the other side in the learned and godly world.

Nevertheless, a very great use is to be made of the spectral impressions upon the sufferers. They justly introduce and determine an inquiry into the circumstances of the person accused and they strengthen other presumptions.

When so much use is made of those things, I believe the use for which the great God intends them is made. And accordingly you see that the excellent judges have had such an encouraging presence of God with them as that scarce any, if at all any, have been tried before them against whom God has not strangely sent in other, and more human, and most convincing testimonies.

If any persons have been condemned about whom any of the judges are not easy in their minds that the evidence against them has been satisfactory, it would certainly be for the glory of the whole transaction to give that person a reprieve.

---

[20] Roman Catholic.

Cotton Mather to John Foster, Aug. 17, 1692, in *Transactions of the Literary and Historical Society of Quebec* 2 (1831): 313–16.

It would make all matters easier if at least bail were taken for people accused only by the invisible tormentors of the poor sufferers and not blemished by any further grounds of suspicion against them.

The odd effects produced upon the sufferers by the look or touch of the accused are things wherein the devils may as much impose upon some harmless people as by the representation of their shapes.

My notion of these matters is this. A suspected and unlawful communion with a familiar spirit is the thing inquired after. The communion on the Devil's part may be proved while, for aught I can say, the man may be innocent; the Devil may impudently impose his communion upon some that care not for his company. But if the communion on the man's part be proved, then the business is done.

I am suspicious lest the Devil may at some time or other serve us a trick by his constancy for a long while in one way of dealing. We may find the Devil using one constant course in nineteen several actions and yet he be too hard for us at last, if we thence make a rule to form an infallible judgment of a twentieth. It is our singular happiness that we are blessed with judges who are aware of this danger.

For my own part, if the holy God should permit such a terrible calamity to befall myself as that a specter in my shape should so molest my neighborhood as that they can have no quiet, although there should be no other evidence against me, I should very patiently submit unto a judgment of transportation,[21] and all reasonable men would count our judges to act as they are, like the fathers of the public, in such a judgment. What if such a thing should be ordered for those whose guilt is more dubious and uncertain, whose presence yet perpetuates the miseries of our sufferers? They would cleanse the land of witchcrafts and yet also prevent the shedding of innocent blood, whereof some are so apprehensive of hazard. If our judges want any good bottom[22] to act thus upon, you know that besides the usual power of governors to relax many judgments of death, our General Court can soon provide a law.

Sir, you see the incoherency of my thoughts, but I hope you will also find some reasonableness in those thoughts.

In the year 1645 a vast number of persons in the county of Suffolk[23] were apprehended as guilty of witchcraft, whereof some confessed. The Parliament granted a Special Commission of Oyer and Terminer for the trial of those witches, in which commission there were a famous divine or two, Mr. [Samuel] Fairclough particularly, inserted. That excellent

---

[21] Exile.
[22] Basis.
[23] A county in England.

man did preach two sermons to the court before his first sitting on the bench, wherein having first proved the existence of witches, he afterwards showed the evil of endeavoring the conviction of any upon defective evidence. The sermon had the effect that none were condemned who could be saved without an express breach of the law. And then, though 'twas possible some guilty did escape, yet the troubles of those places were, I think, extinguished.

Our case is extraordinary. And so you and others will pardon the extraordinary liberty I take to address you on this occasion. But after all, I entreat you that whatever you do, you strengthen the hands of our honorable judges in the great work before them. They are persons for whom no man living has a greater veneration than

Sir,

Your servant,

C[otton] Mather.

83

Letter from Robert Pike to Jonathan Corwin
August 9, 1692

Honored Sir,

According as in my former [letter] to you I hinted that I held myself obliged to give you some farther account of my rude[24] though solemn thoughts of that great case now before you, the happy management whereof do so much conduce to the glory of God, [as well as] the safety and tranquility of the country, besides what I have said in my former and the enclosed [memorandum[25]], I further humbly present to consideration the doubtfulness and unsafety of admitting spectral testimony against the life of any that are of blameless conversation and plead innocent, from the uncertainty of them and the incredulity of them; for as for diabolical visions, apparitions, or representations, they are more com-

---

[24] Inexpert.

[25] The lengthy and learned memorandum that accompanied Pike's letter is not included here.

Robert Pike to Jonathan Corwin, Aug. 9, 1692, in Charles W. Upham, *Salem Witchcraft*, 2 vols. (Boston: Wiggin and Lunt, 1867), 2:538–44.

monly false and delusive than real, and [it] cannot be known when they are real and when feigned,[26] but by the Devil's report; and then not to be believed, because he is the father of lies.

1. Either the organ of the eye is abused and the senses deluded, so as to think they do see or hear some thing or person when indeed they do not . . .

2. [Or] the Devil himself appears in the shape and likeness of a person or thing when it is not the person or thing itself; so he did in the shape of Samuel.

3. And sometimes persons or things themselves do really appear, but [we may wonder] how it is possible for anyone to give a true testimony, which possibly did see neither shape nor person but were deluded; and if they did see anything, they know not whether it was the person or but his shape. All that can be rationally or truly said in such a case is this, that I did see the shape or likeness of such a person, if my senses or eyesight were not deluded, and they can honestly say no more, because they know no more (except the Devil tells them more); and if he do, they can but say he told them so. But the matter is still incredible: first, because it is but their saying the Devil told them so; [and second,] if he did so tell them, yet the verity[27] of the thing remains still unproved, because the Devil was a liar and a murderer (John 8.44) and may tell these lies to murder an innocent person.

But this case seems to be solved by an assertion of some that affirm that the Devil does not or cannot appear in the shape of a godly person to do hurt; others affirm the contrary and say that he can and often has so done, of which they give many instances for proof of what they say; which if granted, the case remains yet unsolved, and yet [this is] the very hinge upon which that weighty case depends. . . .

Now, that the only wise God may so direct you in all, that he may have glory, the country peace and safety, and your hands strengthened in that great work, is the desire and constant prayer of your humble servant, R. P., who shall no further trouble you at present.

[26] Pretended or counterfeited.
[27] Truth.

84

Letter from Thomas Brattle to an Unnamed Clergyman

October 8, 1692

Reverend Sir,

Yours I received the other day, and [I] am very ready to serve you to my utmost . . .

First, as to the method which the Salem justices do take in their examinations, it is truly this. A warrant being issued out to apprehend the persons that are charged and complained of by the afflicted children (as they are called), said persons are brought before the justices (the afflicted being present). The justices ask the apprehended why they afflict those poor children, to which the apprehended answer [that] they do not afflict them. The justices order the apprehended to look upon the said children, which accordingly they do; and at the time of that look (I dare not say by that look, as the Salem gentlemen do), the afflicted are cast into a fit. The apprehended are then blind[fold]ed and ordered to touch the afflicted; and at that touch, though not by the touch (as above), the afflicted ordinarily do come out of their fits. The afflicted persons then declare and affirm that the apprehended have afflicted them, upon which the apprehended persons, though of never so good repute, are forthwith committed to prison on suspicion for witchcraft. . . .

I cannot but condemn this method of the justices, of making this touch of the hand a rule to discover witchcraft, because I am fully persuaded that it is sorcery and a superstitious method[28] and that which we have no rule for, either from reason or religion. The Salem justices, at least some of them, do assert that the cure of the afflicted persons is a natural effect of this touch; and they are so well instructed in the Cartesian

---

[28] Brattle was referring to the similarity between this touch test and countermagic, which apparently undid a bewitchment by transmitting the occult harm back onto the witch responsible. Ministers argued that countermagic relied on a diabolical agency and so was morally equivalent to the original act of witchcraft.

Thomas Brattle to unnamed clergyman, Oct. 8, 1692, in George Lincoln Burr, ed., *Narratives of the Witchcraft Cases, 1648–1706* (New York: Charles Scribner's Sons, 1914), 169–90.

philosophy and in the doctrine of *effluvia*[29] that they undertake to give a demonstration how this touch does cure the afflicted persons; and the account they give of it is this, that by this touch the venomous and malignant particles that were ejected from the eye do, by this means, return to the body whence they came and so leave the afflicted persons pure and whole. I must confess to you that I am no small admirer of the Cartesian philosophy; but yet I have not so learned it. Certainly this is a strain that it will by no means allow of.

I would fain know of these Salem gentlemen, but as yet could never know, how it comes about that if these apprehended persons are witches and by a look of the eye do cast the afflicted into their fits by poisoning them, how it comes about, I say, that by a look of their eye they do not cast others into fits and poison others by their looks, and in particular tender,[30] fearful women who often are beheld by them and as likely as any in the whole world to receive an ill impression from them. This Salem philosophy some men may call the new philosophy, but I think it rather deserves the name of Salem superstition and sorcery, and it is not fit to be named in a land of such light as New England is. . . .

Secondly, with respect to the confessors (as they are improperly called), or such as confess themselves to be witches (the second thing you inquire into in your letter), there are now about fifty of them in prison, many of which I have again and again seen and heard; and I cannot but tell you that my faith is strong concerning them that they are deluded, imposed upon, and under the influence of some evil spirit, and therefore unfit to be evidences either against themselves or anyone else. I now speak of one sort of them, and of others afterward.

These confessors (as they are called) do very often contradict themselves, as inconsistently as is usual for any crazed, distempered person to do. This the Salem gentlemen do see and take notice of; and even the judges themselves have at some times taken these confessors in flat lies or contradictions, even in the courts, by reason of which one would have thought that the judges would have frowned upon the said

---

[29] A theory relating to the flow of invisible particles, developed by influential French thinker René Descartes. According to Cartesian physics, apparently empty space was actually filled with "effluvia," or "subtle matter," material particles that could not be perceived by touch or sight; these particles could be used to conduct energy from one body to another. Cotton Mather also reported that the magistrates "had some philosophical schemes of witchcraft, and of the method and manner wherein magical poisons operate, which further supported them in their opinion" (Cotton Mather, *Magnalia Christi Americana*, ed. Kenneth B. Murdock [Cambridge, Mass.: Harvard University Press, 1977], 331).

[30] Frail and vulnerable.

confessors, discarded them, and not minded one tittle[31] of anything that they said; but instead thereof (as sure as we are men), the judges vindicate these confessors and salve[32] their contradictions by proclaiming that the Devil takes away their memory and imposes upon their brain. If this reflects anywhere, I am very sorry for it: I can but assure you that upon the word of an honest man it is the truth and that I can bring you many credible persons to witness it who have been eye and ear witnesses to these things. These confessors, then, at least some of them, even in the judges' own account, are under the influence of the Devil; and the brain of these confessors is imposed upon by the Devil, even in the judges' account. . . .

The indictment runs for sorcery and witchcraft, acted upon the body of such an one (say M[ary] Warren) at such a particular time (say April 14, 1692) and at divers other times before and after, whereby the said M[ary] W[arren] is wasted and consumed, pined, etc. Now for the proof of the said sorcery and witchcraft, the prisoner at the bar pleading not guilty,

1. The afflicted persons are brought into court and after much patience and pains taken with them do take their oaths that the prisoner at the bar did afflict them. And here I think it very observable that often, when the afflicted do mean and intend only the appearance and shape of such an one (say G[oodman] Proctor), yet they positively swear that G[oodman] Proctor did afflict them and they have been allowed so to do, as tho[ugh] there was no real difference between G[oodman] Proctor and the shape of G[oodman] Proctor. This, methinks, may readily prove a stumbling block to the jury, lead them into a very fundamental error, and occasion innocent blood, yea the innocentest blood imaginable, to be in great danger. Whom it belongs unto, to be eyes unto the blind and to remove such stumbling blocks, I know full well; and yet you and every one else do know as well as I who do not [do so].[33]

2. The confessors do declare what they know of the said prisoner and some of the confessors are allowed to give their oaths, a thing which I believe was never heard of in this world, that such as confess themselves to be witches, to have renounced God and Christ and all that is sacred, should yet be allowed and ordered to swear by the name of the great God! This indeed seemeth to me to be a

---

[31] A minute amount.
[32] Smooth over.
[33] Brattle was referring to the magistrates presiding over the trials.

gross taking of God's name in vain. I know the Salem gentlemen do say that there is hope that the said confessors have repented; I shall only say that if they have repented, it is well for themselves; but if they have not, it is very ill for you know who. But then,

3. Whoever can be an evidence against the prisoner at the bar is ordered to come into court; and here it scarce ever fails but that evidences of one nature and another are brought in, though, I think, all of them altogether alien to the matter of indictment; for they none of them do respect witchcraft upon the bodies of the afflicted, which is the lone matter of charge in the indictment.

4. They are searched by a jury and as to some of them the jury brought in that [on] such or such a place there was a preternatural excrescence.[34] And I wonder what person there is, whether man or woman, of whom it cannot be said but that in some part of their body or other there is a preternatural excrescence. The term is a very general and inclusive term. . . .

The Salem gentlemen will by no means allow that any are brought in guilty and condemned by virtue of spectral evidence (as it is called), i.e. the evidence of these afflicted persons, who are said to have spectral eyes; but whether it is not purely by virtue of these spectral evidences that these persons are found guilty (considering what before has been said), I leave you and any man of sense to judge and determine. When any man is indicted for murdering the person of A.B. and all the direct evidence be that the said man pistoled the shadow of the said A.B., though there be never so many evidences that the said person murdered C.D., E.F., and ten more persons, yet all this will not amount to a legal proof that he murdered A.B.; and upon that indictment the person cannot be legally brought in guilty of the said indictment, [except] it must be upon this supposition, that the evidence of a man's pistoling the shadow of A.B. is a legal evidence to prove that the said man did murder the person of A.B. Now no man will be so much out of his wits as to make this a legal evidence; and yet this seems to be our case; and how to apply it is very easy and obvious. . . .

Many things I cannot but admire[35] and wonder at, an account of which I shall here send you.

---

[34] The Devil's mark, a third teat from which demonic familiars sucked blood.
[35] Feel surprise or astonishment.

1. I do admire that some particular persons, and particularly Mrs. [Margaret] Thacher of Boston, should be much complained of by the afflicted persons, and yet that the justices should never issue out their warrants to apprehend them, when as upon the same account they issue out their warrants for the apprehending and imprisoning many others. This occasions much discourse and many hot words, and is a very great scandal and stumbling block to many good people; certainly distributive justice should have its course without respect to persons; and although the said Mrs. Thacher be mother-in-law to Mr. Corwin, who is one of the justices and judges, yet if justice and conscience do oblige them to apprehend others on the account of the afflicted's complaints, I cannot see how, without injustice and violence to conscience, Mrs. Thacher can escape, when it is well known how much she is, and has been, complained of.

2. I cannot but admire that Mr. H[ezekiah] U[sher] (whom we all think innocent) should yet be apprehended on this account and ordered to prison by a mittimus under Mr. [Joseph] Lynde's hand, and yet that he should be suffered for above a fortnight to be in a private house, and after that to quit the house, the town, and the province, and yet that authority should not take effectual notice of it. Methinks that same justice that actually imprisoned others and refused bail for them on any terms should not be satisfied without actually imprisoning Mr. U[sher] and refusing bail for him, when his case is known to be the very same with the case of those others. If he may be suffered to go away, why may not others? If others may not be suffered to go, how in justice can he be allowed herein?

3. If our justices do think that Mrs. [Elizabeth] C[ary], Mr. [Phillip] E[nglish] and his wife, Mr. [John] A[lden], and others were capital offenders and justly imprisoned on a capital account, I do admire that the said justices should hear of their escape from prison, and where they are gone and entertained, and yet not send forthwith to the said places for the surrendering of them, that justice might be done them. In other capitals[36] this has been practiced; why then is it not practiced in this case, if really judged to be so heinous[37] as is made for?

---

[36] Capital cases.
[37] Wicked and abominable.

4. I cannot but admire that any should go with their distempered friends and relations to the afflicted children to know what their distempered friends ail, whether they are not bewitched, who it is that afflicts them, and the like. It is true, I know no reason why these afflicted may not be consulted as well as any other, if so be that it was only their natural and ordinary knowledge that was had recourse to; but it is not on this notion that these afflicted children are sought unto, but as they have a supernatural knowledge, a knowledge which they obtain by their holding correspondence with specters or evil spirits, as they themselves grant. This consulting of these afflicted children, as above said, seems to me to be a very gross evil, a real abomination, not fit to be known in New England. . . . Good husbands, who, having taken up that corrupt and highly pernicious opinion that whoever were accused by the afflicted were guilty, did break charity with their dear wives upon their being accused and urge them to confess their guilt; which so far prevailed with them [the accused wives] as to make them say, they were afraid of their being in the snare of the Devil; and which, through the rude and barbarous methods that were afterwards used at Salem, issued in somewhat plainer degrees of confession and was attended with imprisonment. [*The following sentence was added by Brattle in the margin of his letter.*] You may possibly think that my terms are too severe; but should I tell you what a kind of blade was employed in bringing these women to their confession, what methods from damnation were taken, with what violence urged, how unseasonably they were kept up [awake through the night], what buzzings and chuckings of the hand were used, and the like, I am sure that you would call them, as I do, rude and barbarous methods. . . .

5. I cannot but admire that the justices, whom I think to be well-meaning men, should so far give ear to the Devil as merely upon his authority to issue out their warrants and apprehend people. Liberty was evermore accounted the great privilege of an Englishman; but certainly, if the Devil will be heard against us and his testimony taken to the seizing and apprehending of us, our liberty vanishes, and we are fools if we boast of our liberty. . . .

But although the chief judge and some of the other judges be very zealous in these proceedings, yet this you may take for a truth, that there are several about the [Massachusetts] Bay, men for understanding, judgment, and piety inferior to few (if any) in New England, that do utterly condemn the said proceedings and do freely deliver their judgment in the case to be this, viz. that these methods will utterly ruin and undo poor New England. I shall nominate some of these to you, viz. the honorable Simon Bradstreet, Esq[uire][38] (our late governor); the honorable Thomas Danforth, Esq[uire] (our late deputy governor); the Reverend Mr. Increase Mather; and the Reverend Mr. Samuel Willard. Major N[athaniel] Saltonstall, Esq[uire], who was one of the judges, has left the court and is very much dissatisfied with the proceedings of it. Excepting Mr. Hale, Mr. Noyes, and Mr. Parris, the reverend elders[39] almost throughout the whole country are very much dissatisfied. Several of the late justices, viz. Thomas Graves, Esq[uire], N[athaniel] Byfield, Esq[uire], [and] Francis Foxcroft, Esq[uire], are much dissatisfied; also several of the present justices; and in particular, some of the Boston justices were resolved rather to throw up their commissions than be active in disturbing the liberty of their Majesties' subjects merely on the accusations of these afflicted, possessed children. Finally, the principal gentlemen in Boston and thereabout are generally agreed that irregular and dangerous methods have been taken as to these matters. . . .

I am very sensible that it is irksome[40] and disagreeable to go back when a man's doing so is an implication that he has been walking in a wrong path; however, nothing is more honorable than, upon due conviction, to retract and undo (so far as may be) what has been amiss and irregular. . . .

What will be the issue of these troubles, God only knows. I am afraid that ages will not wear off that reproach and those stains which these things will leave behind them upon our land. I pray God pity us, humble us, forgive us, and appear mercifully for us in this our mount[41] of distress. Herewith I conclude, and subscribe myself, reverend sir,

Your real friend and humble servant,

T[homas] B[rattle].

---

[38] The title *Esquire* was given to those regarded as gentlemen, including as a matter of course all magistrates.

[39] Ministers.

[40] Annoying or distressing.

[41] Mountain.

85

Letter from William Phips to William Blathwayt, Clerk of the Privy Council in London

October 12, 1692

Sir,

When I first arrived, I found this province miserably harassed with a most horrible witchcraft or possession of devils, which had broke in upon several towns. Some scores of poor people were taken with preternatural torments, some scalded with brimstone, some had pins stuck in their flesh, others hurried into the fire and water, and some dragged out of their houses and carried over the tops of trees and hills for many miles together. It hath been represented to me much like that of Sweden about thirty years ago, and there were many committed to prison upon suspicion of witchcraft before my arrival. The loud cries and clamors of the friends of the afflicted people, with the advice of the deputy governor and many others, prevailed with me to give a Commission of Oyer and Terminer for discovering what witchcraft might be at the bottom, or whether it were not a possession. The chief judge in this Commission was the deputy governor and the rest were persons of the best prudence and figure that could then be pitched upon.[42] When the court came to sit at Salem in the county of Essex, they convicted more than twenty persons of being guilty of witchcraft. Some of the convicted were such as confessed their guilt. The court, as I understand, began their proceedings with the accusations of the afflicted and then went upon other human evidences to strengthen that. I was almost the whole time of the proceeding abroad in the service of their Majesties in the eastern part of the country and depended upon the judgment of the court as to a right method of proceeding in cases of witchcraft, but when I came home I found many persons in a strange ferment of dissatisfaction, which was increased by some hot spirits that blew up the flame, but on enquiring into the matter I found that the Devil had taken upon him the name and shape of several persons who were doubtless innocent

[42] Selected or decided on.

William Phips to William Blathwayt, Oct. 12, 1692, in George Lincoln Burr, ed., *Narratives of the Witchcraft Cases, 1648–1706* (New York: Charles Scribner's Sons, 1914), 196–98.

and to my certain knowledge of good reputation, for which cause I have now forbidden the committing of any more that shall be accused without unavoidable necessity, and those that have been committed I would shelter from any proceedings against them wherein there may be the least suspicion of any wrong to be done unto the innocent. I would also wait for any particular directions or commands, if their Majesties please to give me any, for the fuller ordering [of] this perplexed affair. I have also put a stop to the printing of any discourses one way or other that may increase the needless disputes of people upon this occasion, because I saw a likelihood of kindling an inextinguishable flame, if I should admit any public and open contests. And I have grieved to see that some who should have done their Majesties and this Province better service have so far taken counsel of passion as to desire the precipitancy[43] of these matters. These things have been improved[44] by some [so as] to give me many interruptions in their Majesties' service, and in truth none of my vexations have been greater than this, that their Majesties' service has been hereby unhappily clogged, and the persons who have made so ill improvement of these matters here are seeking to turn it all upon me. But I hereby declare that as soon as I came from fighting against their Majesties' enemies and understood what danger some of their innocent subjects might be exposed to, if the evidence of the afflicted persons only did prevail either to the committing or trying any of them, I did before any application was made unto me about it put a stop to the proceedings of the court and they are now stopped till their Majesties' pleasure be known. Sir, I beg pardon for giving you all this trouble; the reason is because I know my enemies are seeking to turn it all upon me and I take this liberty because I depend upon your friendship and desire you will please to give a true understanding of the matter if anything of this kind be urged or made use of against me, because the justness of my proceeding herein will be a sufficient defense. Sir, I am with all imaginable respect,

Your most humble Servant,

William Phips.

---

[43] Acting or doing something hurriedly and without due deliberation.
[44] Made use of or exploited.

5

Aftermath

Governor William Phips wrote in February 1693 that "people's minds, before divided and distracted by different opinions" concerning the trials, were now "well composed."[1] Phips was presenting a rather rose-tinted perspective on the aftermath of the witch hunt. Two fundamental problems had yet to be addressed. First, a flood of accusations, imprisonments, convictions, and executions had left local inhabitants frightened, angry, and in some cases bereaved; the accusers and the accused, their families, and their friends now had to find a way to coexist. Samuel Parris, the minister in Salem Village who had played such a central and inflammatory role in the witch hunt, now cast himself in the rather implausible role of peacemaker (Document 86). But many villagers—especially the families and friends of those who had been accused—distrusted and even hated Parris. His continued presence proved to be a serious obstacle to reconciliation (Document 87). Parris and his supporters fought hard to save his ministry, but he eventually resigned in 1696 and left the village the next year. Fortunately for local inhabitants, the next minister, Joseph Green, would prove extremely effective in promoting a spirit of reconciliation within the village.

The second challenge facing Massachusetts in the aftermath of 1692 arose from the fact that the witch hunt had been made possible by the willingness of magistrates to convict on the basis of evidence that a growing number of critics had judged to be problematic, with the apparent approval of the governor and his council. Containing the potential damage to judicial and political authority while at the same time recognizing that serious mistakes had been made involved some very delicate maneuvering. The remaining documents in this chapter illuminate the

---

[1] William Phips to Earl of Nottingham, Feb. 21, 1693, in George Lincoln Burr, ed., *Narratives of the Witchcraft Cases, 1648–1706* (New York: Charles Scribner's Sons, 1914), 201–2.

steps taken by officials and other participants in the witch hunt to put the tragedy behind them.

The government's announcement of a day of prayer and fasting (Document 88) and the expressions of regret from magistrate Samuel Sewall (Document 89), jurors (Document 90), and one of the accusers (Document 91) all focused on supernatural explanations for what had happened. According to these explanations, God had unleashed the Devil upon New England as a punishment for human sin; those involved in the witch hunt had been duped by Satan. They neatly sidestepped the possibility that human malice and deliberate falsehood may also have played a significant role in the witch hunt. Meanwhile, more practical measures were taken to undo as far as possible what had happened. Convictions, judgments, and attainders (the forfeiture of property and civil rights following conviction) were reversed (Document 92); compensation was awarded to the families of those who had been executed (Document 93); and individuals such as Rebecca Nurse and Giles Corey had their excommunications "blotted out" (Document 94).

In the late 1690s, John Hale, the minister at Beverly, wrote a book that would challenge the very possibility of trying supernatural crimes in a court of law (Document 95). Hale's words expressed eloquently the anguish felt by those involved in the witch hunt as they looked back upon what they had done. In the face of nineteen executions that could not be undone, men like Hale had much to reckon with.

86

Samuel Parris's Meditations for Peace, Read to the Congregation at the Salem Village Church

November 18, 1694

For as much as it is the undoubted duty of all Christians to pursue peace (Psalms 24.14) even unto a reaching of it, if it be possible (Romans 12.18,19); and whereas, through the righteous, sovereign and awful Providence of God, the grand enemy of all Christian peace has of late been

Salem Village Ministers' Record Book, Courtesy Danvers Archival Center, Danvers, Massachusetts.

most tremendously let loose in diverse places hereabouts, and more especially amongst our sinful selves, not only to interrupt that partial peace which we did sometimes enjoy, but also, through his wiles and temptations and our weaknesses and corruptions, to make wider breaches and raise more bitter animosities between too many of us, of one mind for a time and afterwards of differing apprehensions, and at last are but in the dark; upon serious thoughts of all or most of all, and after many prayers, I have been moved to present to you (my beloved flock) the following particulars, in way of contribution towards regaining of Christian concord (if [it] so be [that] we are not altogether unappeasable, irreconcilable, and so destitute of that good spirit which is first pure, then peaceable, gentle, [and] easy to be entreated, James 3.17), viz.

(1) In that the Lord ordered the late horrid calamity (which afterwards, plague-like, spread in many other places) to break out first in my family, I cannot but look upon [this] as a very sore rebuke and humbling Providence, both to myself and mine, and desire so we may improve it.[2]

(2) In that also in my family were some of both parties, viz. accusers and accused, I look [on this] also as an aggravation of the rebuke, as an addition of wormwood to the gall.[3]

(3) In that means were used in my family (though totally unknown to me or mine, except servants, till afterwards) to raise spirits and create apparitions in a no better than diabolical way, I do also look upon [this] as a farther rebuke of Divine Providence. And by all, I do humbly own this day, before the Lord and his people, that God has been righteously spitting in my face (Numbers 12.14). And I desire to lie low under all this reproach and to lay my hand upon my mouth.[4]

(4) As to the management of those mysteries, as far as concerns myself, I am very desirous (upon farther light) to own any errors I have therein fallen into and can come to a discerning of.

In the meanwhile, I do acknowledge, upon after-considerations, that were the same troubles [to afflict us] again (which the Lord of his rich

[2] Learn from and make good use of it.

[3] Wormwood was a plant known for its bitter taste; gall referred to bile (the secretion of the liver) or, figuratively, to any irritation or chafing. Parris was saying that his family's involvement in the crisis as both accusers and accused made a painful situation even more distressing.

[4] Presumably an expression of shame and self-silencing, the latter in contrast to his earlier vocal encouragement of the accusers.

mercy forever prevent), I should not agree with my former apprehensions in all points, as, for instance:

(1) I question not but God sometimes suffers the Devil (as of late) to afflict in the shape of not only innocent but pious persons, or so to delude the senses of the afflicted that they strongly conceive their hurt is from such persons, when indeed it is not.

(2) The improving[5] of one afflicted [person] to inquire by who afflicts the others, I fear may be and has been unlawfully used, to Satan's great advantage. . . .

As to all that have unduly suffered in these matters (either in their persons or relations) through the clouds of human weakness and Satan's wiles and sophistry,[6] I do truly sympathize with them. . . . I am very much in the mind and abundantly persuaded that God (for holy ends, though for what in particular is best known to himself) has suffered the evil angels to delude us on both hands, but how far on the one side or the other is much above me to say. And if we cannot reconcile till we come to a full discerning of these things, I fear we shall never come to agreement, or at soonest not in this world. . . .

In fine,[7] the matter being so dark and perplexed as that there is no present appearance that all God's servants should be altogether of one mind, in all circumstances touching the same, I do most heartily, fervently, and humbly beseech pardon of the merciful God, through the blood of Christ, of all my mistakes and trespasses in so weighty a matter; and also all your forgiveness of every offence in this or other affairs, wherein you see or conceive I have erred and offended; professing, in the presence of the Almighty God, that what I have done has been, as for substance, as I apprehended was duty, however through weakness, ignorance, etc., I may have been mistaken; I also, through grace, promising each of you the like of me.[8] And so again, I beg, entreat, and beseech you, that Satan, the Devil, the roaring lion, the old dragon, the enemy of all righteousness, may no longer be served by us, by our envy and strife (where every evil work prevails whilst these bear sway, Isaiah 3.14–16); but that all from this day forward may be covered with the mantle of love, and we may on all hands forgive each other heartily, sincerely, and thoroughly, as we do hope and pray that God, for Christ's sake, would forgive each of ourselves. . . . Let all bitterness and wrath and anger and

---

[5] Use.

[6] Intentionally misleading but plausible arguments.

[7] In the final analysis.

[8] In other words, Parris promised to forgive others as they forgave him.

clamor and evil-speaking be put away from you, with all malice; and be you kind to one another, tenderhearted, forgiving one another, even as God, for Christ's sake, hath forgiven you. Amen. Amen.

87

Summary of Grievances against Samuel Parris, Read to the Congregation at the Salem Village Church

November 26, 1694

The reasons why we withdrew from communion with the church of Salem Village, both as to hearing the word preached and from partaking with them at the Lord's table, are as followeth:

1. Why we attend not on public prayer and preaching the word, these are [the reasons]: (1) the distracting and disturbing tumults and noises made by the persons under diabolical power and delusions, preventing sometimes our hearing and understanding and profiting of the word preached; we having, after many trials and experiences, found no redress in this case, accounted ourselves under a necessity to go where we might hear the word in quiet; (2) the apprehension of danger of ourselves being accused as the Devil's instruments to molest and afflict the persons complaining, we seeing those whom we had reason to esteem better than ourselves thus accused, blemished, and of their lives bereaved, foreseeing this evil, thought it our prudence to withdraw; (3) we found so frequent and positive preaching up[9] some principles and practices by Mr. Parris, referring to the trouble then among us and upon us, [that we] therefore thought it our most safe and peaceable way to withdraw.

---

[9] Advocating from the pulpit.

Salem Village Ministers' Record Book, Courtesy Danvers Archival Center, Danvers, Massachusetts.

2. The reasons why we hold not communion with them at the Lord's
table are, we esteem ourselves justly aggrieved and offended
with the officer who doth administer, for the reasons following:
(1) from his declared and published principles, referring to our
molestation from the invisible world, differing from the opinion of
the generality of the orthodox ministers of the whole country;
(2) his easy and strong faith and belief of the affirmations and
accusations made by those they call the afflicted; (3) his lay-
ing aside that grace which above all we are required to put on,
namely, charity towards his neighbors, and especially towards
those of his church, when there is no apparent reason for the
contrary; (4) his approving and practicing unwarrantable and
ungrounded methods for discovering what he was desirous to
know referring to the bewitched or possessed persons, as in
bringing some to others, and by and from them pretending to
inform himself and others who were the Devil's instruments to
afflict the sick and pained; (5) his unsafe and unaccountable oath,
given by him against sundry of the accused; (6) his not rendering to the world so fair, if true, an account of what he wrote on
examination of the afflicted; (7) sundry unsafe, if sound, points of
doctrine delivered in his preaching, which we esteem not war-
rantable, if Christian; (8) his persisting in these principles and
justifying his practices, not rendering any satisfaction to us when
regularly desired, but rather further offending and dissatisfying
ourselves.

John Tarbell
Thomas Wilkins
Samuel Nurse

88

A Proclamation
December 17, 1696

By the Honorable Lieutenant Governor, Council, and Assembly of His Majesty's Province of the Massachusetts Bay, in General Court Assembled:

Whereas the anger of God is not yet turned away, but his hand is still stretched out against his people in manifold judgments, particularly in drawing out to such a length the troubles of Europe by a perplexing war and more especially respecting ourselves in this province, in that God is pleased still to go on in diminishing our substance,[10] cutting short our harvest, blasting our most promising undertakings [in] more ways than one, unsettling of us, and by his more immediate hand snatching away many out of our embraces by sudden and violent deaths, even at this time when the sword is devouring so many both at home and abroad, and that after many days of public and solemn addressing of him, and although, considering the many sins prevailing in the midst of us, we cannot but wonder at the patience and mercy moderating these rebukes, yet we cannot but also fear that there is something still wanting to accompany our supplications. And doubtless there are some particular sins which God is angry with our Israel for, that have not been duly seen and resented[11] by us, about which God expects to be sought, if ever he [is to] turn[12] again our captivity.[13]

Wherefore it is commanded and appointed that Thursday January 14 [1697] be observed as a Day of Prayer, with fasting throughout this province, strictly forbidding all servile labor thereon; that so all God's people may offer up fervent supplications unto him for the preservation and prosperity of His Majesty's royal person and government, and success to attend his affairs both at home and abroad; that all iniquity may be put away which hath stirred God's holy jealousy against this land;

[10] Property or material resources.
[11] Regretted.
[12] Reverse or undo.
[13] Captivity in the hands of Satan and his minions.

Proclamation, Dec. 17, 1696, in George Lincoln Burr, ed., *Narratives of the Witchcraft Cases, 1648–1706* (New York: Charles Scribner's Sons, 1914), 385–86.

that he would show us what we know not, and help us wherein we have done amiss to do so no more; and especially that whatever mistakes on either hand have been fallen into, either by the body of this people or any orders of men, referring to the late tragedy raised among us by Satan and his instruments, through the awful judgment of God, [that] he would humble us therefore and pardon all the errors of his servants and people that desire to love his name and be atoned to his land; that he would remove the rod of the wicked from off the lot of the righteous; that he would bring the American heathen, and cause them to hear and obey his voice.

89

Public Apology by Samuel Sewall
January 14, 1697

Copy of the bill[14] [that] I put up on the fast day; giving it to Mr. Willard[15] as he passed by,[16] and standing up at the reading of it, and bowing when finished, in the afternoon:

> Samuel Sewall, sensible[17] of the reiterated strokes of God upon himself and family; and being sensible that as to the guilt contracted upon the opening of the late Commission of Oyer and Terminer at Salem (to which the order for this day relates) he is upon many accounts more concerned than any that he knows of, desires to take the blame and shame of it, asking pardon of men, and especially desiring prayers that God, who has unlimited authority, would pardon that sin and all other his sins, personal and relative; and according to his infinite benignity and sovereignty, not visit the sin of him or of any other upon himself or any of his, nor upon the land; but that He would powerfully defend him against all temptations to sin for the future and vouchsafe[18] him the efficacious, saving conduct of his word and spirit.

[14] Written statement.
[15] Samuel Willard was Sewall's pastor.
[16] As he was entering the meetinghouse and proceeding to the front of the congregation.
[17] Aware.
[18] Grant.

Samuel Sewall Diaries, Massachusetts Historical Society, Boston, Massachusetts.

90

Public Apology by Jurymen
Undated

Some that had been of several juries have given forth a paper, signed with their own hands in these words:

We whose names are underwritten, being in the year 1692 called to serve as jurors in court at Salem, on trial of many who were by some suspected guilty of doing acts of witchcraft upon the bodies of sundry persons:

We confess that we ourselves were not capable to understand nor able to withstand the mysterious delusions of the powers of darkness and prince of the air; but were for want of knowledge in ourselves, and better information from others, prevailed with to take up with such evidence against the accused as on further consideration and better information we justly fear was insufficient for touching the lives of any, Deuteronomy 17.6, whereby we fear we have been instrumental with others, though ignorantly and unwittingly, to bring upon ourselves and this people of the Lord the guilt of innocent blood, which sin the Lord saith in scripture he would not pardon, 2 Kings 24.4, that is, we suppose, in regard of his temporal[19] judgments. We do therefore hereby signify to all in general (and to the surviving sufferers in especial) our deep sense of and sorrow for our errors in acting on such evidence to the condemning of any person.

And do hereby declare that we justly fear that we were sadly deluded and mistaken, for which we are much disquieted and distressed in our minds; and do therefore humbly beg forgiveness, first of God for Christ's sake for this our error; and pray that God would not impute the guilt of it to ourselves, nor others; and we also pray that we may be considered candidly and aright by the living sufferers as being then under the power of a strong and general delusion, utterly unacquainted with and not experienced in matters of that nature.

We do heartily ask forgiveness of you all whom we have justly offended, and do declare according to our present minds, we would none

[19] In this world and now, as distinct from on the Day of Judgment.

Statement by Jurymen, in George Lincoln Burr, ed., *Narratives of the Witchcraft Cases, 1648–1706* (New York: Charles Scribner's Sons, 1914), 387.

of us do such things again on such grounds for the whole world; praying you to accept of this in way of satisfaction for our offence; and that you would bless the inheritance of the Lord, that he may be entreated for the land.

Thomas Fiske (foreman)	Thomas Perly, Sr.
William Fiske	John Pebody
John Batcheler	Thomas Perkins
Thomas Tisk, Jr.	Samuel Sayer
John Dane	Andrew Elliott
Joseph Evelith	Henry Herrick, Sr.

91

The Public Confession of Ann Putnam[20]
August 25, 1706

I desire to be humbled before God for that sad and humbling Providence that befell my father's family in the year about 1692; that I, then being in my childhood, should by such a Providence of God be made an instrument for the accusing of several persons of a grievous crime, whereby their lives were taken away from them, whom now I have just grounds and good reason to believe they were innocent persons; and that it was a great delusion of Satan that deceived me in that sad time, whereby I justly fear [that] I have been instrumental, with others, though ignorantly and unwittingly, to bring upon myself and this land the guilt of innocent blood; though what was said or done by me against any person I can truly and uprightly say, before God and man, I did it not out of any anger, malice, or ill-will to any person, for I had no such thing against [any] one of them; but what I did was [done] ignorantly, being deluded by Satan. And particularly, as I was a chief instrument of accusing of

---

[20] Putnam gave this apology as part of her successful application to become a full member of the church in Salem Village. The confession was approved beforehand by Samuel Nurse, son of Rebecca Nurse, and then read to the congregation by the pastor, Joseph Green. Putnam stood while it was read and then acknowledged it as hers.

Charles W. Upham, *Salem Witchcraft*, 2 vols. (Boston: Wiggin and Lunt, 1867), 2:510.

Goodwife Nurse and her two sisters,[21] I desire to lie in the dust and to be humbled for it, in that I was a cause, with others, of so sad a calamity to them and their families; for which cause I desire to lie in the dust, and earnestly beg forgiveness of God, and from all those unto whom I have given just cause of sorrow and offence, whose relations were taken away or accused.

[21] Rebecca Nurse and her two sisters, Sarah Cloyce and Mary Esty, were accused and formally indicted in 1692. Nurse and Esty were convicted and hanged. Cloyce was still awaiting trial when the witch hunt came to an end and so survived.

92

Reversals of Conviction, Judgment, and Attainder
October 17, 1711

Province of the Massachusetts Bay:

Anno Regni Anna Reginae Decimo [in the tenth year of the reign of Queen Anne]:

An Act to reverse the attainders[22] of George Burroughs and others for witchcraft:

Forasmuch as in the year of our Lord 1692 several towns within this province were infested with a horrible witchcraft or possession of devils; and at a Special Court of Oyer and Terminer, holden at Salem in the county of Essex in the same year 1692, George Burroughs of Wells, John Proctor, George Jacobs, John Willard, Giles Corey and [Martha] his wife, Rebecca Nurse, and Sarah Good, all of Salem aforesaid, Elizabeth How of Ipswich, Mary Esty, Sarah Wilds, and Abigail Hobbs, all of Topsfield, Samuel Wardwell, Mary Parker, Martha Carrier, Abigail Faulkner, Ann Foster, Rebecca Eames, Mary Post and Mary Lacey, all of Andover, Mary Bradbury of Salisbury, and Dorcas Hoar of Beverly

[22] Forfeiture of property and loss of civil rights as a consequence of being sentenced to death or outlawed.

Essex County Court Archives, vol. 2, no. 136, from the Records of the Court of Oyer and Terminer, 1692, Property of the Supreme Judicial Court, Division of Archives and Records Preservation, on deposit at the Peabody Essex Museum, Salem, Massachusetts.

were severally indicted, convicted, and attainted of witchcraft, and some of them put to death, others lying still under the like sentence of the said court, and liable to have [that sentence] executed upon them.

The influence and energy of the evil spirits, so great at that time, acting in and upon those who were the principal accusers and witnesses, proceeding so far as to cause a prosecution to be had of persons of known and good reputation, which caused a great dissatisfaction and a stop to be put thereunto, until their Majesties' pleasure should be known therein.

And upon a representation thereof accordingly made, her late Majesty Queen Mary the Second of blessed memory, by her royal letter given at her court at Whitehall [on] April 15, 1693, was graciously pleased to approve the care and circumspection therein, and to will and require that in all proceedings against persons accused for witchcraft or being possessed by the Devil, the greatest moderation and all due circumspection be used, so far as the same may be without impediment to the ordinary course of justice.

And some of the principal accusers and witnesses in those dark and severe prosecutions have since discovered themselves to be persons of profligate and vicious conversation.[23]

Upon the humble petition and suit of several of the said persons and of the children of others of them whose parents were executed.

Be it declared and enacted by his Excellency the Governor, Council, and Representatives in General Court assembled and by the authority of the same that the several convictions, judgments, and attainders against the said George Burroughs, John Proctor, George Jacob, John Willard, Giles Corey and [Martha] Corey, Rebecca Nurse, Sarah Good, Elizabeth How, Mary Esty, Sarah Wilds, Abigail Hobbs, Samuel Wardwell, Mary Parker, Martha Carrier, Abigail Faulkner, Ann Foster, Rebecca Eames, Mary Post, Mary Lacey, Mary Bradbury, and Dorcas Hoar, and every of them be and hereby are reversed, made and declared to be null and void to all intents, constructions, and purposes whatsoever, as if no such convictions, judgments, or attainders had ever [been] had or given. And that no penalties or forfeitures of goods or chattels be by the said judgments and attainders or either of them had or incurred. Any law, usage, or custom to the contrary notwithstanding.

And that no sheriff, constable, jailer, or other officer shall be liable to any prosecution in the law for anything they then legally did in the execution of their respective offices.

---

[23] A reckless and depraved way of life.

93

The Massachusetts General Court Makes Restitution

December 17, 1711

By His Excellency the Governor:
Whereas the General Assembly in their last session accepted the report of their committee appointed to consider of the damages sustained by sundry persons prosecuted for witchcraft in the year 1692, viz.

	£	s.	d.		£	s.	d.
Elizabeth How	12	0	0	John Proctor and wife	15	0	0
George Jacobs	79	0	0	Sarah Wilds	14	0	0
Mary Esty	20	0	0	Mary Bradbury	20	0	0
Mary Parker	8	0	0	Abigail Faulkner	10	0	0
George Burroughs	50	0	0	Abigail Hobbs	10	0	0
Giles Corey and wife	21	0	0	Ann Foster	6	10	0
Rebecca Nurse	25	0	0	Rebecca Eames	10	0	0
John Willard	20	0	0	Dorcas Hoar	21	17	0
Sarah Good	30	0	0	Mary Post	8	14	0
Martha Carrier	7	6	0	Mary Lacey	8	10	0
Samuel Wardwell and wife	36	15	0				
	309	1	0		269	11	0
					309	1	0
					578	12	0

I do by and with the advice and consent of Her Majesty's Council hereby order you to pay the above sum of five hundred seventy eight pounds and twelve shillings to Stephen Sewall, Esq., who, together with the gentlemen of the committee that estimated and reported the said damages, are desired and directed to distribute the same in proportion as above to such of the said persons as are living, and to those that

Essex County Court Archives, vol. 2, no. 138, from the Records of the Court of Oyer and Terminer, 1692, Property of the Supreme Judicial Court, Division of Archives and Records Preservation, on deposit at the Peabody Essex Museum, Salem, Massachusetts.

legally represent them that are dead, according as the law directs, and for which this shall be your warrant.

Given under my hand at Boston,

Joseph Dudley

94

Reversals of Excommunication at the Church in Salem Town

March 6, 1712

March 2, 1712: After the sacrament, a church meeting was appointed to be at the teacher's[24] house at two of the clock in the afternoon on the sixth of the month, being Thursday.

On which day [March 6] they accordingly met to consider of the several following particulars propounded to them by the teacher, viz.

1. Whether the record of the excommunication of our sister Nurse (all things considered) may not be erased and blotted out, the result of which consideration was:

That whereas on July 3, 1692 it was proposed by the elders and consented to by an unanimous vote of the church that said sister Nurse should be excommunicated, she being convicted of witchcraft by the court, and she was accordingly excommunicated; since which the General Court having taken off the attainder, and the testimony on which she was convicted being not now so satisfactory to ourselves and others as it was generally in that hour of darkness and temptation; and we being solicited by her son Mr. Samuel Nurse to raise[25] and blot out of the church records the sentence of her excommunication. This church, having the matter proposed to it by the teacher and having seriously considered it, doth consent that the record of said sister Nurse's excommunication be accordingly raised and blotted out; that it may no longer be a reproach to her memory and an occasion of grief to her children,

---

[24] Minister's.
[25] Remove or rescind.

Richard D. Pierce, ed., *Records of the First Church in Salem, Massachusetts, 1629–1736* (Salem, Mass.: Essex Institute, 1974), 218–19.

humbly requesting that the merciful God would pardon whatsoever sin, error, or mistake was in the application of that censure and of that whole affair through our merciful high priest, who knoweth how to have compassion on the ignorant and those that are out of the way.[26]

2. It was proposed whether the sentence of excommunication against our brother Giles Corey (all things considered) may not be erased and blotted out, the result of which was:

That whereas on September 18, 1692 it was considered by the church that our brother Giles Corey stood accused of and indicted for the sin of witchcraft, and that he had obstinately refused to plead, and so threw himself on certain death, it was agreed by the vote of the church that he should be excommunicated for it. And accordingly he was excommunicated. Yet the church having now testimony in his behalf, that before his death he did bitterly repent of his obstinate refusal to plead in defense of his life, do consent that the sentence of his excommunication be erased and blotted out.

[26] Misdirected or lost.

95

John Hale on "Hidden Works of Darkness"
1702

The holy scriptures inform us that the doctrine of godliness is a great mystery, containing the mysteries of the kingdom of heaven, mysteries which require great search for the finding out. And as the Lord hath his mysteries to bring us to eternal glory, so Satan hath his mysteries to bring us to eternal ruin, mysteries not easily understood, whereby the depths of Satan are managed in hidden ways. So the Whore of Babylon makes the inhabitants of the earth drunk with the wine of her fornication by the mystery of her abominations, Revelation 17.2. And the man of sin hath his mystery of iniquity whereby he deceiveth men through the working of Satan in signs and lying wonders, 2 Thessalonians 2.3,7,9.

John Hale, *A Modest Enquiry into the Nature of Witchcraft* (Boston, 1702), 8–9, 162–64, 165–68, 175–76.

And among Satan's mysteries of iniquity, this of witchcraft is one of the most difficult to be searched out by the sons of men, as appeareth by the great endeavours of learned and holy men to search it out, and the great differences that are found among them in the rules laid down for the bringing to light these hidden works of darkness. . . .

Q. But by what way may such divinations and sorceries be proved?

Ans. In the same way that murder, theft, and such like crimes are provable. As (1) By the testimony of two witnesses that the party suspected hath used sorcery, etc. (2) Confession may in some cases be taken in this crime as well as others, as hath been above showed, if the persons be "compotes mentis"[27] and give as clear demonstration of their guilt of the fact. . . . (3) The testimony of partners in the crime, in some cases. . . . (4) Circumstances antecedent to, concomitant with, or suddenly consequent upon such acts of sorcery have like force to fasten a suspicion of this crime upon this or that person, as the like circumstances have to fasten a suspicion upon any for another crime attended with them. . . .

Objection: But is it not, then, according to the principles laid down above, impossible to prove any person to be a witch, seeing the workings between Satan and them are so secret? How can they be discovered?

Answer: Other malefactors work secretly and in the dark, hoping never to be discovered. Job 24.14,15,16,17. The murderer, thief, [and] adulterer say, "No eye shall see me," and disguise their faces, dig in the dark, etc. But the Lord searcheth out such malefactors. . . . So the Lord can and doth discover sorcerers, magicians, and all sorts of witches, when and as oft as he pleaseth; and sometimes leaves them to discover and betray themselves; and sometimes overrules their master whom they serve, to entrap and deceive them. . . .

We may hence see ground to fear that there hath been a great deal of innocent blood shed in the Christian world by proceeding upon unsafe principles in condemning persons for malefic[28] witchcraft. . . . But to come nigher home, we have cause to be humbled for the mistakes and errors which have been [made] in these colonies, in their proceedings against persons for this crime, above forty years ago and downwards, upon insufficient presumptions and precedents of our nation[29] whence

---

[27] Of sound mind.
[28] Malevolent.
[29] Hale was referring to England.

they came. I do not say that all those were innocent that suffered in those times upon this account, but that such grounds were then laid down to proceed upon which were too slender to evidence the crime they were brought to prove; and thereby a foundation laid to lead into error those that came after. May we not say in this matter, as it is [in] Psalm 106.6, "We have sinned with our fathers"? And as [in] Lamentations 5.7, "Our fathers have sinned and are not, and we have born their iniquities"? And whether this be not one of the sins [that] the Lord hath been many years contending with us for is worthy our serious enquiry. If the Lord punished Israel with famine three years for a sin of misguided zeal forty years before that, committed by the breach of a covenant made four hundred years before that, [as in] 2 Samuel 21.1,2, why may not the Lord visit upon us the misguided zeal of our predecessors about witchcraft above forty years ago, even when that generation is gathered to their fathers?

But I would come yet nearer to our own times, and bewail the errors and mistakes that have been [made] in the year 1692, in the apprehending too many we may believe were innocent, and executing of some [who], I fear, [ought] not to have been condemned; by following such traditions of our fathers, maxims of the common law, and precedents and principles which now we may see, weighed in the balance of the sanctuary, are found too light. . . . I am abundantly satisfied that those who were most concerned to act and judge in those matters did not willingly depart from the rules of righteousness. But such was the darkness of that day, the tortures and lamentations of the afflicted, and the power of former precedents, that we walked in the clouds and could not see our way. And we have most cause to be humbled for error on that hand which cannot be retrieved, so that we must beseech the Lord that if any innocent blood hath been shed in the hour of temptation, the Lord will not lay it to our charge, but be merciful to his people whom he hath redeemed, Deuteronomy 21.8, and that in the day when he shall visit, he will not visit this sin upon our land, but blot it out, and wash it away with the blood of Jesus Christ. . . .

It was a glorious enterprise of the beginners of these colonies to leave their native country to propagate the gospel, and a very high pitch of faith, zeal, and courage that carried them forth to follow the Lord into this wilderness, into a land that was not sown. Then was New England holiness to the Lord, and all that did devour them, or attempted so to do, did offend, and evil did come upon them. And the Lord did graciously remember this kindness of their youth and love of their espousals, in granting them many eminent tokens of his favor by his presence with them in his ordinances[30] for the conversion of souls, and edifying and comforting the hearts of his servants, by signal answering [of] their prayers in times of difficulty, by protecting them from their enemies, by guiding of and providing for them in a desert. And the Lord will still remember this their kindness unto their posterity, unless that by their apostasy[31] from the Lord they vex his Holy Spirit to turn to be their enemy, and thereby cut off the entail[32] of his covenant mercies, which God forbid. Oh that the Lord may be with us, as he was with our fathers; and that he may not leave us, nor forsake us!

[30] Religious practices and rituals (including the Lord's Supper).
[31] Spiritual desertion.
[32] Promised inheritance.

A Chronology of the Salem Witch Hunt, 1692–1712

1692 *Mid-January*   Girls in Salem Village begin to have strange fits.

February 29   Warrants issued for the arrest of Tituba, Sarah Good, and Sarah Osborne.

March 1–5   Preliminary examinations of the accused take place.

March 20   Deodat Lawson preaches in Salem Village.

March 27   Samuel Parris delivers statement condemning the use of countermagic.

May 10   Sarah Osborne dies in prison of natural causes.

May 14   Governor William Phips arrives in Massachusetts.

May 27   Phips establishes the Court of Oyer and Terminer.

June 2   Trial of Bridget Bishop takes place.

June 10   Bridget Bishop executed.

June 15   "The Return of Several Ministers" submitted to the governor and council.

June 28–29   Trial of Sarah Good takes place.

July 19   Sarah Good, Elizabeth How, Susannah Martin, Rebecca Nurse, and Sarah Wilds executed.

August 5   Trial of George Burroughs takes place.

August 5   Trial of John Proctor takes place.

August 19   Martha Carrier, George Burroughs, George Jacobs Sr., John Proctor, and John Willard executed.

September 6   Trial of Dorcas Hoar takes place.

September 22   Martha Corey, Mary Esty, Alice Parker, Mary Parker, Ann Pudeator, Wilmot Reed, Margaret Scott, and Samuel Wardwell executed.

October 29   Governor Phips dissolves the Court of Oyer and Terminer.

1693 *January 4* Trials resume, resulting in three convictions (all three reprieved).

May 9 Indictment against Tituba rejected by Grand Jury.

1696 Samuel Parris resigns as minister of Salem Village.

1697 Samuel Parris departs; his successor, Joseph Green, arrives.

1711 Convictions, judgments, and attainders reversed.

1712 Excommunications at the church in Salem Town reversed.

Questions for Consideration

1. What can we learn from these documents about the ways in which colonists in New England made sense of extraordinary occurrences and crises in their lives, especially in terms of the relationship between the natural and supernatural worlds?

2. According to Documents 10–13, how did Samuel Parris and other inhabitants of Salem Village react to the "fits" that spread through the community in early 1692? What clues do the documents give as to why these "distempers" began? How did the villagers' strategies for dealing with the afflictions change over time? Why was Parris so angry when he discovered what Mary Sibley was doing in an attempt to help her niece?

3. What made the accused women and men featured in Documents 14–75 seem to be likely witches? What kinds of evidence were offered against the accused and in their defense? How did conflicts between neighbors figure in these accusations? Did the defendants help or damage their cases by their behavior under examination?

4. Reconstruct the events of 1692 from the perspective of (a) the afflicted girls and their families, (b) other witnesses against the accused witches, (c) the accused, their families, and their friends, (d) the magistrates presiding over the trials, (e) other New England magistrates who were observing the proceedings, (f) Samuel Parris, (g) other ministers in the region, and (h) Governor Phips. How does this exercise change or complicate your understanding of what happened that year?

5. What kinds of emotion (such as fear, hatred, suspicion, and doubt) are voiced or referred to in the documents? What role did physical violence play in the witch hunt?

6. To what extent were the afflicted girls and young women performing for their neighbors and the court officials? If they were, does that mean that their testimony was necessarily false? Are there alternatives to accepting their claims at face value or dismissing them as falsehoods?

7. What can we learn from the statements made by recanting confessors in Documents 77–80 about (a) the procedures used by officials

in 1692 and the atmosphere that prevailed in the courtroom, (b) the ways in which defendants and their families responded to the accusations against them, and (c) the influence of religious belief on those responses?

8. On what grounds did "The Return of Several Ministers" (Document 81) object to the court's proceedings? What strategies did Cotton Mather suggest in Document 82 for dealing with the challenges facing the court? How did the perspectives offered by Robert Pike (Document 83) and Thomas Brattle (Document 84) differ from those of the ministers?

9. How did Governor Phips seek to explain and excuse his role in the witch trials (Document 85)?

10. What do Documents 86 and 87 tell us about the position that Samuel Parris found himself in following the end of the witch crisis?

11. In Documents 88–95, many of those involved in the witch hunt expressed regret for what had happened. How did they account for their actions, and what were the implications for future witch prosecutions?

Selected Bibliography

PRINTED PRIMARY SOURCES

Boyer, Paul, and Stephen Nissenbaum, eds. *Salem-Village Witchcraft: A Documentary Record of Local Conflict in Colonial New England.* 1972. Reprint, Boston: Northeastern University Press, 1993.

———, eds. *The Salem Witchcraft Papers: Verbatim Transcripts of the Legal Documents of the Salem Witchcraft Outbreak of 1692.* 3 vols. New York: Da Capo Press, 1977.

Breslaw, Elaine G., ed. *Witches of the Atlantic World: A Historical Reader and Primary Sourcebook.* New York: New York University Press, 2000.

Burr, George Lincoln, ed. *Narratives of the Witchcraft Cases, 1648–1706.* New York: Charles Scribner's Sons, 1914.

Cooper, James F., and Kenneth P. Minkema, eds. *The Sermon Notebook of Samuel Parris, 1689–1694.* Boston: Colonial Society of Massachusetts, 1993.

Hale, John. *A Modest Inquiry into the Nature of Witchcraft.* 1702. Reprint, Bainbridge, N.Y.: York Mail-Print, 1973.

Hall, David D., ed. *Witch-Hunting in Seventeenth-Century New England: A Documentary History, 1638–1693.* Boston: Northeastern University Press, 1991, 1999.

Mather, Cotton. *Wonders of the Invisible World.* Boston, 1692 (deliberately misdated as 1693 on the title page to evade the governor's ban on publications relating to the witch panic).

Mather, Increase. *Cases of Conscience Concerning Evil Spirits Personating Men.* Boston, 1692 (deliberately misdated as 1693 on the title page to evade the governor's ban on publications relating to the witch panic).

Rosenthal, Bernard, et al., eds. *Records of the Salem Witch-Hunt.* New York: Cambridge University Press, 2009.

Willard, Samuel. *Some Miscellany Observations on Our Present Debates Respecting Witchcrafts.* Philadelphia, 1692 (place of publication actually Boston, a ploy to evade the governor's ban on publications relating to the witch panic).

WITCHCRAFT IN SEVENTEENTH-CENTURY NEW ENGLAND

Abbot, Elinor. *Our Company Increases Apace: History, Language, and Social Identity in Early Colonial Andover, Massachusetts.* Dallas, Tex.: SIL, 2007.

Boyer, Paul, and Stephen Nissenbaum. *Salem Possessed: The Social Origins of Witchcraft.* Cambridge, Mass.: Harvard University Press, 1974.

Breslaw, Elaine G. *Tituba, Reluctant Witch of Salem: Devilish Indians and Puritan Fantasies.* New York: New York University Press, 1996.

Butler, Jon. *Awash in a Sea of Faith: Christianizing the American People.* Cambridge, Mass.: Harvard University Press, 1990.

Caporael, Linnda R. "Ergotism: The Satan Loosed in Salem?" *Science,* Apr. 2, 1976, 21–26.

Craker, Wendell D. "Spectral Evidence, Non-Spectral Acts of Witchcraft, and Confession at Salem, 1692." *Historical Journal* 40 (1997): 331–58.

Demos, John. *The Enemy Within: 2,000 Years of Witch-Hunting in the Western World.* New York: Viking, 2008.

———. *Entertaining Satan: Witchcraft and the Culture of Early New England.* New York: Oxford University Press, 1982.

Godbeer, Richard. "Chaste and Unchaste Covenants: Witchcraft and Sex in Early Modern Culture." In *Wonders of the Invisible World, 1600–1900,* edited by Peter Benes. Boston: Boston University Press, 1995.

———. *The Devil's Dominion: Magic and Religion in Early New England.* New York: Cambridge University Press, 1992.

———. *Escaping Salem: The Other Witch Hunt of 1692.* New York: Oxford University Press, 2005.

Gragg, Larry. *A Quest for Security: The Life of Samuel Parris, 1653–1720.* New York: Greenwood Press, 1990.

Hall, David D. "Middle Ground on the Witch-Hunting Debate." *Reviews in American History* 26 (1998): 345–52.

———. *Worlds of Wonder, Days of Judgment: Popular Religious Belief in Early New England.* New York: Knopf, 1989.

Hansen, Chadwick. "Andover Witchcraft and the Causes of the Salem Witchcraft Trials." In *The Occult in America: New Historical Perspectives,* edited by Howard Kerr and Charles Crow. Urbana: University of Illinois Press, 1983.

———. *Witchcraft at Salem.* New York: Braziller, 1969.

Harley, David. "Explaining Salem: Calvinist Psychology and the Diagnosis of Possession." *American Historical Review* 101 (1996): 307–30.

Hoffer, Peter Charles. *The Devil's Disciples: Makers of the Salem Witchcraft Trials.* Baltimore: Johns Hopkins University Press, 1996.

Heyrman, Christine Leigh. "Specters of Subversion, Societies of Friends: Dissent and the Devil in Provincial Essex County, Massachusetts." In *Saints and Revolutionaries: Essays on Early American History,* edited by David D. Hall, John M. Murrin, and Thad W. Tate. New York: Norton, 1984.

Karlsen, Carol F. *The Devil in the Shape of a Woman: Witchcraft in Colonial New England.* New York: Norton, 1987.

Kences, James E. "Some Unexplored Relationships of Essex County Witchcraft to the Indian Wars of 1675 and 1689." *Essex Institute Historical Collections* 120 (1984): 179–212.

Konig, David. *Law and Society in Puritan Massachusetts: Essex County, 1629–1692.* Chapel Hill: University of North Carolina Press, 1979.

Le Beau, Bryan F. *The Story of the Salem Witch Trials: "We Walked in Clouds and Could Not See Our Way."* Upper Saddle River, N.J.: Prentice Hall, 1998.

Mappen, Marc. *Witches and Historians: Interpretations of Salem.* Malabar, Fla.: Krieger, 1980, 1996.

McWilliams, John. "Indian John and the Northern Tawnies." *New England Quarterly* 69 (1996): 580–604.

Norton, Mary Beth. *In the Devil's Snare: The Salem Witchcraft Crisis of 1692.* New York: Knopf, 2002.

Reis, Elizabeth. *Damned Women: Sinners and Witches in Puritan New England.* Ithaca, N.Y.: Cornell University Press, 1997.

Robinson, Enders A. *The Devil Discovered: Salem Witchcraft, 1692.* New York: Hippocrene Books, 1991.

Rosenthal, Bernard. *Salem Story: Reading the Witch Trials of 1692.* New York: Cambridge University Press, 1993.

Spanos, Nicholas P., and Jack Gottlieb. "Ergotism and the Salem Village Witch Trials." *Science,* Dec. 24, 1976, 1390–94.

Upham, Charles W. *Salem Witchcraft.* 2 vols. Boston: Wiggin and Lunt, 1867.

Weisman, Richard. *Witchcraft, Magic, and Religion in Seventeenth-Century Massachusetts.* Amherst: University of Massachusetts Press, 1984.

WITCHCRAFT IN EARLY MODERN ENGLAND AND EUROPE

Apps, Lara, and Andrew Gow. *Male Witches in Early Modern Europe.* Manchester, U.K.: Manchester University Press, 2003.

Clark, Stuart. *Thinking with Demons: The Idea of Witchcraft in Early Modern Europe.* New York: Oxford University Press, 1997.

———, ed. *Languages of Witchcraft: Narrative, Ideology, and Meaning in Early Modern Culture.* New York: St. Martin's Press, 2001.

Deacon, Richard. *Matthew Hopkins: Witch Finder General.* London: Frederick Muller, 1976.

Gaskill, Malcolm. *Witchfinders: A Seventeenth-Century English Tragedy.* London: John Murray, 2005.

Golden, Richard M., ed. *Encyclopedia of Witchcraft: The Western Tradition.* Santa Barbara, Calif.: ABC-Clio, 2006.

Kent, Elizabeth J. "Masculinity and Male Witches in Old and New England, 1593–1680." *History Workshop Journal* 60 (2005): 69–92.

Larner, Christina. *Enemies of God: The Witch-Hunt in Scotland.* Baltimore: Johns Hopkins University Press, 1981.

———. *Witchcraft and Religion: The Politics of Popular Belief.* Oxford, U.K.: Basil Blackwell, 1984.

Levack, Brian P. *The Witch-Hunt in Early Modern Europe.* 3rd ed. New York: Pearson, 2006.

Macfarlane, Alan. *Witchcraft in Tudor and Stuart England: A Regional and Comparative Study.* London: Routledge and Kegan Paul, 1970.

Marwick, Max. "Witchcraft as a Social Stress-Gauge." In *Witchcraft and Sorcery: Selected Readings,* edited by Max Marwick. Harmondsworth, U.K.: Penguin, 1970.

Thomas, Keith. "Anthropology and the Study of English Witchcraft." In *Witchcraft Confessions and Accusations,* edited by Mary Douglas. London: Tavistock, 1970.

———. *Religion and the Decline of Magic.* New York: Scribner's, 1971.

Acknowledgments (continued from p. iv)

Document 1: *Publications of the Colonial Society of Massachusetts* 39 (1961): 9–10

Document 12: Rev. Samuel Parris Sermons, 1689–1695, Ms 100740. Connecticut Historical Society, Hartford, Connecticut.

Documents 13, 86, 87: Courtesy Danvers Archival Center, Danvers, Mass.

Documents 14, 15, 16, 17, 18, 19, 20, 21, 22, 23, 24, 25, 26, 30, 31, 33, 34, 35, 36, 37, 38, 39, 40, 41, 42, 43, 44, 45, 46, 47, 48, 49, 50, 51, 52, 53, 54, 55, 56, 57, 58, 59, 60, 62, 65, 66, 68, 71, 72, 73, 74, 75, 80, 92, 93, 94: From the records of the Court of Oyer & Terminer, 1692, property of the Supreme Judicial Court, Division of Archives and Records Preservation. On deposit at the Peabody Essex Museum, Salem, Massachusetts.

Document 27: Courtesy of the Trustees of the Boston Public Library/Rare Books.

Documents 28, 29. 61, 64: Miscellaneous Collections, U.S. States and Territories, Massachusetts. Manuscripts and Archives Division. The New York Public Library. Astor, Lenox, and Tilden Foundations

Document 63: Samuel Parris, "Examination of Geo. Burroughs 1692 May 9–11," 9 May 1692, Photostats Collection, Massachusetts Historical Society.

Document 67: Mary Walcott against George Burroughs, 9 May 1692, Salem Witchcraft Papers, Massachusetts Historical Society.

Document 69: Abigail Hobbs, Deliverance Hobbs, and Mary Warren against George Burroughs and others, 1 June 1692, Salem Witchcraft Papers, Massachusetts Historical Society.

Document 70: Mary Webber against George Burroughs, 2 August 1692, Salem Witchcraft Papers, Massachusetts Historical Society.

Document 76: SC1/Series 45X, Massachusetts Archives Collection, Volume 135, page 39.

Document 89: Samuel Sewall, diary, 14 January 1697, Samuel Sewall Diaries, Massachusetts Historical Society.

Index

Abbey, Mary, against Good, 78
Abbey, Samuel, against Good, 78
"Abigail Hobbs, Deliverance Hobbs, and Mary Warren against George Burroughs and Others," 137
"Abigail Williams against John Proctor," 94
"Abigail Williams against Sarah Good, Sarah Osborne, and Tituba," 74
accused
    compensation for, 168, 179–80
    confessions of, 4–5, 28–29, 143, 145–46 (see also confessions)
    groups hostile to, 66
    Lawson's remarks about, 60–61
    perceived as outsiders, 19
    reversals of conviction, 168, 177–78
    reversals of excommunication, 168, 180–81
afflicted girls
    accusations made by, 2–3, 9, 52, 53, 55–59, 160, 163, 165
    analysis of motives of, 21–23
    Brattle on consulting of, 160, 163
    disruption of sermon, 22, 55
    fortune-telling and, 51, 53–54
    Lawson's remarks about, 59–60
    as orphans, 23
    spectral testimony from, 4, 29, 143–45, 152–57, 160, 161, 165–66
    violence and anguish of fits, 2, 52, 54–58
    See also Elizabeth Hubbard; Mercy Lewis; Elizabeth Parris; Ann Putnam Jr.; Susannah Sheldon; Mary Walcott; Mary Warren; Abigail Williams
aftermath of trials, 5, 30, 167–84
    fundamental problems faced during, 167–68
    Hale on, 181–84
    impact on judicial and political authority, 167–68, 173–76, 177–80
    Parris's Meditations for Peace, 168–71
    proclamation of day of prayer, 173–74
    public apology by jurymen, 175–76
    public apology by Sewall, 174
    public confession of Ann Putnam, 176–77
    restitution granted to families, 179–80
    reversals of excommunication, 180–81

reversals of conviction, judgment, and attainder, 177–78
    summary of grievances against Parris, 171–72
Alden, John, 162
Allen, William, against Good, 72–73
Andros, Edmund, 17–18, 19, 47, 139
Anglicanism, 17–18, 38
animals
    as familiar spirits, 24, 27, 55, 56, 57, 59, 84–85, 86, 112–113, 118, 144, 161
    mysterious illness or death of, 9, 13, 76, 78, 79, 109–10
    See also familiar spirits; witch's teat
"Ann Putnam Jr. against Dorcas Hoar," 121–22
"Ann Putnam Jr. against George Burroughs," 139
"Ann Putnam Jr. against Sarah Good," 72
"Ann Putnam Jr. against Tituba," 91
"Arrest Warrant for Sarah Good," 68–69
"Arrival of a Comet and the Death of a Star Preacher, The," 39

Balch, David, 123
Barker, Abigail, recanting of confession, 148–49
Barker, William, Sr., confession of, 145–46
Batcheler, John, 176
Batchelor, Jonathan, against Good, 79
"Benjamin Hutchinson against George Burroughs and Others," 130–31
Bermuda, witch trials in, 6
Bernard, Richard, 26–27, 28, 153
Bibber, Sarah, 32n, 55, 71, 72, 74–76, 118, 119, 120, 122, 132
Bishop, Bridget
    alleged poppets of, 102, 107, 110
    examination of, 102–5
    personal history of, 101–2
    physical examination of, 108–9
    sentencing and execution of, 4, 143, 185
    testimonies against, 105–7, 109–16, 137
    trial of, 29, 101–16, 185
Bishop, Edward, 101
Bishop, Sarah, 102n

195